A LITERARY FRIENDSHIP

Editor's Note

Just a couple of weeks before Gordon's sudden and unexpected death, we had a telephone conversation about this book, where I suggested that for the sake of readers much younger than ourselves, we ought to provide more annotation for references to situations and persons outside the memory of a younger generation. Gordon agreed wholeheartedly, but expressed no enthusiasm for the task, which I agreed to take on. We assumed, of course, that Gordon would be able to check and approve these added notes. In the sad event of his not being able to do so, I've gone with two styles of annotation: footnotes, as they were in Gordon's manuscript, but using Roman numerals for the small number of notes that were already part of the text, and endnotes with Arabic numerals for the additional notes I have written. Occasionally, Gordon left other references embedded in the text in square brackets and I have left these as they were. Otherwise, editorial changes to the text Gordon sent have been minimal – except for obvious typos and correcting a few misquotations.

In documenting the persons referred to, some several times, I've put them alphabetically in an appendix which, as far as possible, considers the context in which they are mentioned, but does not attempt any kind of biographical completeness. The first mention is identified with an asterisk.

Gordon described himself as a born pessimist and he writes in the memoir about "the culture of terminality", the "immense indifference of things" and the "traditions of discontinuity" within Caribbean culture. The appendix is offered as a very modest gesture made against the process of forgetting and a reminder of the vast network of people amongst whom Gordon and Kamau Brathwaite played connective roles.

I'm conscious that with the best of intentions the additional endnotes and the appendix become a kind of commentary as well as an intended aid, but this is too rich a document not to provide references for readers interested in understanding more about its context and brief cues for following up on them. That includes the music that both KB and GR listened to and related to their literary activities, though I can only guess at their particular preferences. Please do send corrections for any errors you may find.

Jeremy Poynting

GORDON ROHLEHR

A LITERARY FRIENDSHIP:
SELECTED NOTES
ON THE KAMAU BRATHWAITE (KB)
GORDON ROHLEHR (GR)
CORRESPONDENCE

PEEPAL TREE

First published in Great Britain in 2024
by Peepal Tree Press Ltd
17 King's Avenue
Leeds LS6 1QS
England

ISBN13: 97818452325840

Supported using public funding by
ARTS COUNCIL
ENGLAND

CONTENTS

AUTHOR'S PREFACE & ACKNOWLEDGEMENTS

This book is my effort to shape into a coherent narrative over five decades of conversation between Kamau Brathwaite (KB) and Gordon Rohlehr (GR). This conversation took the form of letters, phone calls, e-mails and tapes of conferences where both protagonists were involved. Data concerning long-forgotten encounters has been exhumed from GR's notebooks. KB's contributions to the discourse are more frequent than GR's, whose carbon copies of early letters were few; but despite all of its flaws and potholes, a sort of narrative has emerged.

I had thought of calling this mega-narrative "The Fragments W/hole" or "All Dem Travellin' Years: A Chronicle". After much contemplation, I decided to retain "A Literary Friendship: Selected Notes on the Kamau Brathwaite(KB) Gordon Rohlehr (GR) Correspondence." Excerpts from "A Literary Friendship" have appeared in *Small Axe 67*.

The last two texts published by Gordon Rohlehr have been dedicated to no one. "A Literary Friendship" acknowledges, remembers and is dedicated to some of the persons who have helped me publish the many things that I've written over the years. Roberto Marquez, the first publisher of "My Strangled City"; Lloyd Best of *The Trinidad & Tobago Review*; Ken Jaikaransingh of Lexicon, and more recently, Jeremy Poynting of Peepal Tree Press.

Over the years, I have been supported by my spouse, Betty Ann Rohlehr, who has typed and typeset most of what I have written and done her best to keep me alive. Endless love to her.

"A Literary Friendship" has been an unruly text for all sorts of reasons. Janice Edwards wrestled with the typing and formatting of the first version. I messed up much of the final thing. I hope, nonetheless, that it is read by my few remaining friends. My Bookman's eye acknowledges Lawrence and Cecile Carrington and Aggrey Burke in the frontline of this small band. There may be a few others lost in the midst of the mist.

Letter #1:   KB – GR, 10th January, 1967.

This first letter sent from 47 Mecklenburgh Square, London WC1, dates our first meeting as having taken place at the second meeting of the Caribbean Artists Movement (CAM)* at Orlando Patterson's* apartment in London. CAM had recently been formed by Kamau, John La Rose* and Andrew Salkey,* as a gathering of poets, novelists, painters, sculptors, intellectuals, people interested in Caribbean letters, musicians, most of whom were either permanently resident in England or were like Kamau, Patterson and me, doing postgraduate work at universities there. Sympathetic and active members of CAM included Louis James,* a British professor who had briefly taught at UWI, Mona, Jamaica, and Anne Walmsley* who had taught English in the Caribbean and now worked as a publisher's agent specializing in textbooks for Caribbean schools.

   The topic discussed at that second meeting of CAM was whether there was "a Caribbean Aesthetic", and if so, how to identify it. Kamau, George Lamming,* Aubrey Williams* the Guyanese painter, Orlando Patterson and other great names and brains all had their say. I listened until I was challenged to make my input. I told them that I thought they were adopting the wrong approach. My assumption was that any group of persons anywhere would have their own modes of creative expression as well as their own notions on how to assess what they had created. The Caribbean which was made up of many islands and was multi-ethnic, multi-religious and founded on differences of race, colour and class, probably had not one, but several ideas about an "Aesthetic". The way to proceed was (1) to acknowledge the divisions (2) to select representative samples of cultural artistic expression in individual islands and by reading these samples together try to determine what they taught us about the inhabitants of those islands. Jamaica, for example, had produced Louise Bennett* and mento, poetry, 'labrish', Roger Mais,* Rastafari, Don Drummond* and the Skatalites. Why not consider these different expressions as emanations from a single society and determine what collectively they taught us about Jamaicans' residence on earth?

Trinidad would provide us with a different spread of cultural expressions. Why not 'read' the calypso, alongside the novels and stories of Selvon,* Naipaul,* or the music of the evolving steelband?

We should end up with a different amalgam from what we would in the case of Jamaica.

When we had done a number of these readings, we could compare results identifying common elements and differences. What we ended up with would tell us something about the Caribbean Aesthetic we were trying to define.

The assembly, eager to improvise an agenda that would keep the conversation alive, decided that I would prepare a paper on an as yet unnamed topic, and deliver it on April 7th, 1967 at the WI Students' Union. Kamau first suggested the title "Selvon, the Calypso and the Creolisation of Experience." After acquiring, via Maureen Warner,* a copy of Sparrow's recently published *120 Calypsos to Remember*, I recognised that calypso was a complex universe that was larger than either Selvon or Naipaul, and my address evolved towards what was eventually named (by Kamau again) "Sparrow and the Language of Calypso".[1]

In his first letter, Kamau described how he differed from Orlando Patterson who he said seemed

> to see our area as a desert from which nothing can be expected; a society of hostile, marginal, atomized individuals.

He, however, saw "salvation" as lying "in a kind of creole négritude, a concept dismissed out of hand by Patto," and avoided by Rohlehr in favour of "the individual talent." Already KB had identified what were to become the central elements of a polemic that he was to maintain throughout his five or six decades as historian, man of letters and poet. He contested notions of:

(1) The Caribbean as desert, [Naipaul's, Patterson's wilderness] from which nothing has been or can ever be created.[2]
(2) The Caribbean as a society of hostile, marginal, atomised individuals.

Countering these notions he placed not just hope, but "salvation" in "a kind of creole négritude." He would try to quarrel down anyone who did not fully or enthusiastically share his dream of 'salvation' in 'creole négritude'. But paradoxically, he would promote an image of African Diasporan history as a perpetual journey across a metaphorical Sahara, towards what he would come to term *Dis*, the Virgilian/Dantesque Hell. Creole négritude or not, the wandering half-crippled Nummo of *Islands* would in the middle of his journey, declare: "But my island is a pebble... It will slay/ giants,// but never bear children."[3]

It would require a great deal of sympathetic thought to distinguish between Kamau's desert and those of Patterson and Naipaul.

Letter #2: KB – GR, 6th March, 1967.

Rights of Passage, whose "Prelude" telescopes several cycles of travel, travail, arrival, departure, construction, reconstruction, was published on January 12th, 1967, and read at a CAM meeting on the first Friday of February, 1967. In my initial response, I raised what was to be a near eternal issue when I ventured a comparison between Kamau's poetry and Derek Walcott's.* KB advised/admonished me:

> No point, I think, comparing *Rights* with Derek's method; he, after all, writing short lyrics, so that each poem concentrated, carrying its own world each time on its back of metaphor like a snail.

Walcott's response to Brathwaite's method of filtering the I-narrator's voice through various protagonists was that Brathwaite was a writer of lyrics who was abandoning the lyrical for the narrative style.[i]

The launching of *Rights* led to a debate about poetry as 'personal' or 'impersonal' utterance. Kamau argued in Letter #2, 6th March, 1967, that

> The lyrical-metaphysical – Auden – Lowell* – Walcott line isn't the only one. In any case, all three of them are beginning to loosen their styles and their metaphors.

Brathwaite was already assuming an embattled stance, warning *me*, whom he identified as another one of "you critics", that there was room for a variety of approaches to the idea of poetry.

Letter #5: KB – GR, 11th April, 1967.

While listening to the tape-recorded version of "Sparrow* and the Language of Calypso", Kamau picked out the passage on Sparrow's "rhythmic organization of language which our poets have not yet discovered – or if they have, have not yet exploited."

He, who had generalized about "you critics" 'took me up' on my generalisation re "our poets." He argued that Walcott, Dennis Scott,* Lorrimer Alexander* and Wordsworth McAndrew* had all successfully employed speech rhythms, and that his *Rights of Passage* "was committed to this approach right down the line. [...] "Academic critics" tended to keep

i. See "Tribal Flutes," *Sunday Guardian Magazine*, March 19th, 1967.

separate their discussions of poets like Walcott and Brathwaite and artists such as Sparrow.

Letter #8: KB – GR, 27th March, 1968.

I had returned to Guyana via New York, Ohio, Jamaica, Antigua, Barbados and Trinidad, where on 19th February, 1968, I'd presented "Sparrow and the Language of Calypso" at the Town Hall.

In Letter #8, Brathwaite commended me for "The Ironic Approach", my essay on Naipaul published in Louis James, ed. *The Islands in Between*.[4]

> Really writing to tell you how much I enjoyed your Naipaul piece in Louis James Book. For me, the best thing in the book; though it *good* to have that book.

CAM, he said, was in "plenty trouble." I'd foreseen this as I noted CAM's rapid expansion in spite of its lack of a financial base or an administrative structure. Kamau and Doris were running CAM while Kamau was completing his thesis on *The Development of Creole Society in Jamaica*, publishing *Rights of Passage* and *Masks* and recording versions of these long poems with Argo. In order to complete the thesis, he had to return to Jamaica in 1968 to consult documents in the Spanish Town Archives. He seized the opportunity to visit Barbados on invitation of the Arts Council and there did a week of readings and lectures.

CAM could not survive as an amorphous body with largely improvised agendas and a membership caught up in the West Indian/Caribbean/ Diasporan syndrome of constant movement; of transitionality. Rohlehr and Marina Maxwell,* had returned to the Caribbean. Kamau Brathwaite would do so after finishing his thesis. John La Rose was busy, establishing New Beacon Bookshop. There were also the emerging/ideological situations generated by issues such as Vietnam and Black Power. CAM was virtually overtaken by Black Power activists, who lacked and probably shunned the Afro-Saxon gentility that had driven CAM to prioritise the issue of a Caribbean Aesthetic, or Kamau's Creole Négritude which, whether declaimed by Aimé Césaire,* or eulogised by Senghor,* or derided by Soyinka,[5] was viewed by this new generation as a thing of the past.

Letter #11: KB – GR, 6th November, 1968.

CAM was a memory, deprived of the effort and energy of Kamau and Doris Brathwaite.* Kamau returned to Jamaica just before the Jamaican

Government barred Walter Rodney* from re-entry into Jamaica to establish courses in African history. In Trinidad, I co-edited (in fact co-owned) *MOKO*, a four-page newspaper (fortnightly) that grew out of a need to inform Trinidad and Tobago of what had been happening in Jamaica. After reading *MOKO* #1, Kamau commended me for "keeping the faith" a faith, he said, that needed to be kept more than ever. He wondered, as one who had experienced the bankruptcy of CAM, how *MOKO* was being funded and offered a contribution.

CAM Caribbean, he felt, ought to be based on a magazine which would be one way of "getting around the cliques which are the distinction of our so-called intellectual society." Home confronted the returned stranger with more cliques than existed among diasporan Caribbean folk in the UK who, feeling a common need for conversation, supported CAM (once they did not have to do the collective work necessary to shape a strong organisation).

Returned, Brathwaite now faced the problem – or so he imagined – of building a Caribbean version of CAM. He viewed me as a possible co-builder and thought that we needed to meet to plan how we were going to achieve this larger dream. My co-editing and co-ownership of *MOKO*, along with my prior membership of CAM and ongoing dialogue with Kamau via our exchange of letters, suggested that I was just the person to share in the construction of a Caribbean CAM. But *MOKO* was born out of the particular situation of the banning of Rodney from Jamaica, and out of my own personal friendship with Walter. *MOKO*, moreover, was partially and at times substantially funded out of my meagre bachelor's income and would collapse for three reasons:

1) *MOKO* could not survive on revenue derived from sales. In fact, some of the grassroots vendors simply pocketed whatever they made out of selling the paper; and *MOKO*, so my partner James Millette insisted, must carry no advertisements.

(2) *MOKO* ran for sixteen issues between 1968 and 1969, and juddered towards a halt when the Vanguard, printing press of the OWTU, demanded payment in advance for the next issue. At that point,

(3) Millette and a small committee of enthusiasts, the 'friends of *MOKO*,' decided that *MOKO*'s survival lay in its transition into becoming the organ and voice of an as yet nonexistent political party, the United National Independence Party (UNIP) that Millette was going to lead.

I withdrew from *MOKO* which grew into an 8-pager, then a 12-pager (with ads); and after 1970 into a weekly journal that imitated in some respects Patrick Chookolingo's* *The Bomb*.[6] This final version of *MOKO* ran for over 100 issues under the editorship of a Chinese journalist who termed himself 'the Yellow Peril'.

MOKO could never be part of Kamau's dream of a resurrected Caribbean CAM. But there was the *New World Quarterly** pioneered since the mid-sixties by Lloyd Best,* Norman Girvan,* George Beckford,* David de Caires,* Miles Fitzpatrick* and other academics either rooted in the Institute of Social and Economic Research, UWI, Mona, or scattered in various island homelands of the Caribbean and in Guyana. Best as economic adviser to Jagan's* PPP government had edited fifty issues of the *New World Fortnightly* in the early 1960s.

New World was a better site for a Caribbean CAM, particularly after Best returned home to Trinidad, challenged Millette for the leadership of New World (c.1968) and one year later founded the Tapia House Movement* with its newspaper *Tapia*. *Tapia* paid significant attention to literature and the arts, and became the major location, after 1970, of my welter of essays and articles on history, poetry and the calypso. Much of what I wrote on Kamau's work, including substantial chunks of what was in 1981 to become *Pathfinder, Black Awakening in the Arrivants of Edward Kamau Brathwaite*, first appeared in *Tapia*. Tapia/New World was doing what CAM set out to do, that is create and provide an outlet for the concerns and creative ideas of a regional community. But New World wasn't Kamau's baby, and he never acknowledged it as dreaming his dream. Besides, New World wasn't particularly concerned with Kamau's Creole Négritude.

CAM Caribbean, Brathwaite dreamed (in Letter #11, 6th November, 1968), ought to be based on a magazine, which would be one way of "getting around the cliques which are the distinction of our so-called intellectual society." He realised very early that:

> One of the problems of small society criticism, clearly, is that you can lose your friends too easily if you attempt to initiate criticism or challenges of entrenched positions.

Letter #13: KB – GR, 8th February, 1969.

KB wrote this after Louis James, one of the stalwarts of CAM, objected to Brathwaite's review of *The Islands in Between*. (See *Southern Review*.)[7] James planned to write a rejoinder.

Generating controversy, Kamau grew to resent critics who disagreed with his own ideas and vigorous promotion of them. He found himself caught up in a fight against what he termed "the Academic Establishment", and the "status crow". He saw himself as an "intellectual guerilla," and because he had early identified me as a soldier fighting in his war, he did everything he could to get my essays published in whatever journals existed: *Caribbean Quarterly*, *Caribbean Studies*, *Jamaica Journal*, *BIM*. Since a substantial amount of the articles he promoted was directed towards the illumination of his poetry, one can say that in promoting Rohlehr, KB was also promoting KB.

He was the leading spirit in the publication of *Savacou** in 1969, and put me on the Editorial Board of that journal, though I had little time to do more than I had undertaken (*MOKO*, calypso research; all those essays, reviews etc.). Besides his correspondence with me, he often wrote other colleagues and complained when they did not reply.

Letter #18: KB – GR, 27th November, 1969.

> We can't expect trans-Carib co-op [eration] if we don't learn to reply to each others letters and queries. Communication remains in almost every sense a problem.

Communication, trans-Caribbean and between the Caribbean and the rest of the world, was a major Brathwaitean value. It drove him during those 'early' years in the late 1960s and continued well into the new millennium.

Letter #20: KB – GR, 2nd October, 1970.

He'd heard from 'Boots', historian James Carnegie*, about a diary I'd kept during the Black Power 'revolution' of 1970.[8]

> Boots tell me 'bout de Diary. Think it great great great. I int see it yet, you got to settle down now, ole man, and give we a book. No fuckin' collection of articles. You got to write a Book. A long book, wid everything horganize an put in perspective. If necessary GET LEAVE TO DO DIS.

> There is so much I feel we have to do and say an try, I feel an' wish I cd jes EXPLODE, BLOW UP. Like the whole SOUL scene man. The things that Aretha Franklin* doing. You hear – I mean HEAR "Think" and the new album, *Spirit in the Dark*. Coltrane INT DEAD. An now Roberta Flack* makin' music to make me cry. An we reggae boys got rhythmic complexities (I only realize this when I listen to the music in de States) that pushing everything still further forward.

All of this was packed into a single paragraph which I have divided into two; the first highlighting KB's insistence that I wrote a book "wid everything horganize an put in perspective"; the second drawing excited attention to the exploding dimensions of Black sound and song; reggae in the Caribbean, Afro-American Soul in the USA, whose new high priestesses/muses/ loa, Aretha and Roberta had taken command of the stage. The third and senior voice, Nina Simone,* was still alive and driven by the assassination of Martin Luther King, the 'King of Love', was growing deeper, darker and more embittered – and preparing to emigrate to France, as Sidney Bechet* had done two generations earlier.

While Kamau pushed me towards a big text that would organize and put into perspective *everything* (politics, kaiso, the young poetry of the 'revo'), he was himself trying to do the same thing and exploding because of the narrowness of both space and time that the prison of academia – (i.e. fixed and still 'colonial' syllabi, teaching norms, the enormous stone of essay reading and examinations) – imposed on us both, two Sisyphuses or Sisyphi (?) grinding upwards on our respective slopes.

There was really no way to place in perspective the vast "everything" of the perpetually expanding and travelling diasporan vision, voice, sensibility. This vision could not be contained or adequately defined in phrases like "Creole négritude" as KB knew, or was about to find out. There was no measuring of our faring forward from, and caught in the relentless cycle of *zamani*, towards long gone undead ancestors – the John Coltrane* whose energy still lived in our never-returning but still potentially alive ancestors.

Kamau thought that we, he and I, were both trending towards illumination of the "everything" of our heritage, and he tried to maintain a steady dialogue through which we would exchange experiences and visions. He thought that 1970 was "as important as "Morant Bay"[9] even though he confessed that he had never been to and did not know Trinidad at all. I was his gateway into a Trinidad that I myself was in the process of discovering.

[Kamau made his first visit to Trinidad six years after 1970, when his main mission was to gather material for his expanding "Bio-Bibliography of West Indian poets." In Trinidad he met some of the younger writers like Anson Gonzalez* and Victor Questel.* I took him to a poetry reading at the library in Belmont, where he listened to and commented on Questel's Jazz poem, "Triangles of Sound." My wife and I took him on a drive along the North Coast Road, where we visited Blanchisseuse, the Paria River and the Swing Bridge. In letter #57, KB-GR, 1st Sept., 1976, he thanked us for our hospitality. He had stayed at our place.]

I very much appreciate all the trouble you took looking after me and showing me some of Trinidad. I'll never forget the bridge over the River Kwai and our swim at the river mouth and the drive into the Northern Range. That was really a special thing for me. And just being with you all for a bit was good.

We were involved in a typical Caribbean experience, with Brathwaite, a Barbadian, married to a Guyanese (part Amerindian-ancestored), resident in Jamaica and learning that whole huge island daily; and Rohlehr, a Guyanese, married to a Trinidadian, resident in Trinidad and entering into its labyrinthine cultures via kaiso, the emerging voices of its youthful poets and its Afro-Saxon intellectuals from J.J. Thomas* to Eric Williams.* Both Brathwaite and Rohlehr were travelling souls faring forth bravely and intuitively at two ends of the same wilderness.

Letter #21: KB – GR, Saturday 3rd October, 1970.

From reading the diary KB ["White Fridays in Trinidad"] concluded that I had not been fully committed to a movement whose "built-in failure" I'd foreseen. He didn't quite appreciate my outsider status in a fragile newly independent (only eight years old) former Crown Colony. Regional Caribbean institutions such as UWI were frail structures in the face of Jamaican, Trinidadian, Barbadian or Guyanese nationalism. 'Nationalism' defined and built boundaries around 'nationals' who belonged and non-nationals who did not. I, among many others, had trouble renewing my work permit, and little or no sympathy from my Trini colleagues on campus. So, I couldn't be fully committed to anything political: NJAC*, *MOKO* or *Tapia*. Was Jamaica more broad-minded or pliable? The Rodney, Colin Moore,* Clive Thomas* debarments suggested otherwise.

More important than the issue of my commitment to the 'revo' was Brathwaite's observation that the February marches could be located in a wider history of ancestral nomadism and quest for oasis and home. He wrote in Letter #21:

> What struck me first, of course, was that the whole thing took place during harmattan – drought – the most significant time for Africa and the Caribbean, time of the wilderness, time of the slave ship, time of the slave rebellion, time of the drought. The sky is clear, the mind is clean; debilitating humidity is purged from the air. And so it happened at that time in Trinidad. The time too of greatest opposition and paradox of elements – Derek's loveliest in drought,[10] which you quote. I have a whole new sequence called Harmattan Poems[11] written during that same drought. I see it took you back to Eliot and the Wasteland.

It was undoubtedly Kamau who, long before the American Weather Satellite, had identified the link between the Sahara and the Caribbean Archipelago via the Harmattan, what today everyone terms the Sahara

Dust. In his Harmattan poems KB expands on what he had written in *Islands* about the Caribbean dry season. Brathwaite's Harmattan blows between Xmas and Easter. It is thus Lent, Wilderness and bestows a legacy of bush fire, conflagration & slave rebellion. Brathwaite builds the metaphor until the Harmattan emerges as the terrible refiner's fire that comes with the rebirth of Christ/*Osiris*; the anticipated day of vengeance, the *Dies Irae*, sung about even in the Methodist Hymnal.

I had remarked on how the march to Caroni in 1970, with its hope for green oasis somewhere south of the city,[12] reminded me of Brathwaite's "Volta"[13] where El Hassan is lost in the wilderness and his dream to build a new kingdom with villages, markets and community recreational spaces peters out. In a sense, I saw the march to Caroni through the eyes of Kamau's poetry, while he saw it through my February 1970 Diary. But I was as distant from the action as Kamau in Jamaica. I had foreseen the collapse of both march and 'Revo'.

Kamau also commented on my criticism of the 'Revo' as 'quixotic' in its desire/hope for immediate melding between Afros and Indos despite 'centuries of mistrust'.

> We have to accept, Gordon, that we are made up of several cultures, each culture must build itself truly, in terms of its own traditions, on this soil. Only after this can we think of coming together. But the myth of the multi-racial society purveyed by the Colonial Office on the eve of Independence, and taken up by our Govts, gets in the way. WE ARE ONLY MULTI-RACIAL ELITES. Those boys should have stuck to Black/African Power and left the Indians to join them – as I'm sure they wd. have done.

Here Kamau seemed to acknowledge the 'plural' nature of Caribbean societies (though elsewhere he had dismissed the pluralist formulations of M.G. Smith* and Raymond Smith*). He recognised, but avoided the implications of pluralism for his own dream of islands interlinked by 'Creole négritude', and he was certainly wrong in his assertion that the Indians would have joined the Black Power movement on their own terms if left to build their own traditions.[14] He was also wrong in his assertion that the Revo would have succeeded if its leaders had possessed a deeper surer sense of African culture and had gone "underground where the cultural secrets are." No true intro-racial or inter-tribal harmony existed anywhere in Africa. Kamau himself had written in *Masks* about the bloody wars that had led to the formation and collapse of African empires: Benin, the Zulus, the Ashanti. As for

---

ii.   Kamau Brathwaite, "The Contribution of M.J. Herskovits to Afro-American Studies", in African Studies Association. of the West Indies (*ASAWI*) *Bulletin* No. 5, December 1992, 85-94

the notion that a knowledge of "the organization of Shango, of vodun" could supply the foundation of "something organic" in Caribbean communities in revolt or resistance, he had only to consider the situation of Haiti (as he must have been doing as, at that very moment, he was writing his introduction to Herskovits' *Life in a Haitian Valley*).[ii]

Meanwhile in Jamaica, two cultural performances were coinciding: (1) Marina Maxwell's* production of *Rights of Passage* under the sponsorship of the National Theatre Trust, and (2) a discussion of the recently staged Walcott play *In a Fine Castle* at the Creative Arts Centre, UWI, Mona. Walcott's play evoked criticism from Trevor Munroe, George Beckford, Richard Small and Bobby Hill. They wondered at Walcott's preoccupation, not with the Black Power Revo, but with its impact on the White Creoles. Kamau writes [Letter #23, KB – GR, 18th November, 1970].

> But de trouble wid de play *in dis day an age* was that it was concern wid de whites (ok) and give us all the old stereotype shit bout de niggers; that he int know he culture; that he like castle; that he really want white meat; that he role is silence.

Walcott had ignored the entire tradition of slave rebellion and its continuity in Bogle, Bedward, Garvey, Caribbean négritude.

> An when our leading poet and playwright ignore this, at this time, he slappin' we in we face, man. *Dream on Monkey Mt.;* now this; it too much there; that to understand the WI, we have to understand *fantasy*; Carnival is one big fantasy etc. In the castle of my skin, you the shepherd, I the swineherd. Makak the ape.[15] He ent existential, he just traditional.

Brathwaite wrote that "the whites, to a man and a woman *defend* the play." Something was coming to a head – or to the several hydra heads of the young, newly independent Caribbean societies. 'The February Revolution' of 1970 was 'the visibility trigger' of a new era, the moment of fission that had propelled into visibility the various traumatised and terrified consciousnesses that Caribbean people had suppressed for so long. So the whites completely empathized with Walcott's portrayal of the exploding society and his vision of black apes thirsting for revenge. The 'black' activists, most of them 'socialist', could not understand plays written out of such stereotypes. The 'mulattos' (character Brown in the play) found themselves caught in the middle.

The next grand staging of all of these exploding issues, was the Association of Commonwealth Language and Literature Studies (ACLALS) conference of January 1971, held at the Creative Arts Centre, UWI, Mona.[16] Naipaul, who spoke about the almost nonexistent "phantom literature" of a traditionless Caribbean and mocked at the recent embrace of the folk by an emergent intelligentsia, was treated with discourtesy by a few of the militant Black nationalists, one of whom said that the assembly should forgive "Brother Naipaul" who had become estranged from his region of origin, while another voice recommended that he should be shot. Kenneth Ramchand* began his contribution with an attempt to disparage my prior "Literature and the Folk" keynote address. He wasn't going, he said, to 'folk-up' his own criticism.

A few days later, in an address entitled "Blacker than Me", Ramchand fired his first open broadside at Brathwaite's Creole Négritude. Naipaul had dismissed "Ogun" as an absurd attempt to mythologise an illiterate carpenter. Following suit, Ramchand would in "Edward Brathwaite."[iii] parody "Negus" by rendering Brathwaite's repeated drum-beat:

> "It
>> it
>> it
>> it is not"

as the ridiculous

> Pit
>> pit
>> pit
>> pit is pot.

One remembered Kamau's description of the Barbadian literary elite as an establishment whose custom was to destroy by mockery the nonconformist or the creator of new sound. Earnest, experimental and aggressive, Kamau wanted most of all to be taken seriously. He viewed with great concern the prospect of my having to deal with a combination of Ramchand, Pat Ismond* and Wayne Brown* in the years after ACLALS. He needn't have worried.

In the Letter #25, GR – KB, September 15th, 1971, I described the state of discourse in Trinidad and Tobago which may have been quite similar to what was happening at Mona, but involved both interracial, interclass and inter-generational quarrelling that rendered relatively unimportant the snipes and gripes of my perceived antagonists. I wrote:

Trinidad is undergoing a period of terrible self-laceration. There is verbal savagery going on all the time, which takes the form of picong, self-righteous attempts to rationalize personal cowardice, a sickening ritual

---

iii.   *An Introduction to the Study of West Indian Literature* (London: Thomas Nelson & Sons, Ltd, 1976).

of play-acting and an impotence of action... In this atmosphere, the easiest thing to do is to look for scapegoats.

My letter, one of very few that I could find, was a long response to Kamau's comments in Letter #24, KB – GR, 6th September, 1971 on "West Indian Poetry; Some Problems of Assessment," *Tapia* No. 20, Sunday, August 29, 1970, pp. 11-14.[18]

It's the finest literary response and criticism that I've so far read in our part of the world. Every one of the words in my cable were (sic) carefully meant.

He'd cabled me – those were pre-internet times – "Your review broad, deep, generous grounded with it. We come of age. Peace. Eddie."

Since "West Indian Poetry: Some Problems of Assessment" began as a response to Eric Roach's* severe dismissal of the new poetry in *Savacou* 3/ 4, Brathwaite immediately appropriated it as the beginning of "The *Savacou* Debate." That is, he placed the essay as an extension of the issues that had emerged at Mona and peaked during the ACLALS conference. In those days, he kept encouraging me to become editor of a Southern Caribbean version of *Savacou*. I had no time for that kind of ordeal.

For all the fulsome praise, Kamau was deeply disturbed by what he termed my Walcottian paragraph at the end of the essay which I'll now quote.

In answer to Mr. Roach's question about the possible fate of today's generation of 'soap-box bards', I'd venture that in twenty years' time, their fate may be no worse than his. The experience of living in the West Indies is sufficiently chastening to temper most rhetoric into reticence. Carter burned out in five years into the sad blue "Poems of Shape and Motion" whose doubt was more movingly shaped into poetry than his earlier oratorical commitment. The weight of compassion, life and time which those poems contain tells me as clearly as anything how our lives will, from generation to generation, be denuded slowly into grief, tiredness and silence. In twenty years, if spared by ganja, soul, cacapool rum and the widening barbarity of our politics, most of today's youth will be respectable citizens, without illusions, and terribly afraid of tomorrow's children, whose ears they will try to fill with fables of the swinging seventies.[19]

Kamau commented:

If 20 years is all we have; if the erosion is so killing as you claim; then it seems that we still have not learned to adapt to our environment; which means, that we still don't accept, and therefore don't understand it. i am much more hopeful. i think we are learning, slowly, painfully, but learning; and that there will be more than 'grief, tiredness and silence'.

My closing paragraph proved to be prophetic. Kamau termed it "Walcottian", this pessimistic (but accurate) response to Roach's question of what the current generation would be saying and doing in twenty years' time. I 'predicted' that most of them would, like Roach himself, be "denuded into silence" (NB Kamau's phrase – *The Arrivants*, p. 61). I cited Martin Carter,* who had transitioned from the revolutionary rhetoric of *Poems of Resistance* to the reticence of what came later.

In Letter #25, GR – KB, 15th September, 1971, I attempted a full answer to Kamau's query about the final paragraph. I said many of the things I felt about Walcott, Roach and Naipaul that would become public in a later essay such as "My Strangled City" (1976/1977)[20] and in "Between Negations",[21] the interview Selwyn Cudjoe* conducted with me in 1981. I tried in Letter #25 to address Brathwaite's comments on the final paragraph.

I argued that Roach in his savaging of the current generation was acting as if his generation had successfully established a foundation that the youth were trying to destroy, when, in fact, his generation had only just begun a struggle and were making it hard for the younger ones to continue. Williams and his followers had retained a Crown Colony type of authoritarianism that had bred protest similar to what was common in previous generations. These protests were now being squashed by traditional methods of repression.

I explained that I read current political situations in the West Indies against the template of "the Guyanese experience and doom in my bones." Guyana I described as being in a state of pure confusion: "gestures of anti-imperialist radicalism accompanied by mamaguism, teefin and repression." I cited as evidence the University of Guyana Council, now shorn of its independence and fully controlled by the Party in power, especially with respect to appointments and arbitrary dismissals.[22]

I next challenged Brathwaite with his own pessimism:

But my island is a pebble ....

...... It will slay giants

But never bear children.
["Pebbles," *The Arrivants*, 196]

I told Kamau that he himself sounded pretty "despairing" (I did not say Walcottian) in a passage like that and continued:

I too sing my songs of the skeleton, gloom counter-pointing humour, blues providing a dense mudsill for rebellion. At times, I believe, my mind oscillates pretty close to nihilism, at others there is this tunnelling to tap roots, this delving to inner ground...

I never really dwell at despair or hope. These two [extremes] seem to me to be part of the same feeling about life, the one emerging naturally from the other. You see my final paragraph as an end, but it is no more so than your own "But my island is a pebble." It is but another point of departure. I don't give the society only twenty years, I am merely commenting on a fact of life here, which is that twenty years is what the society seems to give itself before it loses contact with its youth. Cipriani* lasted twenty. There were Butler* and Gomes*. Now we have Williams catching his ass after fourteen (1956 – 1970). Williams, reinstating Cipriani in his pantheon of significant nation-builders, said the same things about Gomes as today's youth are saying about Williams.

Similarly, there were always many Eric Roaches at each period of transition, who failed to recognize the continuity of things; eternal recurrence of rebirth, reburial, blues, rebellion, slavery, emancipation. For me it isn't a matter of simple hope or simple despair but one of continuing to live despite the perpetually encroaching absurdity and the sterility of the time. That a sense of people as people can provide a wall of courage, is one of my beliefs, as it is of yours.

I finally cited Marc Matthews'* poem "For Cuffee"[23] which focused on a Guyanese convict of the 1950s who bore the same surname as that of the Republic's national hero, a famous Akan leader of the 1763 slave rebellion. I wondered what the poet meant. Was it that the spirit of rebellion has always dwelt in figures like both the historic and the contemporary Cuffee, though seldom in the leaders of society even when such leaders elevate the rebel to the status of 'national hero'? Who resurrects these spirits into heroes after they are good and dead? Who hunts them down while they are alive and kicking and talking back? How should one view such ironies? [Before the decade was through there would be Maurice Bishop* and Walter Rodney. How should one respond to this eternal recurrence? With hope that there will always be heroes or unhope that such spirits are always reduced in their time until their resurrection into national holidays?].

KB never responded to Letter #25.

In August 1972, a little while before CARIFESTA, 1972, I found myself in Barbados where I delivered two talks at the Centre for Multi-Racial Studies, Cave Hill, one entitled "Lamming: Then and Now" and the other "New Bearings in Popular Art Forms and Poetry".[24] The lecture on Lamming examined his transition from the early *In the Castle of My Skin* to the later allegorical/symbolic *Water with Berries* and *Natives of My Person*, both published between 1971 and 1972. The lecture on poetry, illustrated by taped performances of the poems discussed, quoted Brathwaite's state-

---

iv. "Timehri", *Savacou* 2, Sept. 1970, 35-44.

ment in his essay "Timehri" about his effort to write poetry rooted in imagery derived from the Barbadian landscape and speech rhythms drawn from Barbadian and other Caribbean oral tradition. Brathwaite wrote of the influence of the emerging prose fiction of his fellow-writers on his own efforts to write an indigenous poetry:

> ...in 1953 George Lamming's *In the Castle of My Skin* appeared and everything was transformed. Here breathing to me from every pore of line and page, was the Barbados I had lived. The words, the rhythms, the cadences, the scenes, the people, their predicament. They all came back. They all were possible.[iv]

Kamau's mother, who thought I'd said that Kamau had copied Lamming, interjected that even as a boy Kamau was always writing poems and stories in an exercise book. i.e. Kamau was an original. He didn't have or need literary ancestors.

Kamau hadn't attended the lecture but later heard about his mother's intervention and provided his own melodramatic account of something he hadn't witnessed. His mother, according to him, had simply "taken over" the session. He had transmuted the incident into family folklore: prelude, perhaps, to his later divinization of the Mother figure in *Mother Poem* and his mythologization of the island of Barbados.

The Cave Hill showdown between Rohlehr and Mrs Brathwaite was closely followed by CARIFESTA (the Caribbean Festival of Creative Arts) held in Guyana between August 26th and September 15th, 1972. Rohlehr, a specially invited homecoming celebrity, was housed in a new bungalow three miles outside the city and two hundred metres away from his family home. The Committee had provided him with a chauffeur and the capacity for easy access to anywhere and anything he and his spouse should need.

Kamau was housed in CARIFESTA VILLAGE, an entirely new housing area built to accommodate the 4,000 artists hailing from 22 provinces, including Brazil, Venezuela, Haiti, the Dominican Republic, Mexico and Cuba as well as most of the islands of the cricket-playing West Indies. CARIFESTA '72 was, for Kamau what he would later term a "Golokwati" moment: a moment of coming together, a meeting place for creators, ideas; a convergence of pathways of the scattered diasporan tribes, that was never quite to be repeated even though a dozen or more CARIFESTAS were to follow over the years. Kamau wrote a diary: a magnificent though virtually unknown account and assessment of the three weeks pageant. It was serialized in the *Advocate* in Barbados though nowhere else (that I know of).

My part in CARIFESTA'72 was to deliver the keynote address: "The

v. See "Between Literature and History", *Transgression, Transition, Transformation: Essays in Caribbean* Culture (Trinidad: Lexicon Trinidad Ltd., 2007), 338-373.

Creative Writer and Society in the Caribbean". Focusing on the relationship between historic consciousness and creative writing, I (in)famously
neglected to include the great pioneer work of Norman Cameron* (my
former principal (ag) and mathematics teacher at Queen's College between
the late 1950s and early 1960s). Cameron, then University of Guyana
Professor and winner of Guyana's highest award, was in the audience. At
the end of my address he arose and upbraided me for not having said a word
about him. ("Not one word about N.E. Cameron, the man who started it
all. Not one word!!"). He then stalked out of the lecture theatre, having
reduced my "celebrity status" to nothing. I've written about this grand
moment in "Between Literature and History."[v]

Cameron's important and foundational *The Evolution of the Negro* was
republished (I hear without Cameron's permission) by G.K. Hall of
Boston. It had been, in 1972, unavailable for nearly forty years. It was a
symbol of the fate of the self-published author (as I was myself due to
become) – not to be widely read because mainly of poor distribution.
Neglected, erased, irrelevant to the chain of discourse, regarded as an
oddity by ever-younger generations of the ignorant, Cameron could not be
satisfied, nor could his pain be assuaged, by any sort of merely national
award. He needed to be acknowledged, recognized, bowed down to all the
time; over and over.

Would this happen to Kamau? To CLR? Did it happen to me? And does
this sense of having simply fallen out of the line of contributors to tradition
fuel a furious narcissism and a need, as the cycle of one's time closes, to
archive at least one's self, the articles and particles of one's achievement?

Kamau saw CARIFESTA 1972 as Caribbean self-affirmation and
summed up the experience in Sam Selvon's words:

"Look man it doan matter how we do things here: is our thing and we
goin' do it our way, unnerstan?"

The Caribbean was 'playing itself' as we say in Trinidad and Tobago.
Kamau begins his "Carifesta Journal"[25]:

The slave masters were absent. There were no whips at Carifesta. No
foreign magistrates of taste or art. No missionaries or sergeant-majors.
No one had to shoe-shine-boy, shimmy or show his teeth at the sun
over his shoulder. There were no Euro-American camera crews, no dotty
anthropologists taking notes.[vi]

---

vi. *Carifesta Journal*, p.1,
vii. *Carifesta Journal*, p. 1.

CARIFESTA 72 offered a way of seeing and being that went beyond the various types of play-acting that Brathwaite himself portrayed in *Rights of Passage*. It opened up new perspectives for an independent Caribbean only a decade old in Jamaica and Trinidad and Tobago, only six years old in Guyana and Barbados.

> Carifesta was Emancipation Day come true; collective Declaration of Independence; first ever meeting of the Caribbean people.[vii]

This was not true. There had been in 1958 the *Festival of Arts* (Trinidad) that marked the opening of the West Indian Federation. Its scope was narrower than CARIFESTA's three-week pageant, but it was still a significant preliminary moment, which included Walcott's pageant *Drums and Colours*.[viii]

After this introduction, Kamau traces the history of CARIFESTA, the wonder of its happening at all in a region so fragmented geographically, ideologically, and culturally. He is forced to recognise the problems posed by multiethnicity and multiculturalism, the factors of race and colour, differences in language, the common history of cultural imperialism, erosion, and the possibly permanent damage caused by the submergence of both indigenous (i.e. Native Caribbean/Amerindian) and captive African cultures.

He doesn't, in spite of this, focus on the quite significant 'war' taking place in Guyana over Burnham and his government – the 1968 'rigged'/frigged elections, the farcical cooperative republic, accusations about 'ethnic cleansing': (the phrase was not yet common but the reality it implied was quite evident). Guyana, declared independent like Barbados in 1966, had emerged out of real fires and genocidal omens. [See Cheddi Jagan, *The West on Trial*].[26] Burnham needed something like CARIFESTA to gain, or rather save face in the community of nations, both in the Caribbean and in the world.

Kamau mentions, but does not explore, the controversy that had arisen over Burnham's reassignment of the residue of funds that had since 1948 been paid for the repatriation of indentured Indians. The majority of these had chosen to stay in Guyana and the more militant of their spokespersons felt that the repatriation funds should be paid out to them. Burnham viewed these funds as having become the property of all Guyanese and used some of it to pay for the construction of a National Assembly Hall where the opening ceremony of CARIFESTA would be held. His political/racial

---

viii. See Gordon Rohlehr, "A Scuffling of Islands, the Dream and Reality of Caribbean Unity in Poetry and Song," in *A Scuffling of Islands Essays on Calypso* (Port-of-Spain, Trinidad: Lexicon Trinidad Ltd., 2004), 22-101.

opponents propagated a strategy: Indians would buy out most of the tickets for the inaugural ceremony and then not attend. It did not work. The event and most others over the three weeks were sold out. Some Indo-Guyanese did participate in face of criticism from the militants.

Kamau did not focus on this crucial Guyanese issue. He was interested rather in his disputed themes of 'African' resurgence into visibility, and of the African 'folk' base that had survived slavery and the plantation experience to become the basis for Caribbean culture in this post-colonial, post-Independence era. Yet KB must have sensed the inherent shakiness of his position as he surveyed what was being performed at CARIFESTA. He recognised that what he was witnessing was, for the better part, not "authentic folk", but folk cleaned-up and watered down by a validating black and brown bourgeoisie. The CAM debate about a Caribbean aesthetic was still very much alive in 1972, and CARIFESTA was really an illustration of the spectrum of possibilities open to the peoples of the Caribbean,

Brathwaite's main argument in the "Carifesta Journal" was that most of colonial education had been directed towards the stigmatization and censorship of the African element, even though that element was the base and bedrock of Caribbean and a substantial part of North American culture. His most unequivocal affirmation was for the Jamaican National Dance Theatre Company's* Kumina which, he noted with sardonic pleasure, was rejected weeks later by a reviewer when the Company performed in England. Kumina was totally outside of eurocentric modes of understanding or evaluation. It was too far away from what they had indoctrinated the colonial to become. It was, one British critic wrote, "religious frenzy... evoked by rhythmic drum... and forceful singing... expressed through groups of stamping and gyrating dancers." It wasn't Bolshoi or Tchaikowski enough.

Kamau, whether commenting on dance, music, painting or sculpture, sought out Caribbean folk authenticity or lack thereof in what various artists were presenting as iconic of their nations. For example, Catelli All Stars, a leading steelband from Trinidad, rendered European Classical music and seemed to be proudly representing the fact that Pan had travelled 'so far' – that is, in the direction of 'real' (i.e. European concert) music in such a short time since the dustbins, 'iron' and biscuit tin do-dups of World War II.

Philip Pilgrim's* oratorio, The Legend of Kaieteur, was regarded with equal

---

ix. See Gordon Rohlehr, "Drum and Minuet: Music, Masquerade and the Mulatto of Style" in Transgression, Transition, Transformation, Essays in Caribbean Culture, 82-88, for a detailed discussion of Pilgrim's Legend of Kaieteur.

scepticism because there was little that was Guyanese about it: this, despite the inclusion of a steelband alongside its two-piano orchestra.[ix]

Ray Luck,* my Chinese contemporary at Queen's College, a brilliant pianist, well aware of the CARIFESTA occasion, did not play any European music in his individual contribution. But was what he did play part of a "Caribbean Aesthetic"? Kamau shook his head. He also ruefully disparaged the Barbadian contribution as the strangest and most uncertain with respect to its Caribbean identity, (even though one item in the Bajan performance was a dance rendered to a rhythmic reading of Kamau's "The Dust".)

Still, KB enjoyed the coming together of so many souls: Shake Keane*, Dobru (the Surinamese Robin Ravales),* Errol Hill,* Sam Selvon among others. He regretted the absence of Lamming, John La Rose and Andrew Salkey, pillars of CAM who had helped plan CARIFESTA in 1970.[27] Walcott, deeply sceptical about such a gathering, was at the time in New York. Yet Kamau ends the journal on a positive note:

> all these things are ours. This festival, to my mind, represents not only a coming-together of the Caribbean peoples, but is in many respects, a home coming for us all. We in the Caribbean may not 'dare to dream to change the world' but we can dream to change our world.

Finally, Kamau always suggests that the things "I dream about" survive beyond the things I sing, I shout, and I groan. So CARIFESTA becomes one of these ultimate times of dreaming where

> John Figueroa* danced to Rasta reggae, Martin Carter moved to Shake Keane's flugel-horn; the Djuka master drummer Basilius Baille* invoked the gods of earth and water and created congo patterns under Dobru's verse. And there was always music: the cha-cha-cha, mosquito violin, hoarse voice of Yoruba, sharp Hindustani and the power of Zapow.* And within the music went our words: origins: clusters of stars; discovered people: Errol Hill embracing Samuel Selvon, Lavinia Williams* telling us of Haiti; Brazilian Neuza Saad* dancing till her feet were burned to blood by stage of board and drum; the pace and glitter of St Lucia's Banjo Man;[28] the people coming off the street to see what Stanley Greaves had painted*; Cheddi Jagan talking after Rohlehr's lecture: "And not a word of Norman Cameron, the first of them all."

The CARIFESTA of Festival City was a different and more profoundly moving experience than the several items performed on the stage over three weeks. It marked both the climax of Brathwaite's fiercely articulated pronouncements of the 1960s and his transition towards the wider, more ambiguous prospects of the rest of the 1970s into the bitterness of the

1980s. The "Carifesta Journal" would lead to the more tightly structured *Contradictory Omens* (1974), whose assumption was that the Caribbean is torn between centripetal and centrifugal forces, and that this tension leads to a series of 'omens', dark signals of disunity, unhealing fractures, energies pitted against and seeking to negate each other. Though *Contradictory Omens* reads like a revisitation and summary of too simple positions (e.g. the Creole négritude) of the late 1960s, it is clear that the issues and discourse were changing.

There was my own "My Strangled City" with its focus on urbanization and the emptying out of the "folk" mind as it encounters, first the crampedness and lack of opportunity in the Caribbean town, and then the anonymity and harshness of the northern city. Then there was the UNESCO Conference of 1978 held in Bogota. The main document – one of the best I've read – that emerged from these ten days of the gathering of Caribbean and Latin American intellectuals and cultural administrators, was entitled:

UNESCO: Final Report of the Inter-governmental Conference on Cultural Policies in Latin America and the Caribbean, 10-12 January, 1978.[29]

Rex Nettleford,* a major though restrained participant in shifting cultural debates of the 1960s, was Jamaica's prominent representative at the Bogota conference. He was editor of *Caribbean Quarterly*, head of the Extra-Mural Studies Department, Director of the National Theatre Dance Company and their main dancer-choreographer. Nettleford was also a sort of unofficial moderator of the Walcott vs. Brathwaite cultural polarization, and an avuncular witness of Kamau's rage against what he termed the Academic and Cultural Establishment, and the 'status crow' of the Mona Campus.

After Bogota, the phrase 'Caribbean Aesthetic' had to contend with the notion of the Caribbean as crossroads between North and South America and the question of whether it was possible to design a cultural policy for this region of small explosive and powerless states in a rapidly globalizing world. "Cultural Policy" was bigger than "Caribbean Aesthetic", though it would be impossible to chart the former, if one could not come to some workable definition of the latter. The CAM issue was not dead but it had been overtaken.

One of the major triumphs of Brathwaite's mission to identify linkages between the Caribbean and Africa remained his recognition of the harmattan as the weather system that pervaded the dry season and the trade winds that had facilitated trans-Atlantic voyaging for centuries. In Letter #39, KB – GR, 12th January, 1974, Kamau noted with satisfaction that the scientists at last saying what i say long time (on back of argo *rights*) that carib weather is affected by sahara dust. I lookin forward to the day when our met maps will include Africa in their forecast maps. Can you image [sic] the effect that will have when it come pun television? At the moment, as you know the forecast maps confine to north america.

But the harmattan, also celebrated though as yet unnamed in Martin Carter's magnificent line: "is air dust and the long distance of memory"[30] would not save Brathwaite from the scepticism of commentators whose instinct had always been to deny connections with Africa as ancestral metaphorical "Mother". Some questioned the authenticity of his personal experience of Africa. The great omniscient seer, C.L.R. James, for example, viewed KB as "at best a talented poseur and adroit craftsman."[x] Brathwaite, wrote CLR, works very hard. Parts of his poems "seem to come straight from Aimé Césaire's *Cahier d'un retour au pays natal.*"

As for Brathwaite's advocacy of linkages between the Caribbean and Africa, James thought little of it

> There is something artificial about Brathwaite. He goes to Africa to find out then writes about it. Poets don't do that... [He] goes working hard, goes to Africa, picks up this, reads about that. I don't think his poetry is genuine and spontaneous.[xi/31]

CLR also thought my work inferior. I had never sat at his feet and, like Kamau, I was simply a hardworking journeyman, picking up this, reading about that.[xii]

Kamau deeply resented all reactions to his African experience as inauthentic, and to his poetry as either inferior to Walcott's or derivative of Césaire's. Pat Ismond, whom he would never forgive, had since 1971 begun the invidious comparison between Walcott's Western (Eurocentric) "humanism" and Brathwaite's efforts to restore or awaken the virtually dead gods of Africa in the vagrant diasporic consciousness.

> ...Walcott's awareness of man in search of fulfilment and man the victim of adversity follows the patterns evolved in the Western Imagination. Western philosophy, going as far back as Plato, conceives of man as a creature endowed with the capacity for Truth and Beauty through which

---

x. Samuel Omo Asein, World *Literature Written in English*, Spring 1981, 96-104.

xi. Asein, ibid.

xii. See Sunitha, Kathyra, Byrappa – Transcription of interview with C.L.R. James, 12th April 1983, London.

he can attain transcendence over the dark forces that threaten to undermine his humanity. African wisdom follows another angle of approach. Arising out of the exigencies of the African experience, it sends the African Imagination in search of a more precipitate contact with Evil. The spiritual energies are engaged in a direct placating of Evil that involves an absorption in its darker mysteries – something of what Conrad perceives in his *Heart of Darkness*. Brathwaite captures the essence of this philosophy in the following lines, hinting at the significance of the fetish for the African…

[…] In the Western imagination the thrust is upwards; in the African downwards.[32]

Commentary varied between CLR's and others, which dismissed Kamau's work for its 'inauthenticity' and a derivativeness that verged on plagiarism, and Ismond's that recognized and reacted against a 'darkly' shamanistic quality in the poetry. Both rejected the 'Creole négritude' that Brathwaite believed was the achievement and salvation of diasporan Africans. He sent along with Letter #46, [KB – GR, January 1975, Mona] a package with the scripts of *Pageant of Ghana* and *Edina* which had been rejected by Evans Bros, who anticipated difficulties in marketing those 'plays'. *Odale's Choice*, on the other hand, was "going into the Nigerian school system." Four schools in Jamaica had performed it in the schools' drama festival. All won prizes. Kamau boasted that the Akan Childrens' Theatre that he co-founded with Efua Sutherland* in Ghana, had (in 1960) already reached "where Ti Jean is NOW."

Those who thought his use of Akan language and rituals to have derived from his reading of Nketia* or Rattray* were informed otherwise.

But to understand me and Ghana and then *Masks* you will have to watch the DIARY me keep of that first traumatic journey ACROSS the river, from the coastlands into akan, at the time of the YAM FESTIVALS and then you will have to know that the person who teach me to drive became one of my best friends for all the years there. He name TABI TWENEFOR. that I spent most of my time as an education officer, visiting PRIMARY SCHOOLS, and living out there, in places where white men don't normally visit: certainly no west indians, who is mostly confine to capitals and coastal towns.

He next described his friendship with the omanhene and amankrado of a village named AHAMANSU, "where I live for nearly a year as registration officer for the United Nations plebiscite." From 1956 to when he left, his interpreter Stephen Agyeman became his protégé, attaching himself to the household as was the custom. He helped Agyeman to become a teacher – then to enter teachers' college and university. Through Efua he met Kwabena Nketia, a musicologist who wrote *The Music of Africa* (New York:

Norton, 1974). He invited Nketia to Barbados in 1975.

He never expanded about his 'first traumatic journey' across the river, but claimed to have grown ("grow, GROW, GROW") in Ghana. He also wrote "a whole archive of letters to Erika Ritter* and Frank Collymore.*"

Early in 1975 [Letter # 47, KB – GR, 28th February, 1975] Kamau began to write "some kinda black criticism ting" for the University of Pennsylvania. It turned out to be a text that grew longer and longer – a chronicle of the CAM and UWI, Mona experiences that contained sections on Elsa Goveia*, Sylvia Wynter* and Gordon Rohlehr.

> i find that you sorta like you linkin the whole thing together: i mean CAM – Sparrow – politics – rebellion – blues – pressure – sounds – black Fridays – eric roach – *Savacou* and so on. hence I call it the love axe/l.

I understood everything there except the word "hence". What did the fact of my linking these different things together have to do with the idea of 'love' or that of axle(?) axe/l? Kamau would eventually proclaim that:

> The constant, I would say consistent fabric and praxis of my work, has been to connect broken islands, cracked broken words, worlds, friendships, ancestories.

This statement defines or describes the axle and axis around which revolved the fabric (i.e. the tangible visible elements of his work, the poems, essays, things that are manufactured, spun out, woven). Fabric suggests what is *fabricated*. It can be seen and touched; but yet there is something unstructured (?) insubstantial (?) fluid (?) about "fabric"; as if the fabric of KB's work is constantly in the making, constantly being spun out. KB senses that his work, though broad and enormous, is not *monumental* in the sense of what is solidly built in stone, fixed.

His work, all of it, is constantly in the process of being made. Praxis suggests movement, becoming, performance, process. Praxis, as defined in the *Shorter Oxford Dictionary* (p. 1562) is

(1) Action, practice, doing... accepted practice, custom, and

(2) An example or collection of examples to serve for practice in a subject, esp. in grammar, a practical specimen or model.

"Praxis" as "action, practice, doing" comes nearest to Kamau's usage of the word in the quotation above. What KB makes and has always been making (fabric) and how he makes it (praxis) his style in the act and performance of making, have together worked towards the fulfilment of his multidimensional axial objective, which is (1) to connect broken islands (2) cracked broken words. Hence, the recurrent issue of lost, broken, changed, eroded languages, fragmented, intangible meanings; lost metaphors and the possibility or impossibility of reconnecting diasporan people with ancestral world views and meanings from which they have become disconnected. KB's "fabric and praxis" are both the results of the effort *and* the failure or the only partial success in reconnecting.

Kamau also speaks of reaching out beyond the Caribbean. He envisages the connection of "worlds"; and while at this stage of his evolution he seems to disparage the European aesthetic that still occupies the centre of Eurocentric Caribbean minds (i.e. Ismond's "Western Imagination"), Kamau is himself a product of Chalkstick's school, a maybe unwilling "hostage" of his Latin and Greek Mediterranean histories, myths, grammars and values. The exclusion from or distorted inclusion of "Africa" on Chalkstick's curriculum becomes the constant target of Kamau's attack; the reclamation of "Africa", wherever feasible, becomes his undying mission.[33]

Brathwaite in his mission statement also speaks of "connecting friendships". That is what the ceaseless correspondence has been about. I am only one of many people he kept in touch with; over and over he would complain of not having heard from me. He was able, via keeping in touch with my own 'interlinkage' of CAM, Sparrow, politics, blues, rebellion, etc. to partially fulfil one of his main objectives: the connection of broken islands. Sometimes it seemed that the friendships were a convenient means of fulfilling or facilitating the larger objective of seeing the fragments of islands w/hole.

Brathwaite said in 1975 that *The Love Axe/l* would have a large index and produced a checklist of my publications that included all that he knew of what I had written, but excluded a considerable number of items he had never seen. His checklist, however, provided him with a basis for locating my work in his grand schema. He never quite accommodated himself to the fact of my work's variety and its resistance to being boxed into anyone's schema. Kamau's mindset had begun to move towards the creation of boxes, schemae, even as it widened out to embrace a universe of space and time and histories. The history of *The Love Axe/l* is the history of this paradoxical process of widening out and yet, creating neat archival categories. The document kept expanding to what it became in the late 1990s: about 800 pages.[34]

1975 marked the halfway line between Kamau's return to the Caribbean from Ghana and his resignation from his substantive post of Professor of Social and Cultural History at UWI, Mona. There is a hint that he was negotiating a transfer from Mona to Cave Hill in 1975. In Letter #50, KB – GR, 29th September, 1975, he stated that he had been 'seconded' to Cave Hill. The packers had estimated $5000 to move "the things in my house", but UWI, Cave Hill was not prepared to pay more than $500 (Ja). Doris had resigned from her job, Michael had been taken from school and they had sold "we lil piece o lann."

This was, to all appearances, a serious move; a return to the native land. Yet Brathwaite had applied for only one year's 'secondment' and now everything had crashed. There has always been this confusion, this lack of certainty in KB's travelling life: this urge to move from one place to another. This quest for ubiquity had consequences. Kamau did not/could not travel light. He needed all of his impedimenta and that was a problem. Roots were temporary; movement, or the urge to move, permanent. In addition, projects were always popping up. The Jamaican Government had commissioned him to write the justification of Nanny and Sam Sharpe[35] as national heroes and to submit it by October 7th 1975. The papers on Sharpe were in London and KB was going there next day – i.e. September 21st, and returning on October 5th or 6th.

His agenda was simply too jam-crammed. One can understand his frequent use of the word "improvisation" to explain his work: the late and sudden changes he might demand of a publisher when a manuscript was on the verge of being published, for example. His life itself was being constantly improvised. This made for whim, spur-of-the-moment adoption of concepts, inventiveness, a tendency to make it up as one went along – Jazz. *The Love Axe/l* which began as "a commentary based on the talk I gave at Philadelphia" was rejected by Pennsylvania University Press [Letter #52, KB – GR, 6th December, 1975]. Kamau was simultaneously working on "a monster Bibliography of WI Poetry" [Letter #52].

Letter #55, KB – GR, 7th May, 1976 was written on a sheet of paper adorned with the letterhead of the Afro-American Studies Center, Boston University where KB had been spending part of the 1975-1976 academic year after his collapsed secondment at Cave Hill. He had just returned to Boston from Los Angeles and New York and was due back in Mona, Jamaica on 15th June, 1976. He had signed a contract with G.K. Hall, Boston, to publish his Bibliography of West Indian Poetry. He wrote in Letter #61, June 21, 1977 that he was again in Boston, finalizing his Bibliography.

Six years later [Letter #88, KB – GR, 21st July, 1983] in a letter written on the Library of Congress stationery, KB disclosed that he had been at the University of Worcester since January (1983) and was due to return to Jamaica in September. His Bibliography on poetry was "now awesome." But he was still having issues with G.K. Hall. In his next letter [#89, KB – GR, 9th September, 1983] he was on the verge of flying to Kingston via Miami, with 3,500 [!!] pages of the "Bio-Bibliography." He was mistrustful

---

xiii. See *MR I* and *MR II*.

of the publishers and their new editor. He was still working on the Bibliography during the summer vacation of 1984 [Letter # 94, KB – GR, 7th July, 1984] when in October, 1984 [Letter #95, KB – GR, 22nd October, 1984] G.K. Hall terminated (by phone call) the contract.

He resolved to publish it himself but I don't think he ever did or could; though he did publish a number of checklists based on the Bibliography.[36] He turned to other projects, like trying to interest the Afro-American Studies department of UCLA to publish *History of the Voice*,[37] and venturing into the new and current field/ (enthusiasm/fad) of '*Magical Realism*'. CASA de las Americas, publisher of his prizewinning *Black + Blues* (1976), would also publish *Roots* (1986) a prizewinning anthology of KB's essays (1957-1981), and later would award Brathwaite with his third prize for his *Magical Realism* exploration.[xiii]

It can be concluded that the two decades of KB's return to the Caribbean were a period of growth in several directions – poetry, polemic, the development of Caribbean Studies, the editing of *Savacou*, publication of his own work, an enormity of research such as the unpublished Bio-Bibliography of West Indian Poets, and constant travelling mainly to North American academic institutions. His work was facilitated by Fulbright (1982-1983; 1987-1988) and Guggenheim (1972-1973) fellowships. He achieved a sort of 'Academic celebrity' that was rivalled only by the equally stellar dancer, choreographer, orator, essay writer, labour relations expert and UWI administrator Rex Nettleford. But KB's celebrity was counterpointed by a personal unease towards both the Caribbean and the American landscapes of his achievement. Both UWI, Mona and US Academia were perceived by him as habitats for "the status crow". Hence the pitched battles in which he engaged "the academic establishment" and his 'untrustworthy' colleagues in the History and English Departments. Hence, too, his suspicion, already visible during his Jamaican years but blatantly obvious during his two decades at New York, that he was being surveilled and undermined by unseen and malevolent agencies of (?) (?) (?). He never quite identified them, but he knew they existed and were at work against him.

Throughout the 1970s and into the eighties, Kamau via his poetry ("Wings of a Dove" (1967),[38] "Negus" (1969),[39] "Starvation" (1974)[40], "Good Friday 1975: Kingston in the Kingdom of the World" (1975),[41] "Stone, for Mikey Smith" (1983)[42] projected a vision of what he would later call DIS – i.e. Hell.[xiv] Kingston, like Le Roi Jones'/Amiri Baraka's Newark in *The System of Dante's Hell*, becomes the Caribbean version of *DIS*. This portrait of Kingston, accurate as it indeed was, probably angered Kamau's Jamaican colleagues who, patriots of a young nation, wanted to see balance – an equal focus on the positive and affirmative aspects of their society.

---

xiv. See *Trench Town Rock*, "5. Short History of Dis or Middle Passages Today", 61-74

Brathwaite was an outsider, a man estranged – despite the things he dreamt about – from the community, one who made the mistake of letting felt truths fly out of his mouth uncensored.

The most profound of all the poems that expressed Kamau's alienation from Jamaica and sense of the failure of his mission was "Good Friday 1975: Kingston in the Kingdom of this World." There the Voice is that of (1) a Christ figure (2) any one of the reduced black visionary vagrants of Kingston's streets (3) a Dogon Nummo/Sun God – cast down and out and forced to wander crippled with his vision of rehabilitation and redemption. His monologue takes place in his prison cell where he awaits judgement (Herod, high priest, Pilate). Here Kamau creates his version of a recurrent figure in Caribbean literature: the alienated poetic Voice, the Outsider, Bookman; Walcott's Spoiler,[43] Mutabaruka's vagrant sitting on the wall,[44] David Rudder's madman lahaying on the wall.[45] The I, Eye, Voice is Kamau's and more than Kamau's; it is Kamau as Shaman caught or catching himself at a moment when he is least acknowledged by the congregation he thought he was saving. Before the decade of the 1980s expired, Kamau had become the Shaman he'd imagined into existence and created. He'd learned in the process that "finding home did not mean being at home" [Letter #83, KB – GR, May 1981].

Letter #98: KB – GR, 31st May, 1986
Kamau sent me *X/Self* which he said like *Rights of Passage* (1967) and *Black + Blues* (1976) had been written in drought, his now mythologised season of the Harmattan. He also told me of "Doris's continuing illness" and warned that "the prognosis looks bad." Doris died on September 7th 1986, the day of her sixtieth birthday. Kamau first sought to cope with her death by renewing his agenda of travelling. In Letter #103 [KB – GR, Irish Town, 14th October, 1986] he informed me:

Dear Gordon,

Now know I the salt, the wasteland.

Tomorrow morning I go to Ohio for some lecture/readings of *History of the Voice*, and then to London for Caribbean Focus (literature). Wish me strength, wish me luck.

Later in November I go to B'dos (Independence?) to a Writers' Group there, to Dominica – Writers' Group there invited the i; and since I wish to go see D's people in New Amsterdam & take some of her ashes

xv. *The Visibility Trigger*, Cahiers de Louvain, Belgium, 1986 (60 pages) and *Jah Music*, Savacou, Kingston, 1986, (60 pages).

to her mother's grave, have I suggested to AJS that I would like to read in G/town... a kind of thank you to Guyana for having produced and loaned me for a too short while this special woman.

After fulfilling this strenuous schedule of travelling and reading in America, the Caribbean and across the Atlantic in London, Kamau undertook his first public appearance and performance in Jamaica on Friday 21st November, 1986. The event which took place at UWI, Mona before an audience of mainly KB's academic colleagues, was a book launch of two of Kamau's publications.[xv]

After the launch, Brathwaite returned to his home in Irish Town and penned on November 22nd 1986, a letter addressed to the Mona community that was simultaneously a personal howl and scream, and magnification of 'the poet' (i.e. himself) as an individual whose life must be read as a metaphor of the catastrophe and anomie in which the wider society terrifyingly abides.

Brathwaite's letter began with an indictment of his colleagues for their having inflicted on him "brutal and frightening neglect." He seemed to blame them for "the violent and emotional internal hemorrhage which has been going on [and] is now black clotted & massive." He referred to a statement he had made at the book launch: "I have been becoming my own poem to Mikey Smith."

To what extent had Brathwaite hidden "centre-self" in the various "I" narrators of his poems throughout the two trilogies and the intermediate *Black + Blues/Third World Poems*? Winnifred Risden* had complained of being unable to locate a genuine personal voice behind the ever-shifting congregation of narrators from Uncle Tom to Ogun. Was Brathwaite all of these voices, or none of them?

Here in his 'letter of indictment' (my title), EKB was claiming a closeness, almost a sameness and total self-identification with such brutally sacrificed and murdered scapegoats as Mikey Smith, Walter Rodney and even Christ.[xvi] Could one trust such self-identification with archetypal victims, or should one see it as another kind of exploitation, a sort of spirit-theft in which the slain hero-victim is reduced to the narrating voice of a narcissistic poet? Ultimately, was the reader being asked to forget Rodney or Smith or Christ and contemplate, instead, Kamau in his dungeon of raw suffering; (suffering which he would later half-acknowledge, to have brought on himself)?

Beneath this Letter of Indictment, and the *Zea Mexican Diary* that soon followed, lay a confession of guilt in a Lammingesque Ceremony of Souls,

---

xvi. See "Good Friday", 1975. "Kingston in the Kingdom of this World," and "Stone: for Mikey Smith."

that varied from the original Haitian ritual in that there was no community, no houngan, no dancers, no drums; only the individual poetic Voice, beating its drum and dancing itself and wailing in its own self-created *hounfort*.

Kamau understood the reluctance of his real/imagined colleagues to come closer and offer whatever comfort they could to him, who had been, even in his vision of creating a community of sensibility, an isolated creature. While he had always claimed that the picture of him as an *isolato*, i.e. as one who sought isolation and often put distance between himself and visitors to his College Common and Irish Town sanctuaries, was untrue, there were witnesses to this accusation that one had no reason to doubt.

In his Letter of Indictment, indeed, Kamau quotes (?) a friend he meets in a supermarket who explains the neglect that Kamau now suffers:

> When something like this happen, evvabody is brought face to face wid dem own mortality & we don't want to get inna dat.

The bereaved man becomes a sort of threat, a spectre of what will happen to everybody else; not quite a scapegoat, but an untouchable from whom one needs to establish spiritual distance, lest one somehow invokes onto oneself the same fate before its due time. So leave him alone. Dead people and those marked by death, seek the consolation of company. '*Solamen miseris socios habuisse doloris.*'

Another response was less sympathetic and more judgemental.

> All yu friends think you spoil & you must face the lonely all alone & learn to stann up on you own two feets.

Kamau would 'process' this second response in *4th Traveller*, one of the *Dream Stories* in which he narrates his inward journey from " the dark village of the dead" to the state of i/sol/ence where, like a turtle, he protects his "i" by retreating into the lonely sunshine of his shell.[xvii]

The third indictment comes from an overtly judgemental witness, one without empathy:-

> No No my fwend, now you is being punish far being a recluse/far shutting yourself away from us & writing poems poems poems (when you shudda been one a de boys in de Coffee Room or SCR Bar or at parties parties patties.)

Kamau's mockery of the philistine SCR Voice here suggested that he

xvii. See Gordon Rohlehr, "Dream Journeys," in *Transgression, Transition, Transformation: Essays in Caribbean Culture* (Port of Spain, Lexicon Trinidad Ltd., 2007), esp. 432-438.

saw himself as an outsider in this still foreign nation where he had already lived two and-a-half decades. He remained a stranger, despite his mission which he next described as

> helping to organize a situation where there might still not be the death but birth/continuation of our poetry. For what really is to us a poem/ poetry? How much it mutter, eh? Where comes it from and how? from what dark engine years of salt & wilderness created it?

Subtly shifting the line of his narrative he portrayed himself as a sacrificial offering.

> Ah yes, I offer up i/self in writing this to pity, your superior, your susu, patronage, your self-esteem, complacency, indifference, even perhaps concern. But (yes) gwine say it write it set um down here so as to try to make you/help you understand our culture has lost certain crucial eyes in this its Middle Passage.

Returning to his poem, "Stone", he presented it as having grown out of the failure of the Jamaican nation, and said that his launching of and reading from *Jah Music*

> was perhaps a desperate act, a cry for help, a warning to a community… that kills a thousand of our/selves each year. & I have seen the dead man bleeding face down in the gutter blunted blunted dented in by the hobnailed police officer's boot kicking it over & in as if that once man's head was a dead discarded water coconut rolled over in the dutty water.

So, having almost shifted the focus from his personal grief and ordeal of isolation to more startling images of social brutality, Kamau emerged as shaman and preacher

> to a community that harbours books gives lectures on our poetry writes crit creates models talks of paradigms has & has had several of our poet/ people with us & among us/artists and writers/those who create the crits. But do we ever stop to think of where those metaphors come from/ how they come from/what source & sauce of energy How plants the seeds How waters the stem How cares the blossom from the dragons teeth?

Kamau's Letter of Indictment ends with a dreadful premonition of catastrophe: the erasure of his and maybe the region's cultural archives; those objects of our societies' indifference and neglect and targets of either Man's or Nature's malice.

Preparing for the launch up here in Irish Town, I looked around a thousand years of manuscripts of efforts to help say how we stay how we say what we say when we stay so & I asked iself what now Here all alone so suddenly all alone without thought perhaps for the morrow *What happens* if hurricane blow all these embryonic fish tales of ideas away if fire catches & teks away the voice of Dobru of Mrs. Herskovits & Sterling Brown* & Walcott & Miss Queenie* & Eric Williams, & Shake Keane & Paule Marshall & Alice* & Toni* & Sparrow & Atilla the Hun.*

The hurricanes did blow, the fires did burn – the *Tapia* Archives, the San Fernando Library, the Folk Research Centre in St. Lucia that I helped open in 1993; Lakshmi Kallicharan* incinerated in her flat in Georgetown, Andaiye's* Archive in Guyana, and so onwards, upwards to Queen's College Guyana in 1997.

So Kamau's Letter of Indictment of November 22nd, 1986, moves from self-indulgence towards his real topic: the collapsing, neo-colonial Caribbean community; the absence or failure of a cultural policy driven by the necessity for collection, archiving, preservation, education, and building on identifiable traditions. It is this recognition of a failure of cultural policy in the post-independence Caribbean that leads to Kamau's intuition or dreams of future destruction by fire, flood and hurricane (see e.g. "Dream Chad" in *Dream Stories*).

Kamau's "Letter of Indictment" ends as it began

I am only one symptom of what is happening to our society: we are so bombed out, burnt out, raped out, knifed out, shot up, robbed out that I wonder if we are a society at all/whether if called on to defend ideas, ideals, structure, family or dreams/nation? we'd be able to do it Or have we not found ourselves, without perhaps knowing it, into another Babylonian Captivity (lock stock & prison); but one now without the whips & the physical bars/scars; a psychological wasteland; victims of the 21st century as we have been victims of the 18th 19th & 20th. And victims because we have been too passive and too passive because we haven't had/or lost the heart to love each other/caritas.

Early in March, 1987, Kamau sent me a draft of The *Zea Mexican Diary*. I scribbled notes that were soon incorporated into Letter #104, GR – KB, 6th March, 1987.

How does one relate author to work?

It shattered the afternoon, your diary: "7 Sept to 7 Sept 60 yrs. Afterwards."

ANR Robinson* won the election on the date of his 60th birthday, 16th December, 1986: 30 years after Eric Williams won the 1956 elections on his birthday.

Cycles: the first, i.e. Doris's birth/death, private/personal; the second, ANR's/Eric's/the PNM's, public.

The *Zea Mexican Diary* destroyed my musing. So many things in my head. Such Pressure.

Extraordinary; unimaginable, unique. C.S. Lewis* once wrote *A Grief Observed* about how he tried to cope with the death of his wife. I must now read him again. But I doubt if anything so close to the moment of anguish exists.

And the irony …. Your writing in Irish Town, she, the subject of your writing, dying in Mona.

You write of your inability to accept void and your hoping for a sign, a message. What messages do the dead send?

This Diary may be your best poem – if poetry is naked truth to feeling. I'd be afraid to write it; though I probably would if the urge seizes me, as in 1970, as with Grenada.

These notes were incorporated into Letter #104 of 6ᵗʰ March, 1987.

Dear Eddie Kamau,

Thanks for the privilege of your diary. It shattered me, the evening I received it. I've never read anything quite like it; and though I once wrote my diary and still occasionally do, I doubt if I could write anything at all under similar circumstances. I kept asking myself : "Is this healthy? therapeutic? Is the death being converted into theatre? Poetry? Is this in fact, Eddie's best and most compelling poem? Doesn't it reveal too much?"

I mean I wouldn't let *anyone* into my nakedest self. Not even myself! I'd smother that nakedest and most vulnerable and, perhaps, truest self by work or the gulf of activity, the vortex of doing. The thing astounded me precisely because you'd always submerged the Ego in the general mask. Now, at this moment of crack and howl. This act of terrible naked bravery.

And you felt the guilt of a dedication to converting that demon of death into an act of saying, even as Doris lay dying. The inexorable pull between love and art; and the fear of terrible self-knowledge that, perhaps, art was more important than the love that had nurtured it; and that it had ever been so.

There follows a section of the letter about the delirium caused by the 1986 elections: national bankruptcy, an austerity budget; dismay at the irresponsible publication of the leaked Scott Drug Report with its lists of policemen, magistrates, and respectable solid gold citizens facing possible indictment. The mood in T & T was one of:

> Guarded optimism riding above a deeper substratum of unhope. There is stoicism and bubbling impatience, an indetermination which all sides are trying to turn to their own account:- the Government into a kind of warmly hopeful activity fuelled by the goodwill of a people eagerly seeking participation in the national life; the Opposition cadres into chaos or uncertainty which make people long for the old slackness and thieving.
>
> My struggle is to find space to work and energy to keep at it and faith to continue to affirm as everything grows a bit distant and the joints stiffen with the rust of arthritis, mild but distinct.
>
> Your struggle is, probably, what to do with the too much and too sudden space that has now come into your life.
>
> We'll both have to fight for or against our spaces.

That would have been a wonderful ending to Letter #104. It wasn't. There was a businesslike addendum in which I listed some of the things I'd been doing at my end of the Archipelago:

(1) Seminar Papers on Calypso that I was sending to KB.
(2) The 3-part essay on *Black + Blues* entitled "Songs of the Skeleton";[48] the notes of which, I said, were more fascinating than the review itself.
(3) "Possession as Metaphor", my essay on Lamming's *Season of Adventure*.[49]
(4) News about *Calypso & Society* (which would not be completed until 1990).
(5) Joan Dayan's one-week visit. It was a conversation with her that had inspired my taped readings of Brathwaite's and Walcott's poetry.
(6) The draft of the introduction to the as yet untitled *Voiceprint* (eds. Morris, Stewart Brown & Rohlehr).[50]

Letter #104 signalled my awareness of two Brathwaites:- "The business-as-usual nomad, rooted, unrooted everywhere; and the shattered, decentred Brathwaite seeking catharsis in confession; refashioning his future at age 56 in the middle of the journey.

The main reaction to the Letter of Indictment was Michael Dash's review of *Jah Music* and *The Visibility Trigger* (27th April, 1987). Dash sent KB a copy of his review with a covering note that seemed to anticipate the sort of response that he could receive from the keyed-up Kamau.

Dear Eddy,

Here is a review done for JWIL. I am not sure that I want to hear your response. But perhaps I do.

As always
M.

Dash recognized that

in a way both collections are about death or rather martyrdom. In celebrating the dead poet or musician, Brathwaite enters into his own debate with oblivion. For two short collections, he desperately clings to the word in order not to surrender to silence.[49]

Dash was correct. Brathwaite, dedicating his poems "to assassinated revolutionaries martyred musicians and dead poets" was celebrating "the fallen members of a spiritual avant-garde. Secular litanies contrast poetic authority with authoritarian politics." Dash believed, however, that "Elegiac verse is a difficult genre to handle" and that too often "Great Caribbean poets have produced dismaying verse in service of worthy causes." Césaire, Guillen, Depestre had all failed at writing poetry in this genre. So had Brathwaite with "The Visibility Trigger".

Responding, I think, to Kamau's 'Letter of Indictment' where he accused the campus community of neglecting him, in his moment of catastrophic grief, Dash concluded, (correctly, I think, but cruelly),

Brathwaite is more interested in re-enacting the tragedy than in transcending it. These poems reveal his own sense of vulnerability in the face of an uncaring hypocritical world. There is insecurity here, a fear of slipping, unnoticed, into the void of becoming 'drypool': dead eye...' of suffering.

This certainly was not the consolation or soothing that Kamau was seeking at that time. I understood Dash's 'lash-back' attitude. He had taken it upon himself to be the voice of the offended, the insulted even, Mona Campus community, the responder to the sheer narcissistic rage of Kamau's indictment of colleagues and the whole foundering post-Independence Caribbean, who had not shown any signs of having yet created a new, conscious and compassionate community.

I thought, however, that Dash's reading of the poems was flawed in places, and on Wednesday, July 1st, 1987, wrote in my notebook [#8, p. 201-2] notes that would eventually become "Brathwaite with a Dash of Brown: Crit, the Writer and the Written Life" a Conference paper presented at the Eighth Conference of English Departments, UWI, Mona, May/June, 1988.[50]

Amen, Amen. For Doris: and for Eddie, hollowed out, utterly devastated still by her fading into these hills; by the sense of hurt he carries, the notion of being simply abandoned by his friends. The problem is complex and involves, first of all, the issue of being an outsider in a place with a very fierce sense of itself, especially in these early decades of young nationhood.

I mean the revived *Focus*, edited by Mervyn Morris and Eddie Baugh, didn't even acknowledge Brathwaite's presence in their country for twenty years. His post-1970 portrayals of the devastated Kingston 'manscape' were some of the earliest attempts in contemporary poetry from Jamaica to wrestle with the meaning of "this island now". But *Focus*, a partially nostalgic effort to resurrect the spirit of the founding years of Norman and Edna Manley, had no place for realities such as those that were being explored in Brathwaite's Kingston poems.

One can function as a foreigner anywhere if one has a base or centre. Lacking such, one needs a cocoon of insulation, a *kumbla* – to borrow Lixie's* image – to which one returns when bruised by the rough edges of encounter, or within which one lives. [Kamau would in "4th Traveller," adopt the image of the turtle that withdraws into its hard shell of "i-solence." But in the months following Doris's death (7th Sept., 1986) he hadn't yet been able to grow the hard protective shell or live within his own lonely sunshine (i/sol/ence) that his vulnerable situation of outsider made necessary].

While Doris was alive Doris served as centre and protective kumbla. It is she that brought order to his extraordinarily disordered life, putting up with his tantrums, the rages that implode within the creative spirit, but which can make the poet a very difficult person to tolerate.

How did, how does one create in an incestuous place such as the Mona (or indeed, the St. Augustine) campus? One *has* to retreat from such a vacuum in order to create. Too many lives there press too closely on each other. Too many unfulfilled super – or semi-intelligent egos grazing on and rubbing against each other; too little space altogether. Even when Eddie lived on College Common he tended to withdraw from time-wasters, ole talkers, friends – the well-meaning and mostly affable barflies of the Senior Common Room.

For all the critical acclaim or rejection he'd received as a *public poet*, he was, in fact, the most private of persons. I put this privacy down to an impenetrable Bajunness. It is a feeling I get about Barbados and Barbadians which, perhaps, *Mother Poem* is an attempt to clarify. This secretive Bajunness also finds expression in Lamming's extraordinarily complex people with their layered psyches, tangled motives and their private selves in retreat even from themselves. Lamming's *Natives of My Person* or *Water with Berries*, for example, work from the periphery, the external, towards the shattered centre of the psyche – witness Teeton or the Commandant.

The journey to that centre takes the entire book. In *Natives*, what each man discovers is a fear, a guilt, an incapacity, the vision of which paralyses until in a conscious act of self-deception, each man creates a new mask, an image of self which is false but more favourable: a reconstruction of face. No one really succeeds at such healing self-deception in *Natives*, where each man must live/or die eventually, with his psyche fissured, with truths too startling to accept but too powerful to negate or ignore.

Harris often *begins* with this fissuring of the Psyche, the eye, the self, which is then moved through harrowing processes towards nakedness and regeneration.

Brathwaite differs from Harris, Lamming or Walcott, by offering autobiography as distancing metaphor; as a means of *not dealing directly* with the shattered howl of Ego, the centre-self. Even in *Mother Poem* and *Sun Poem* autobiography is set at a distance as the Ego abandons the centre of the work, which is offered as a symbol of the broader experience of a Caribbean Everyman. Brathwaite in "Timehri" called this process of distancing himself from his experience, – or rather of *withdrawing* the Self from the experience – "egolessness, the Self without I, without Ego".

But beneath all this lay that other side which made occasional appearance in the earlier poems, but spoke only through the various splintered masks of the other poems. Since most of us have been trained to look for that personal I at the centre of the poem, many of us left Brathwaite with a sense of still being stranger to the man behind the multiplicity of masks.

If the poetry denied the reader-access to centre-self, and the poet himself, for all his affability, tended to retreat from certain types of encounter, how did this affect how others saw and reacted to Brathwaite and how he in turn reacted to them? I think that a mutual mistrust developed whose source was multiple.

(a) The quite natural problem of Brathwaite's reconciling his life and sensibility as a poet with the everyday tedium of his job as historian and history teacher. This proved quite a strain, given the fact that the inter-disciplinarian tends to be misunderstood in academic fora. The codes and metaphors that Kamau imposed on the interpretation of history, were viewed as obfuscation by some historians; while his statements on literature were mistrusted by the literati. Baugh, writing on Brathwaite's criticism stated that one had to bear in mind that Brathwaite was a poet whose poetic vision would perforce influence – (for better or worse?) his literary criticism.[51]

Thus, while at one level Brathwaite was much acclaimed (the readings, the admiring applause, the fascinated females at home and abroad, the proliferation and maybe profligacy of the muses and of Brathwaite himself [See the *Zea Mexican Diary*]) at another level he was regarded as an odd-ball crack-pot poet; jack of all spades; too black in an age where negritude had gone out of date and marvellous realism had become the current fad. Kamau was also too polemical, too simple, too complicated; not sufficiently lyrical, too rhetorical, but lacking Césaire's violent energy;

too prosaic, too African or too fakedly so [Jean D'Costa on Kamau's (mis)use of African words, phrases, concepts in *Masks*, a fake poem about a fake return][52] too talkative (Dash).

Brathwaite's reactions were extreme, at times a trifle paranoid; certainly mistrustful of the praise that he in fact cherished and needed, for it was on such praise that his carefully guarded Ego depended for its nurture. Here lies the crux of the problem: the Ego is dependent on the Eye of the Other for appreciation; for an acclaim that needed to be continuous and uncritical. Such an Ego is obviously vulnerable in a land which, as I said earlier, is strenuously involved in its own collective and exclusive self-affirmation, and is unconcerned with the special needs of the Stranger. Such an Ego is doubly vulnerable among similarly self-obsessed egos, all insecure, but most with their base of comfort, their centre of complacency fairly stable.

How will Eddie survive here without Doris? He's living in a remote place – more remote conceptually than in reality. Irish Town is about 40 minutes' drive from Campus. He'll need to make himself or his base more accessible. Doris used to function as a sociable alter-ego who brought out the warm communicable 'other side' of today's morose – (Dash terms his Kingston Poems 'morbid') Kamau.

Grieving at the devastation I see in his face, the uncertainty for the first time of his eyes, the fragility of his hands, I think he should quit this scene altogether, since he clearly is unable to cope with it. To cope will require toughness, not a dependence on acclaim; a better or resigned grasp of one's own life as one slides down the nether curve of the sun's arc into darkness, not hope that any other person will, as Doris used to do, bring order to one's chaos of documents and one's creative rage.

Such was the notebook prelude of July 1987 to what eventually became a Conference Paper in Middlemay 1988. In Letter #102, KB – GR, 22nd May, 1988, Kamau thanked me for the Conference Paper, "Brathwaite with a Dash of Brown."

It kinda unlocked locks, etc. since I never thought anyone wd. NOTICE what Dash had done, far less comment on it! And of course, you went far beyond 'comment' into another example to us all on how to treat our literature with generosity, respect, and a widening sense of whole/soul. This also there in yr, Guyana awards address (i.e. "Trophy and Catastrophe; An Address" *Kyk-Over-Al*, 38, 13-22, June 1988 and *Caribbean Quarterly*, 36(4): 1-8, December 1991)[53] a tremendous journey between three worlds. And I thank you for it.

He had for some time been proposing a *Savacou* print of Rohlehr essays, though he'd heard that Karia Press was on the verge of publishing an anthology of these. Karia never delivered, nor did Hansib, a Guyanese-owned publishing house in the UK which had, via David Dabydeen, received a batch. Longman/Lexicon Caribbean would eventually publish two collections four years later; *My Strangled City & Other Essays* and *The Shape of That Hurt and other Essays* (1992). [Revised and republished by Peepal Tree Press, second decade, new Millennium].

If Kamau eventually thanked me for what I wrote in "Brathwaite with a Dash of Brown", he could not agree with my advice that he leave Jamaica or learn to live in isolation from an academic community that he deeply mistrusted and from which he was in fact disconnected. In Letter #105, KB – GR, Mona Dept. of History, 5th July, 1987, he confessed that his trip to London of late October, 1986 had left him fearful of being on the verge of a stroke or heart attack. He needed "someone who will take me through the whole thing." But "there is nobody, nobody, no body."

He expressed doubts about my recommendation that he should rely on no one and try to grow a shell against his vulnerability.

> I am a great one for 'community' Is not just a writer's concept with me. Is what gave birth to the sort of CAM we had/and what has prevented me from attempting a Caribbean CAM. It helped me wonderfully to sustain this ideal, even though it was intimately different in Ja/with the kind of 'abrasions' you described. But without this sense, this hope, I will have nothing, I can't really go into myself, The 'easy people' which now seems like everybody think that I am already 'into myself alone' by going up to Irish Town. But IT is only a retreat & base for the writing/ or it was with D.

He couldn't "create a new base" as I had suggested, and wasn't sure that if he tried to do this he'd end up with a satisfactory alternative to what he had at present. In Letter #106, KB – GR, 8th July, 1987 he went beyond stating his reluctance to leave Irish Town and provided positive reasons why he intended to remain there.

> Woke up ts morning to look full down into the sun in the green bowl of the valley and realize now I remember now why you spoke about the taciturn, hostile, alien landscape. I do not see it, feel it this way. I *love* it here. Perhaps in the silence, it is the nearest I seem(?) here to Mile & Quarter of *Boy & the Sea*.[54]

> I would prefer to *wait* here and hope to *continue* here and if I can survive towards(?) that hope. What I need is help, practical help, moral support, and some love. What frightens me and stuns me is the lack of those things, Pain(?) the total neglect.

---

xviii. See *Anales de las Americas* #10, 1990, 247-253.

If I *withdraw* as you advise, all the honey of creation will withdraw with me. No – not that, my friend. Not that.

I couldn't remember telling him that the *landscape* was "taciturn, hostile and alien." It was he that had written about the hostility of the villagers who saw him as an intruder living in "a grudgeful great house".[55] But forgetting that, Kamau seemed to be relating nostalgically to the landscape which reminded him of his boyhood in Barbados and his grandfather's farm.

Nature, however, showed her other side when Hurricane Gilbert struck Jamaica almost exactly two years after Doris's death. Kamau, despite his mistrust of American Fulbright students in the Caribbean whom he suspected of being CIA agents, willingly accepted his second one-year Fulbright award between 1987 and 1988, but was back in Jamaica and domiciled at his Irish Town home when Hurricane Gilbert struck. The experience of Gilbert is harrowingly explored in "*Shar.*"[xviii]

Kamau's hurricane attacks first the rootedness of things: fixed established ceiba/cumacka/silk-cotton trees, mythical homes of ancestors and some of the last remaining links to Africa. The hurricane sounds like an immense buzzsaw, chopping limbs, snapping trunks. It chews up galvanize, alu-zinc, the most modern of roofing, as easily as it devours things ancestral. It attacks the very idea of home as it invades the innermost recesses of great house or shanty: bedroom, study, archives. It attacks dreams as the poet lies prone on his sodden bed staring at the spaces where once the roof was and seeing only rotten rafters.

It negates millennia of trans-Saharan journey. It releases the worst and the best – bandits daring the landslides to loot the helpless ruin, and the stoical voices of the poor that via song still can, if not hope, insistently affirm. In one version of *Shar*, the voice of the singing Muse is that of his niece, who dies young.

Such was the poem. There was, however, no such reconciliation in other accounts of the ravages of Hurricane Gilbert. In Letter #197, KB – Vice Chancellor, UWI, 18th November, 1988, Brathwaite described his partially successful fund-raising in the USA for stricken Jamaica sufferers. He stressed that he did not want any of the money he'd raised to be spent towards the rehabilitation of his Irish Town 'Archives' but suggested to the Vice Chancellor "that the Irish Town situation shd be tackled as part of the UWI Rehab Redev Project." The Vice Chancellor connected KB with "Michael Paty of the UNDP attached to UWI" who agreed to visit the IT site on Monday, 21st November, 1988.

KB asked the University to undertake "the entire Irish Tn operation since it is too much of an awesome act of the God of Nature for me to undertake financially, managerially and as a lecturer having to continue the life of a full teaching & research load (14 contact hours per week, not to mention prep of lectures for 2 courses and the correction/discussion of papers for some 200 students.")

KB then itemized what needed to be done: elaborate damage from rainwater and landslide, roof blown off by Gilbert; need to clear access road (track) to main road. The archives were in KB's opinion, crucial to the culture.

> there can be no culture without that care & accumulation, the collection and classification of some of the things that were said, thought and expressed in the time frame each one of us was fortunate to be in.

Hurricane Gilbert was Brathwaite's second catastrophe, one that injected reality into his romantic/idyllic vision of the IT landscape with its endearing prospect of green valleys. Now he had begun to accept that

> No culture can be built on these kinds of landslip, landslide. But I am prepared to make one more effort.

He then listed what was stored in the IT 'Archives' – an amazing/ attractive list of items whose steady diminishment would become the subject/theme of his repeated lamentations over the next three decades. KB regarded as priority a complete descriptive inventory of these IT resources, packed into the single remaining roofed room of his home; a damp leaking place whose wall was built into/against the mountainside. The roof of this room, "growing weary of the struggle against the elements, is beginning to groan & gape its way upwards towards the sky like its ripped brothers have already done."

Brathwaite said that he had had offers "from various centres abroad, for the sale & therefore transfer of some of my material, & since Gilbert, you will appreciate that there has been renewed interest if not pressure." He was disturbed that there had been no offers from either UWI or the Jamaican Institute.

> In any case, Zea & I had visioned this place here at Irish Town as developing into a Caribbean Research Archive Centre & after she died I continued working towards this in her memory – when like the hurricane lick me down but not out – let me tell you.

One significant feature of KB's letter to the Vice Chancellor was its revelation of the variety of 'agencies' with which Kamau had had dialogue.

> Ford, Harvard, Yale, the Caribbean Artists Movement, the U of Phil, the Am Antique Soc, Kent, Warwick, Liège among others.

It seems that KB's extensive and continuous travels had given him a kind of global reach. His poetry, his ideas, cultural paradigms, seemed to have made greater impact internationally than at home where, like his bardic voice in "Kingston in the Kingdom of This World" (1975) he remained awaiting the recognition and respect of his imagined community. His letter, then, was a challenge directed at the leadership of the UWI empire, to heed his sermon.

"Meantime, I need somewhere to live," he declared. This problem was temporarily solved, but not by UWI.

> The Consortium/Ford Foundation, in order to enable me to teach this first term with them, have provided me with three months accommo in Kingston: Nov [88] to January '89.

This is how he came to reside in Marley Manors, the site of his third catastrophe in 1990. In Letter #109, 4th March, 1990, he informed me that AJ Seymour* had died and Aubrey Williams, Guyana's great painter and early member of CAM was "gravely ill." He also thanked me "for that phone call to Barbados on my father's funeral."

In Item #110 he sent me an early version of *Trench Town Rock*, first written in 1990, then republished in *Hambone* 10, Spring, 1991, and reformatted for Lost Road Publishers, No. 40, Providence 1994. Lost Roads advertised *Trench Town Rock* as KB's reconstruction of

> his incendiary, book length poem ... An apocalyptic palimpsest of Jamaican experience, Caribbean patois, topographical expressionism, and documentary accounts of terrifying violence and injustice.

Trench Town Rock, in fact, documented the final of the *trilogy of catastrophes* (my term) which convinced KB that it was time to resign from Mona and put distance between himself and Jamaica.

Trench Town Rock begins with a narrative about the murder of a security guard on 16th July 1990, whose body is discovered at the guard hut of Marley Manors. Brathwaite, who is awakened by two gunshots and a volley of seven, does not witness the murder but undertakes writing a fictional reconstruction of what he imagines has taken place. He adopts the persona of a newspaper reporter familiar with the wider context of urban violence in which this murder at Marley Manors is just another item. The *Sunday Gleaner*, [11 Nov. 1990] reveals 622 violent deaths by the end of October 1990. Another source of statistics records:

> one rape every 8 hours, 1000+ reported cases of abuse & rape last year 44 reported cases of incest all in a population just barely 2.3 plus million [Noon, 10 December, 90, JBC/TV][56]

Kamau attempts wearing the mask of Voyeur, a self-distanced alien, a carnivalesque Bookman whose object is to chronicle the statistics of dystopia; to list the dead and dying. It is a mask he shares with friends, fellow-poets and citizens who pretend an indifference to such signs of social disintegration. But Kamau is – temporarily to be sure – living at Marley Manors, and cannot mask his awareness of "the physical and psychological damage & maiming" that he has been writing about since "Good Friday 1975: Kingston in the Kingdom of This World." That poem falls into context.[57] Kingdom is now fifteen years later rendered "King*doom*", as the myth of "Dis", foretold since 1975, steadily emerged at the closure of the Millennium.

The object of KB's narrative is to shock society back into conscience and consciousness through starkness of Voice and usage, a montage of film clips, taped discourse, Isaiah-like lamentation. Reading each murder as a 'sign', KB records that the 17th August is Marcus Garvey's birthday, the same iconic day that poet Mikey Smith was stoned to death on Stony Hill. Thus, as he is awakened by the two gunshots at the guard hut of Marley Manors, his empathy with the guard, bound hands and feet and shot, and with a young dreadlock shot seven times in the chest from the 'volley' of bullets that succeeded the initial two, becomes complete. He becomes (in imagination) the victims (as Michael Dash had complained in his review of *Jah Music* and *The Visibility Trigger*). Lying in bed at Marley Manors, he worries at the meaning, not only of the gunshots and the victims, but of the silence that follows:

> but now that cry & silence & my worry for him beating in the silence,
> my heart like in my eyes of bandage & beating till it hurt as if my pain
> was his inside my head and bondage.[58]

In Chapter Four (TTR), entitled "My Turn: Foreday Morning" Wednesday October 24, 1990, Kamau narrates how he became victim and witness of what so far, he has only been able to imagine. This episode, catastrophe 3, occurs 90 days after the unsolved murders at Marley Manors. KB returns from Barbados but becomes victim of an attack by two gunmen who break into his flat, hold him up with gun and knife and tie him up with a telephone cord while ransacking his desk, suitcases and study, stealing everything that can be stolen:

> my room like the sea – the debris & litter all over the beaches – bibliography
> files & my poetry manuscript folders all trampled and curled by the
> breakers – books hit by like a hurricane – my life like torn from its moorings
> & something like spiders crawling over my faces [sic]…[59]

Brathwaite employs littoral, edge-of-the-sea imagery: storm-surge, *breakers* and the sensation of life as he used to know it on the beaches of his Barbadian boyhood now having been violently "torn from its moorings." This invasion is the ultimate violation of the concept of "home"; it signals uprootment, points to further vagrancy. Marley Manors where his monumental bibliography, *L/X* and files of new poetry lie trampled and curled, has proven to be just as perilous a refuge as the ruined Irish Town 'Great House'. Life in Jamaica has become reduced to flotsam/jetsam.

Also, KB's person has been attacked by younger men – his 'children' – who keep calling him "bway", as the generations reverse their roles and the sons rule the fathers. The line of natural succession from fathers to sons, the Akan spiritual bloodline of sunsum, kra, mogya on which the psychic balance of the nation is based has been irreparably (?) ruptured. Hence the man-versus-man, yout' versus policeman, man-versus-woman, black-on-black violence of intensifying rapes and murders. The signs of the emergence of DIS are everywhere. In "The Short History of *DIS* or Middle Passages Today," Chapter 5 of *Trench Town Rock*, Kamau itemises the worst of these signs: police boots kicking people; a youtman kicked in the face after he breaks through security at the National Stadium to congratulate Péle who has just scored a goal; man shot by a 'Supercop' outside Tom Redcam Public Library:

> the police came to 'pick him up' – he never bothered stoop down to the brother. stood there & kicked *my head* until he bashed it in, *until the kicking turned my body over.*[60]

For Kamau, an impassive Bookman recording the death, turned Shaman, amidst the silence or futile troubled conversations of newspaper, radio and television commentators, the victim's kicked-in head and body become "my head," "my body," in this current everyday ritual of sacrificial waste. The archivist and 'objective' chronicler in KB locates this barbarity in its historical context:

> Orlando Patto's Dungle of the 60s Sisyphus become the Riverton City (Kingston) Dump of 1992: an image of a city smouldering in garbage & men & women plundering that monstrous HELL of stench & detritus & death. dead rat. live rat. for bread. bone. dead rotting flesh. dead rotting fish, the decomposing contexts of yr kitchen sink & toilet bowl & latrine & what you sweep off from yr floor & doormat tabletop in greasy paper plastic bags.[61]

Chronicling, finally, an episode where a dead UWI lecturer and his female friend are found on the dump,[62] to a chorus of silence from the UWI administration and general community, Brathwaite warns that "the age of Dis, Distress, Dispair & Disrespect, Distrust, Disrupt, Distraction" has overtaken "other Caribbean countries and beyond."

> See Achebe, see Soyinka, see Biko, see Jackson, see Miroslav Holub, see The *Diary of Anne Frank*, see Sun Yet Sun, see all the Disappeared of S. America – see see *see until yu bline*.[63]

Seeing, then, can only go so far. Naipaul in *Guerillas*, *In a Free State* and *A Bend in the River*, particularly the first two, would arrive/had arrived at a similar epiphany: that of the impotence of the writer/traveller as voyeur. But what scope for action beyond voyeurism and outcry really existed? Modern Africa seemed to be very much in the situation of 'black-on-black' violence that was paralysing the post-Independence Diasporan Caribbean, South America with its entrenched guerillism and its destruction of native Amerindian habitats, and civilizations. Anne Frank's Diary pointed one backwards to Nazism and the Jewish Holocaust, and perhaps, offered perspectives of hiding, deception and love. Kamau, surveying the Jamaican manscape saw no hope in the mindless self-destruction – the violence turned inward – of black-on-black murder, which illustrated as the Twentieth Century closed only the dimensions of the prison in which Diasporans were dying:

> And like the victims of our first (that 18th Century) Middle Pass. [disappearing with] no memory of no mourning for this passage.[64]

So Kamau quits Mona and in 1991 is named Professor of Comparative Literature at New York University: a new life, one might say. His most significant communication was the copy of a letter #112, Monday, 15th June, 1992. This quite long letter was sent from Newcastle-upon-Tyne (UK) where he two days later [Letter #113, Wednesday, 17th June, 1992] explained that he had "Been over here about a month now (since c. May 20) on this Arts Council jaunt." His explanation for being in England in midsummer 1992 was that he was making some money to pay off expenses incurred since Hurricane Gilbert. He said he found it ironic to be having to scuffle in that way:

> since these are the years we had hoped to have used (by now/overdue) for my full-time writing. I really can't imagine, looking back, how i have been able for so long to achieve creative fulltime teaching ...w./creative fulltime think/writing.

He wondered at the mélange of my own activities:- Caribbean Studies Moderator, UWI, St. Augustine; Caribbean Examinations Council (CXC)

Chief Examiner (1969-1976) in English B (Literature); the publications since *Pathfinder* (1981), i.e. *My Strangled City* (1992) and *The Shape of That Hurt* (1992). He had long wanted to publish these essays of two-decades as *Savacou* essays, part of what, he had termed the '*Savacou* Debate', and grand extensions of his foundational CAM dream/scheme. He commended

> The *fabulous* body of lit crit of lit history & thought [which] earns you a most honoured place in the Caribbean pan band and my dedication of *Middle Passages* to you (yes is YOU).

He had read "Trophy and Catastrophe" and commented, "What a superb summation of what and where we are. One of your 'wisest' pieces." He was going to send me his letter to Bridget Jones,* (aforementioned as Letter #112, Monday, June 15th, 1992).

In that letter he began with the news that there was to be an ACLALS (Association of Caribbean Language and Literature Studies) Conference in Jamaica in August 1992, and bemoaned the fact that he had not (yet?) received an invitation. He had contacted Eddie Baugh who informed him that he would be informed in due course. He regarded this as a snub, considering that he, KB and John Hearne had been the main organizers of the 1971 ACLALS Conference at Mona:

> a cultural turning point in the Caribbean and I, seen as the INSTIGATOR was made to suffer for it – still am – ref BAUGH and THIS ACLALS.

Bridget Jones, an acting lecturer in the Department of English, UWI, Mona, had asked him for bibliographical data re his own work that he was only too willing to supply. He began by informing her that since 1975 he no longer used 'Edward' or 'Eddie' and that he was currently in the process of getting his name legally changed to 'Kamau'.

> There is a significant diff. between the KAMAU work and the Eddie work ... (clearly the man going WEIRD in ole age!) but there is a signif diff most noticeable from the moment when i sadly began to INSIST on the KAMAU (battles with UWI & Dept of Hist etc etc etc/which is from when Zea Mexican died. And if you look at the work from that time, starting w/X/Self (finished when she was dying) right through to TTR and the MIDDLE PASSAGES, you will, i hope see the diff.

1975 then was viewed by KB as the year when he began to change from the Eddie work to the Kamau work. This was, I found, true. I'd say the 'change' began not so much in his poetry – though *Islands* had posed some problems with its newly minted and indigenised metaphors: a score or more of them. The 'change' had begun with two lectures he delivered in 1975, one of which was later entitled "Afternoon of the Status Crow", [65] It was six years before Jurgen Martini of Bremen offered his assessment of the then still current debate about a Caribbean Aesthetic; "Literary Criticism and Aesthetics in the Caribbean I: E.K. Brathwaite."[66] Martini's main concern was with the implications of a divide opening up between Caribbean-born critics and Eurocentric ones. There were issues of autonomy and authenticity and Martini's biases lay in the same direction as Brathwaite's. While he never accounts adequately for Brathwaite's shifts of position throughout the 1970s, Martini does provide a useful overview of many of the issues that preoccupied critics of Caribbean Literature in the seventies: cultural erasure, amnesia, interculturalization, hybridity, mulatto and mestizo issues of dividedness.

Martini was the main organizer of the Conference at Bremen (1983) at which KB presented his seminal paper "Caribbean Culture: Two Paradigms."[67] Martini edited *Missile and Capsule* (1983)[68] which brought a new dimension of international (mainly European) attention to ideas that were largely ignored as eccentric by Caribbean readers and thinkers. Most of what Kamau says in "Caribbean Culture: Two Paradigms", he had already said in "The Afternoon of the Status Crow" (1975). *X/Self* drew on the Afternoon of the Status Crow/Caribbean Culture: Two Paradigms lectures and was really not the final book of KB's second trilogy, but the first of the "Kamau" as distinct from being the third poem of the second "Eddie" trilogy. Kamau severely edited *X/Self* in order to force it into the restructured framework of *Ancestors*.

Brathwaite reviewed his entire literary career from the Ghana years to the last Mona years. He listed *The Arrivants* (1973), *Black + Blues* (1976), *Ancestors* (1986), *Shar* (1990), The *Zea Mexican Diary* (1992), *Dream Stories* (1994), a work he said that "tunes into certain shall we say SORROWS within landscapes"; *Trench Town Rock* (1990, 1991, 1994) that "contains [an] account of my death in Ja"; *Middle Passages* (1991).

Responding to direct and specific queries by Bridget Jones as to his affinities to Césaire and Guillén and his connections, if any, to Haiti and Cuba, Kamau explained that apart from fragments of Césaire's *Cahier* that had appeared in *Black Orpheus* and a bilingual edition he'd acquired via John La Rose's New Beacon Bookshop, he had never read the *Cahier* "until last month at NYU" i.e. until November 1991. There were differences in structure between his own "Eliot-influenced long poem" and Césaire's *Cahier. Rights of Passage* is a succession of "parts/fragments": Césaire is like a seamless garment."

He then turns to Pat Ismond's essay in *Caribbean Quarterly*, 1981, where the invidious comparison of *Rights* and *Masks* to Césaire's *Cahier* was first made.[69] Having not properly read Rohlehr's *Pathfinder* (1981),[70] Brathwaite tells Bridget Jones[71] in 1991 that "No CRIT of Caribb lit has YET taken her to task." Brathwaite's still bitter criticism of Ismond's essay was that it was full of "self cultural insults & biases & inaccuracies"; and because it had been allowed to exist unattacked, "the INJUSTICE, the cultural insult and the insult to my work REMAINS."

Asked about his relationship with pioneers of Négritude, he said he had never met Césaire, Damas, Senghor or Janheinz Jahn nor, apart from his years in Ghana, visited West Africa. He had spent four weeks in Haiti in 1969 when he met several painters and sculptors and witnessed "real vodun in the Artibonite Valley." *Islands* had been written before his visit to Haiti, "though i might well have revised it after the visit." He began research on Toussaint in 1969 at the University of Port-au-Prince.

Asked about his acquaintance with Cuba, Brathwaite wrote that

> c. 1975 [I] went with a UWI/Mona group to Cuba; greeted by Rétamar etc. won the Casa de Las Americas prize for poetry *Black + Blues* 1976 and again in 1986 for lit. crit. (*Roots*) was at Carifesta '79 and on the Casa Premío lit. jury 1990. & there were sev other visits between 75 and 90. And of course there was Guillen's visit to Mona in 74 when I read my poem to/for him in the Assembly Hall. I read it again with Cuba trans at Carifesta 79 in Havana before a huge stadium crowd that inc. Fidel, but so late (well after midnight) that the ailing ageing Nicolas had left by then.

He also mentioned a "fruitful relationship w/Lit Dept., U of Havana & plenty tapes from Carifesta 79, but most of these stolen the night I was murdered in Ja."

The letter to Bridget Jones served the useful purpose of Brathwaite's self-location as Stranger in a new academic universe. Old hurts remained and would remain unhealed for the remainder of his life. But New York was a "semi-colon" in his restless travels up and down, back and forth through which with Doris now five years deceased, he was constructing his new base over the ruins and occasional rumblings of the old life.

One next meets him at CARIFESTA V (Trinidad & Tobago, August 1992). The Journal of CARIFESTA V, edited by librarian Pearl Eintou Springer, contains a useful tracing of the development of CARIFESTA since its beginning in Guyana in 1972. CARIFESTA 72 had remained in Brathwaite's memory as the yardstick by which he measured the development of the idea of a congregation or community of Caribbean Artists; a major aspect of the CAM dream with which KB had begun his life's mission.

What did CARIFESTA now mean after two decades? To Derek Walcott who had stayed in New York during CARIFESTA 72, CARIFESTA had never meant much.

> CARIFESTA is a cynical exploitation of West Indian artists by West Indian Governments, since they don't have a cultural policy matching the amount

of money wasted in the celebrations ... (the Festival represents two weeks of activity for artists, who are subjected to 50 weeks of inertia and indifference for the balance of the year).[72]

Since Bogata 1978, the issue of a regional, or even several national cultural policies, the UNESCO imperative, had replaced or simply overtaken the quest for a Caribbean aesthetic that had preoccupied Kamau's CAM since 1966. Designing a cultural policy suggested not just definitions or theorizing, but enactment, building and putting into operation, structures; putting ideas to work.

Walcott hadn't seen any such cultural policy emerging, and by 1991 Trinidad and Tobago had become mired in a huge attempt, the third or fourth since Independence in 1962 – to design a cultural policy statement for critical discussion in parliamentary committees. CARIFESTA 1992 was the attempt to put together the ideas of artists and practitioners (eg, Leroi Clarke,* Earl Lovelace* and a score of others); another group working directly with the Minister of Culture; Margaret Walcott,* Derek's former wife, whose job was to read and sort out correspondence from the public as to how they thought CARIFESTA should be shaped; and a group of financiers and business people who, surfacing late, appeared nonetheless to be the driving force beneath the hoped-for festival.

The Muslimeen Coup of 1990 took centre stage a few days after a meeting of all these groups with Prime Minister Arthur Napoleon Robinson. This meeting was the first time all the organisers of CARIFESTA had come together or, in some cases, even heard of the existence of each other. There was, naturally, much confusion and some anger.

After the Coup, CARIFESTA was substantially scaled down. Efebo Wilkinson was called home from CARICOM to organize the festival. Eintou Springer was made coordinator of the Symposium. Margaret Walcott's work was largely ignored, as if to illustrate the correctness of Derek Walcott's acerbic comment since 1981.

So CARIFESTA 1992 – (the original 1991 date had had to be abandoned) – was nothing like CARIFESTA 1972. Kamau Brathwaite was lodged in the Hilton; but either without, or unaware of the sort of VIP access to travel that he had enjoyed in 1972. CARIFESTA 1992 was for him a disappointment, though his "The New Aesthetic and the Nature of Culture in the Caribbean: the Dream Coming in with the Rain", received much praise as one of the keynote addresses.[73]

In the version of this address which appeared in the *Proceedings of the CARIFESTA V Symposium*, August, 1992, Brathwaite began by describing his task as one of compressing a three or four-hour paper into a half hour presentation. What he achieved was an overview of impediments that had barred progress in the articulation of a Caribbean aesthetic. Providing his own working definition of a Caribbean aesthetic as:

a critical communal sense of the essence of one's culture which would involve our awareness of style and how that style became style…

Brathwaite curiously identified all sorts of reasons why, despite four CARIFESTAS since 1972 and multiple conferences on culture, no true aesthetic had emerged.

Barriers against such emergence lay in

(1) a 'remarkably fragmented' history beginning in the genocide of indigenous Amerindian peoples within three decades of Columbus's arrival;
(2) the catastrophic genesis of the landscape itself over 500,000 years;
(3) slavery, predation, erasure as historic continuation of catastrophe, leading to uncertainty about identities and relayed violence in social evolution;
(4) abundant evidence of creativity, yet failure to understand or assess the quality of what the fragmented islands and what their indigenous and indigenized folk have created;
(5) miseducation: resulting in ignorance of landscape and the meaning of our residence on earth, indifference to and disrespect of environment;
(6) easy exploitability by metropoles;
(7) insularity, absence of viable systems of communication, both within and between island communities.

Brathwaite's paper dwelt on these failures (that is, the things that had sent him into this new phase of exile) rather than on the growth of agencies of healing, redress and regional reparation since CARIFESTA '72 and the foundational CAM of the mid-sixties. What redeemed this gloomy retrospective address was Kamau's superb performance of "Angel/ Engine" from his *Mother Poem*. The "Proceedings of the Seminars" derived its name from the last line of "Angel/Engine",[74] a poem about ritual reconnection with submerged ancestral energies that Kamau believes survived the Middle Passage. Recognition of these buried presences, Brathwaite had, against all odds believed, was the beginning of cultural reclamation and building.

This was a fitting conclusion to KB's central text of the thirty years since his return journey across the Middle Passage from Ghana to the Antilles. Yet it did not quite address the cultural exigencies of the contemporary Caribbean, where the tide (tidalectics?) of discourse had changed from the original concern with defining an aesthetic to the current post-Bogota 1978 UNESCO concern with designing a regional cultural policy for the

Caribbean and Latin America. Kamau's old and never-to-be-abandoned preoccupation with the location of Africa in both diasporan and world history had been 'replaced' by the more immediate need of all the fragmented ethnic communities to rewrite histories and relocate identities in the newly independent and emerging 'post colonial' nations. Indeed, the very word 'nation' had become a space for the confrontation of antagonistic ethnic groups and class and colour formations, each with its own sense of 'aesthetic', its own notion of the shape of things to come, and its own thrust towards power, authority and domination, in a context where the market-driven cultures of the globalised world were blindly pursuing new versions of old cultural dominance and identity erasure.

Item #116 is entitled "Programme for Saturday, October 24, 1992, *North South Counterpoint, Kamau Brathwaite and the Caribbean Word*, Hostos Community College, 475 Grand Concourse, New York. This Conference/Symposium that was taking place just two months after Carifesta V, August 1992, was in many respects, the first attempt in the year of Columbus's Quincentennial, to locate Brathwaite in the new North American context of a meeting of the various diasporan communities of the Caribbean and Latin America.

The occasion was organised by Silvio Torres-Sailliant,* a Dominican Professor of Literature who had been previously commissioned by the Phelps-Stokes Fund in 1977 to arrange an interface between Caribbean and mainly African American scholars that culminated in an exchange of experiences and ideas at the Catholic University in Santiago, Dominican Republic. This Symposium at Hostos Community College brought together a similarly cosmopolitan assembly of scholars and artists who spent an entire day discussing Kamau's ideas and achievements. Here, one might say, Kamau and things Kamau had more than thirty minutes, more time to "see the fragments/whole" than he was allowed two months earlier at CARIFESTA V.

The list of contributors included Robert Stewart* of Trinity School; Reinhard Sander,* University of Pittsburgh; Terrence Julien,* La Guardia Community College; Joan Dayan,* University of Arizona; Barbara Webb,* Hunter College; June Bobb,* Queen's College, CUNY; Lawrence Breiner,* Boston U; Mary Morgan,* Kamau's sister, Registrar UWI, Mona; Tom Dent,* Poet, organizer of New Orleans Jazz and Heritage Festival, Civil Rights Activist; Marina Maxwell,* Michigan State U; Elaine Savory Fido,* NYU; Ngugi wa Thiongo,* NYU; Edouard Glissant;* Hollis Liverpool* (calypsonian Chalkdust); Cynthia James,* Andrew Salkey, Lorna Goodison,* Fred D'Aguiar,* Linton Kwesi Johnson.*

This collection of scholars and artists, each with his or her significant dossier of achievement in Caribbean Studies – cultural historians, literary critics, musicians, novelists, poets, all contributors to various elements of new polemical discourse – was an illustration of KB's 'global reach' and following. I delivered the Keynote Address. Kamau spoke on "Caribbean Words" recounting for yet another time the catastrophes that had driven him out of the Caribbean and how the trauma of Hurricane Gilbert especially had reshaped his writing: i.e. *Dream Stories*, the *Zea Mexican Diary*, *Middle Passages*, *Trench Town Rock*, *Shar*. He described Doris's death and the experience of having lived through Hurricane Gilbert and the destruction of his archives as having left him

> in the middle of a rift valley of grief that had to become surreal & the magical realism of *Dream Stories* – the first such contrib. in my contents & the first, it seems to me, looking around, in anglophone Caribb. lit.

'*Magical Realism*' was one of the new areas of discourse that had grown current at UWI during KB's latter days there. Already reeling from Michael Dash's taunt that he had become one of Samuel Beckett's absurd characters from *Waiting for Godot* or the trilogy of novels, who spoke excessively and repetitively because they feared their own inner voids and had nothing new to say, Brathwaite was eager to show that he was, in fact, pioneering into new modes. *Magical Realism* was one of these. KB's wrestle with *MR* had started more than a decade before the 1990s when it first came into public attention.[75]

In Item #83, KB – GR, May 1983 was an overview of the development of West Indian Literature from "the literature of settlement" 1640-1840, through colonial writing (1840-c. 1940) and "the literature of decolonization (c. 1900 -)." The overview was entitled "Firstword". Brathwaite explained that he was not attempting

> a comprehensive history or critical survey of Caribbean Literature in English ... [but] simply one man's record of his growing up in the literature, and growing up with it, not as lover and reader only; certainly not as critic and academic, but as committed participant.

KB then proceeded to evaluate his eight years in Ghana which he said provided him "with the kind of de-education which would result in the poetry since *Rights of Passage* (1967) and *Masks* (1968)" and inspire his "building towards an understanding of *home*: counterpoint to exile."

In this "building towards an understanding of home" he was inspired to write "Jazz and the West Indian Novel"[76] which he now in 1983 called "*the most controversial probe I'd yet attempted.*" There was, in other words, much that was uncertain and open to scrutiny in Kamau's intuitive linking of the

---

xix. KB is quoting Abel Enrique Prieto, *Reason for Being: an Introduction to Carpentier' Thinking Granma*, 24 August 1980, p.5.

African-American revolution in rhythm and sound (Jazz) and the Afro-Caribbean naissance through the explosion of literature in the years since World War II.

> For the first time I was moving from literary criticism in the sense of 'giving marks' in CLR James's phrase, to trying to see *why* these 'things on the page' were the way they were. Did they have a shape, a style; and assuming that they all came out of the same or similar psycho-physical experience, did they (if not why not) similarly express, at least in essence, this shaped experience? In other words, I was beginning to talk about *aesthetics*: the notion of a way of seeing that Lamming had introduced in *The Pleasures of Exile* (1960) and Wilson Harris had raised in "Tradition and the West Indian Novel" ([1964] London: New Beacon, 1967).

He next compared the 'position' that had begun to emerge in his own thinking with Alejo Carpentier's* notion of a *mestizo* aesthetic where "all symbiosis, all intermixture begets the baroque" and "the baroque appears where there is transformation, mutation, innovation... It can be the culmination just as it can be the premonition."[xix]

Kamau was being confronted with the difference between Latin American mestizo aesthetics and his own emerging Afro-centred mulattismo. He never, of course, admitted that what he called "Creole Négritude" was a variety of what I would come to call "mulattitude." Mulattitude in the Anglophone Caribbean tended (cf Walcott) to deny the African ancestor. Kamau's aesthetic worked in the opposite direction by stressing the African component that he saw as base and matrix of Creole sensibility. Yet Kamau, whose Creole négritude was as much a controversial "probe" as his theory about "Jazz and the West Indian Novel" or the connection between the burning of Rome and the beginning of slavery [cf *X/Self*, "Rome burns and our slavery begins"[77]], intuited or imagined an affinity between his "Jazz" and Carpentier's Baroque."

> I like to think that my *jazz* and Carpentier's *baroque* are about the same thing: product/process of interculturation/symbiosis. It is certainly what my writing: prose, poetry, academic, literary, historical: I can make no distinction: has been increasingly about. '*Brother Mais*' (1974) indicates the first *nativization* of the aesthetic, while "The African presence", "The Love axe/l" and "Nation Language" provide the kind of specific examinations which indicate, I hope, that the concern has some root, some grounation, ... some hope.

Such then was Kamau's explanation of the origin of his central thesis of "Creole négritude" even as he observed the abandonment of the concept of negritude in the francophone Caribbean of Césaire, Damas and Depestre who had in their different ways inspired its birth. His 'probe' into the new area of Magical/Marvellous Realism would win him another Casa de las

Americas Award, but *MR* would have to contend with several other parallel discourses that KB almost in consternation itemised in "Firstword." There were:

> plural society" [a hardy perennial] 'creole society', 'plantation model', New World', 'Puerto Rican model', 'Federation' [long departed, yet hanging around, zombie-like], 'Fidelismo' etc.

There was also the Development of Caribbean Studies with Caribbean Literature appended as a sort of tolerated addendum during annual Conferences of the Association of Caribbean Studies. Caribbean Studies produced concepts such as:

> 'plot' as opposed to 'plantation', 'guerilla', cultural gorilla, 'native', 'natty dread', 'dialectic', 'black' (bongo, Bantu), 'folk', 'ital', 'conscious', 'grounds' [root; rhizome; repeating islands].

Kamau survived in this world of multiplying concepts by standing his ground, improvising, creating new concepts – e.g. the notion of 'tidalectics' which caught on though it was just as dubious as earlier KB formulations. As we have seen, he quarrelled a great deal against 'enemies', some of whom actually liked him. He fought many battles that he could not win. While he deeply and sometimes eternally resented negative responses to anything he wrote or said, he tended to take for granted positive responses and often complained, even in the face of all the words I'd written on behalf of his words, that no one had been giving him the attention or respect due to his Sisyphean efforts.

In October 1992, the Nobel Committee requested that I submit a recommendation for Brathwaite who was being considered for the Nobel Prize for the year 1992 – the year that Derek Walcott won the prize (and the battle for world recognition that had for years been taking place between these two super-antagonists). I would again be approached by the Nobel Committee in subsequent years though my testimonials on Kamau's behalf proved unsuccessful.

In 1994, the year when *Dream Stories* was published by Longman and *Barabajan Poems* by Savacou North (i.e. Kamau himself), Brathwaite won the Neustadt International Prize for Literature.[78] The achievement of that award was regarded by some as a stepping stone to the Nobel. *World Literature Today* vol. 68, no. 4 (Autumn 1994), 662-774, contained the most substantial acknowledgement of Kamau's literary achievement to date. Mary Morgan's (Kamau's sister's) "Highway to Vision: the Sea Our Nexus," a paper she had read at the Hostos Symposium two years earlier, signalled that whatever fissure had in 1986 opened up to divide the Brathwaite family, was now healed. "Highway to Vision" was an account of Brathwaite's childhood in the Round House and on Brown's Beach. It counterpointed Kamau's vision of landscape and seascape in *Mother Poem* and *Sun Poem* and was graced by ten portraits from the family album that provided, as nothing else could, images of Kamau's father, mother, grandfather, great uncle, Kamau at 2 yrs (1932), Kamau, Mary and the Round House.[79]

The editors of *World Literature Today* took great pains to locate Kamau in his Barbadian background. The 'Salutation' was rendered by His Excellency Dr. Rudi Webster, Ambassador of Barbados to the United States, who ended his Salutation thus:

> Professor Brathwaite, you are a great human being and a genius in your profession. On behalf of the Government and people of Barbados I salute you and offer you my heartfelt congratulations on your award of the Neustadt Prize.[80]

This was a huge moment that marked the 'international scope' of Brathwaite's achievement even as it affirmed his rootage in Barbados. Kamau's self-anchorage in Africa was signalled by the presence of Ghanaian scholar, Kofi Awoonor who was also one of the Neustadt judges. The keynote address was delivered by Ngugi wa Thiongo (whose grandmother had served as Muse/Priestess at Kamau's naming ceremony in Kenya).[81]

In 1995 the University of the West Indies, Cave Hill, conferred an Honorary Doctorate on KB. Diasporan par excellence, he was also endowed with an Honorary Doctorate by Tougaloo College, Mississippi. Then on August 24th, 1995, Brathwaite received the Carifesta VI Award for Literature, in the Central Bank Auditorium, Port-of-Spain. Brathwaite's award was one of several that bounteous Trinidad conferred on that occasion. Other Awardees were Martin Carter, George Lamming Earl Lovelace, Derek Walcott, Vidia Naipaul, Sylvia Wynter and Moonsammy [Ernest Moutousammy],* a Martiniquan writer totally unknown to the Anglophone Caribbean.

I thought that Trinidad, eager to compensate for what many considered to have been a 'substandard' Carifesta V in 1992, was in Carifesta VI overreaching by honouring everyone they could think of, and a danger existed of dishonouring honorees even in the delirium of honouring them. At the request of the honouring committee, I researched, wrote and delivered four of these commendations: Brathwaite's, Lamming's, Carter's and Lovelace's. As it turned out, the event was a great success and I was proud to have written those commendations, one or two of which were later published in *Caricom Perspectives*.

During the latter half of the 1990s, Kamau kept responding to the constant pull of 'home'. He had already mythologised the Barbados of his childhood in *Mother Poem* and *Sun Poem*. In vacation months he had begun 'sharing' his island with groups of NYU students who saw firsthand Brown's Beach, the steeple of the Roman Catholic Church (the holy carbolic church) peeping over the centre of Round House. He also took them to see the fierce windswept Eastern coast of Bathsheba. One or two of my colleagues in the English Department Cave Hill steupsed at the notion of Kamau as tourist guide and at his romanticising of landscape.

Between 1997 and 2000, Brathwaite had all but returned home. He had purchased a home 'out by the airport' that he called Cowpastor. He had also married Beverley Reid, his Jamaican housekeeper during the Irish Town years. He served on the Barbados Government Commission on Racial Inequality and Reconstruction. During that same period, there arose a hiatus in my correspondence with KB; though I do remember having been in Barbados in one of his early Cowpastor years, and having been driven around in his mini-moke to Brown's Beach. Then in April 1998, I received a letter #117, KB – GR, Tuesday, April 21, 1998.

He had resumed what he now called *LX* (*the Love Axe/l* of yore). It had become an expanding bibliography and he wanted data about my research student, Timothy Crichlow's thesis (1981) on Norman Cameron; the date of Victor Questel's* first appearance in *Tapia*, data on "Sparrow and the Language of Calypso", "Sparrow as Poet", "Literature and the Folk", "The Creative Writer in West Indian Society", – and other things that he had already acquired, but may have misplaced during his North/South peregrinations. He also wanted a "short list of Xpat novels slumming in the WI."

A short letter, full of great demands, #117 was sent from Cowpastor and was a summary of #118, a longer letter written since 7th April, 1998 and making the same requests. From #118 I learned that KB was due back in New York in September, 1998. This was why he was currently struggling to finish *LX* before September. The reason for his request was that "all my precious ACLALS material perish at IT in Gilbert." He wanted many things: data on the connection between Derek Walcott and VS Naipaul; data on the Trinidad & Tobago Theatre Workshop's performance of *Odale's Choice*;[82] data on Williams and C.L.R. James after the return of James in the 1960s; the *Tapia* fire; Pat Bishop's* thesis; the history of *MOKO* that I'd sent long ago; Ken Ramchand's date of birth and the title of his thesis; my articles and books of kaiso.

LX then, had become an effort to repair the breach(es) left by the catastrophes of the 1980s – to fill the gap between the CAM and Mona days and the New York days; to restore as much as possible of what he had lost and imagined I would still have; to reclaim, rebuild and sacralise 'home'. But there was a great deal of new forgetting taking place, even as he re-rooted himself at Cowpastor. And there was the ambivalence of *Ancestors*

---

xx. See *Barabajan Poems*, 1994, 11.

which linked into a trilogy the remembered time of *Mother Poem* and *Sun Poem* and the new journeyings and style of *X Self* – what KB had termed in his letter to Bridget Jones "the Eddie poems" and "the Kamau poems." *LX* was trying to be the ever-expanding archive of everything, changing shape and fonts and creating a Kamau hieroglyph that at times seemed to make difficult what it thought it was clarifying.

In 1999 I delivered the Central Bank of Barbados distinguished lecture: the Sir Winston Scott Memorial Lecture. It was entitled "George Lamming, Kamau Brathwaite: Nationalists, Caribbean Regionalists, Internationalists"[83] and tried to cover how they rendered their island 'home' and birthplace, their self-location as citizens of the Caribbean Archipelago, and how they envisaged themselves and their ideas as relevant contributors to wider international discourse. It was a tall order to compare the careers and polemic of two such artists in a forty-minute address to nodding Friday evening elders. But, as with Carifesta VI, things worked themselves out, and I received for my effort a set of mint silver coins and two small clocks set in crystal – two, because my wife had accompanied me on this venture.

Kamau was in Barbados at Cowpastor, but was, initially, reluctant to attend. He seemed to be apprehensive and suspicious – something like the UWI Mona syndrome. The thing was puzzling, for was this not "home" in a way that Jamaica had seemed only partially to have been? On enquiry I learned that Brathwaite had been engaged in a duel with Barbados officialdom over a choice of the Cowpastor site for a home. Developers and landscapers were in the process of bulldozing the area to construct a golf course – (Gulf curse Kamau called it) – as part of a tourism project. He had years before grumbled that "the hotels are squatting on my metaphors" and this was a deadly example of that quip. So Kamau's Barbados "homecoming" had begun to present as many problems as his departure from Jamaica a decade earlier, and Kamau was as stubborn in his resistance. Paradoxically, he was serving on the Barbados Government's Commission on Racial Inequality and Reconciliation: i.e. he was a servant of the same officialdom that he was fighting over the Cowpastor issue.

It was both this, and what he saw as his family's non-acceptance of Beverley, that made him suspicious of all public events, including even the Central Bank's Open Lecture, to which he had himself previously (2nd December 1987) contributed the Twelfth Sir William Scott Memorial Lecture.[xx] As I remember it, Kamau did attend my address and was very pleased to have attended.

Notebook #12: Sunday, January 09, 2000
I spent the first half of the Millennium Year, 2000 as a visiting professor to Stephen F Austin University in an East Texas town called Nacogdoches,

a quiet, pleasant, but quite isolated place, 150 miles north of Houston and ninety miles south south west of Shreveport Louisiana. I had arrived early in January, when rain and chilly temperatures kept me confined to my room and forced me to begin reading the four or five draft theses that I had brought up from Trinidad, three of which were studies on different aspects of Brathwaite's work. Relaxation took the form of afternoon walks around the Campus and its environs and listening to music, particularly such music as seemed to be exploring aspects of Black identity and African-American self-location in America.

Notebook #12: Thursday, 13th January, 2000
My post was officially entitled "Special Visiting Professor for Promotion of Better Understanding of Race, Ethnicity and Gender" and it was due to run between January 6th and May 15th, 2000, with a Spring break in March. The calypso course attracted only four students, who de-registered from it on the first day. The literature course, which was structured to encourage the parallel reading of Caribbean and African-American texts, was more successful, though it wasn't easy to get the students to recognize points of contact between the two African diasporan situations.

This was partly because they did not recognize links between their own present and past. The emerging notion of artists as being the channels between the current generations and the ancestors, was negated by the discontinuity between the current post-modern generation and all that had gone before. My Nacogdoches literature class had never heard of "Steal Away to Jesus". Not even the three Black ones. It was pointless suggesting that when the singer says "My Lord He calls me, He calls me by the thunder," he or she might be referring to Ogun or Shango disguised under the Bible's Hebraic imagery. The students had, however, heard about the Underground Railroad, where it was common practice to employ spirituals as codes of communication, vehicles of rebellion.

No one knew who Caliban was, he who had become a central figure/metaphor in post-colonial literary discourse, though when I started to tell the plot of *The Tempest* there were a few vague nods of acquiescence. The class hadn't heard of Zora Neale Hurston,* a major connection between the Southern plantation and the Caribbean via both her novels and her pioneer work as an anthropologist. They seemed to have suffered terribly from Derek Walcott's "deep amnesiac blow", yet, happily, they did not know that they were suffering, because they had grown up under another 'norm'.

Something had wiped out everything – besides maybe, Oprah – or somebody wasn't putting anything that was solidly and meaningfully 'Black diasporan', in place. There in Nacogdoches was the same discontinuity that characterised Caribbean life and sensibility; the same near-absolute disjunction between generations, which meant that linkages, Brathwaite's great endeavours, "the constant... and consistent fabric and praxis" of his work, could never be assumed to exist, but had over and over to be taught. It was like me asking my own students at St. Augustine two years previously "Who was Uriah Butler?" No one knew except one girl, an exchange student who had been prepped, but who subsequently died, probably under the weight of such strange and unusual knowledge.

Though I regretted the loss of the Calypso course, I was glad for the space I had gained to read five or six masters and doctoral dissertations, the 'UWI work' that had accompanied me on this safari to the oldest town in Texas. Among these were two MPhils and one Phd thesis on Kamau Brathwaite, ie: Althea Kaminjolo, "The Trilogies of Edward Kamau Brathwaite as Post-Colonial Discourse"; Paula Ellis, "Nation-Builders in the Works of Kamau Brathwaite," and Darren Gaunt, "Mother and Sun: Reading Brathwaite's *Mother Poem* and *Sun Poem*". Kaminjolo and Ellis were MPhils, supervised by me at UWI St. Augustine, while Gaunt was a PhD candidate from Flinders University of South Australia. Reading these theses helped deepen my insight into the expanding Brathwaite narrative, his complicated modes of telling, and his metaphors that, originating in landscape, history and myth, kept growing in complexity over the decades of his saying.

During the semester break, I spent ten intense days travelling in and out of Nacogdoches, first to Jamaica, to sit on the panel of examiners for Curdella Forbes,* who argued that a 'gendered' reading of West Indian literature could transform both perception of neglected, 'invisible' female authors and overvalued (?) patriarchal male ones. Her main focus was on Lamming's and Selvon's novels. I travelled to Jamaica via Shreveport and returned to Nacogdoches via Miami and New Orleans where I renewed my acquaintance with sounds, tastes and the vibrancy of Black celebration that was entirely absent from my temporary 'home' across the extensive swamp that separated East Texas from the very similar Louisiana landscape. New Orleans was recovering from the recently celebrated Mardi Gras, but that city of festivals, so similar to multiethnic carnivalesque Trinidad, was now celebrating St Patrick's Day when the Irish reaffirm their presence and the colour is green, not the gold, green and purple of Mardi Gras. As I moved in my bubble towards Jackson Square with its acrobats, jugglers, portrait painters, palm readers and houses with bold colours of yellow, pink, blue, ochre, I could hear the river-boats playing their steam-whistle melodies of smiling Irish eyes and four-leaf clovers...

Notebook #12: Saturday, 25th March, 2000

xxi. *MOKO*, 16 & 17: June 6th & 10th, 1969.

I returned to Nacogdoches from New Orleans via Shreveport, to find an email from Kamau requesting data on Elsa Goveia. I tried to pull a few memories together out of this vault of time, place and distance. Then I received another email, from Donette Francis,* a PhD student at NYU who had been taught by Kamau. She wanted to interview me on the CAM days. Her thesis was that most West Indian scholars and artists began their quests for their Caribbean identities while in exile. Suddenly the past, which had tracked me down and sniffed me out of my bubble and meander of solitude, had become valuable to a new and dislocated generation in quest of continuity, links in the chain back to ancestors. Suddenly, like Kamau or George or Sam, I had become history.

Apart from Kamau's request and Donette's there was Clinton Hutton's email, requesting a paper on Don Drummond for a symposium that he was in the process of organising. Now Drummond, about whose career and tragic end I had written in "Sounds and Pressure",[xxi] had always been my favourite Jamaican musician – even more than Bob Marley, one of whose memorial lectures, "Me an d'Music" I had delivered at the Creative Arts Centre, Mona Jamaica on 4th February, 1999. But Clinton Hutton's request had found me with only a fortuitous handful of Drummond sounds and *none* of my notes on Jamaican music. Drummond, moreover, was pure sound; no words. What could I say about him that would warrant another return to Jamaica so soon after Curdella's oral?

Notebook #12: Thursday, 27th April, 2000
Before the scheduled date of the Drummond Symposium (May 6th, 2000) another quite tempting opportunity to escape the peaceful stasis of Nacogdoches presented itself. Markus Coester,* a researcher into Caribbean (mainly Jamaican) music stationed at the Johannes Gutenberg University, Mainz, Germany, invited me to present a paper at a Conference on "Transitional Identities" due to take place at Mainz during the last week of April 2000. Coester had interviewed me at UWI, St Augustine on 24th June, 1999, when I was impressed by his extensive knowledge of Caribbean popular music and his description of the archives of this music that existed at Johannes Gutenberg. Nothing like those archives, as far as I was aware, existed anywhere in the Caribbean: not even in the Institute of Jamaica or St Lucia Folklore Research Centre that in 1993 I had launched; not, certainly, in Trinidad and Tobago. So, I 'had was to go' to the intriguingly named Transitional Identities conference in Mainz. Besides, my sister Christina, her German husband, Uwe, and their children, my nephew Sven and niece Nicole, lived in Ulm, a few hours' train ride from Mainz. I hadn't seen them for quite some time.

The Johannes Guttenberg Universitaat, is located in a former military barracks which the occupying French converted into a university. The military severity remains in basement offices containing a printery, the Jahnheinz Jahn African collection, the Department of Ethnology. There is a sense of too little room for all the different collections that the place boasts. But there is also the sense of outreach, of a serious and quite curious embrace (?) of the Other as artifact:– things Black, African; the Ska/Reggae continuum; Haiti; French West Africa, probably the entire Continent.

I asked myself why should the Germans know and seek to know more about Africa and the Caribbean than the East Texans in one-hoss Nacogdoches, the oldest city in Texas. Perhaps, landlocked, their borders crossed everyday from France, Belgium, Austria, Switzerland, the Americans kneeling on their craw, the Germans need to be open, cosmopolitan. Nacogdoches is also landlocked, but apart from the highway that they say will in a few years run from Houston clear into Canada, nothing passes willingly through Nacogdoches. Those who go there HAVE to be going there.

So the town that calls itself a city, remains absolutely insular/insula, total island in its sea of pines and over one hundred varieties of oak. Red River Radio and all the other local radio stations at Lufkin, Shreveport, Grambling University Texas, help preserve the insula from the threat of cosmopolitanism. For though the immensely popular Mexican cuisine is both available and supported by the supermarkets, Hispanic culture is simply another insula, another 'island' in the cluster. These islands – there's an African-American one hidden somewhere – don't really touch each other. They are like planets, each locked into its own orbit after centuries of segregation. And although there are intersecting streets and all the evidence of rurality, there is nowhere the sense of an intimate culture of sidewalks and pavements and dining in the open spaces, the sense of conviviality that the French, and perhaps the Spaniards and Italians have given to Europe, and by extension, to stiff-assed rectilinear Germany.

Notebook #12: Friday, 28th April, 2000
On the train to Ulm I contemplated the range of 'transitional identities' that had been explored and anatomized in the first day of conference papers. E.A. Markham* discussed his adoption of multiple styles, personae and voices, including female ones, in his stories and poems. Mervyn Morris* presented a tape-assisted illustrated discourse on Louise Bennett and her descendants. Gordon Collier* outlined his project: a comprehensive annotated bibliography of Derek Walcott's prose writings: reviews of literature, painting, plays, etc. I was delighted to learn that his inspiration to undertake such monumental work had come from something I had written in the 1970s "*Savacou* Debate". I reminded the conference of

Victor Questel's bibliographies on Walcott from which – Questel deceased – scholars like Bruce King* and Robert Hamner had undoubtedly benefited.

There was a really excellent paper on Dionne Brand and there was a paper that examined autobiographies of Surinamese women decentred by migration to Holland. Dionne Brand, in turn, delivered a paper that was clear and insightful as it revealed the trauma of migration to and indigenization in Canada. Canadians, she said, had defined the landscape as wilderness, and the European presence there as constant conquest and humanization of wilderness. This meant that the entire non-European presence – especially that of Native Canadians – had been 'othered', neutered', erased, equated with a wilderness to be conquered or silenced. Some of these 'othered' groups simply faded into the landscape in two or three generations. Brand's people arrived at a place where, despite the fact of their being a substantialminority – i.e. more than 30% of Canadians – they belonged neither here nor there. Their identity lay in the fact of transition between equally inaccessible and indefinable alternatives.

There was Gilmore,* a white British-educated Barbadian who sought a place for Grainger's* poem on the sugar cane as ancestral West Indian literature. Gilmore, whose real concern was how to locate himself and his ethnic group in today's post-Independence Barbados, disputed Kamau Brathwaite's focus in *Barabajan Poems* on the works of Chapman,* who, according to Gilmore, was an even greater racist than Grainger. Questions were raised about Gilmore's reading of Brathwaite. I felt that Brathwaite, having mythologised both the Barbadian landscape and the peasantry in *Mother Poem* and *Sun Poem* was now involved mainly in mythologising and relocating himself in the vanishing landscape of his origins.

In *Barabajan Poems*[84] and *ConVersations*[85] he not only reworked autobiography but included white Bajans in his mythologised landscape. One of the 'heroes' of *Barabajan Poems* was the white man who swam around the island, nearly perished in its currents and – nice touch this – was welcomed/ received on his emergence from the water by Kamau's sister, who offered him a towel. It was a curious inclusion because Kamau was vicariously entering the body and mind of the white protagonist and appropriating his experience – i.e. treating it almost as if it were *Kamau's* experience.[86] [One may compare his self-identification with the stoned Mikey Smith,[87] or with the assassinated guard and rasta youth gunned down at the porter's lodge of Marley Manor.[88]]

There were also the two poor white women in *ConVersations*,[89] reduced to a worse penury than Miss Own in *Mother Poem*. What are these totally marginalised people doing in *ConVersations* which is, like *Barabajan Poems*, an original taped interview or lecture that is transcribed and expanded via numerous interpolations? Interpolations involve a bringing of new knowledge or concerns to the original lecture or conversation; an expansion of discourse; a 'falsification' of the text in the sense that the interpolation involves not what was said but, perhaps, what the writer might have liked to have said. The interpolations exist as insertions in the text or as endnotes. They are put in boxes, or rendered in a different typeface, or with lines running like vertical margins alongside the text proper.

Kamau for some reason seemed to have grown more inclusive and maybe kinder to Bajan whites. He might have softened with age. Or he might have been embracing the landscape even more closely; forever circling back now to foundational experiences; preparing a mental landscape – largely located in the past – that could enable his final habitation (not death here, but re-entry). One sensed that he had grown tired with New York and was finding it dangerous health-wise to return there. He contracted pneumonia during the winter of 1999 and had in fact been 'home' in Barbados for nearly two years.

Notebook #12: Sunday, 30th April, 2000, Mainz
Today's sessions, Carolyn Cooper's,* my own, went very well. Then there was the plenary session, one disturbing feature about which was that only the Caribbean delegates were featured. Why? I asked. The assumption seemed to be that it was the Third World natives alone, or more than any others, who had insecure, fragile transitional identities that needed shoring-up or being held together. I felt that Europe's and particularly Germany's situation was far less secure than the organisers of the Conference seemed to think it was.

At Nacogdoches I had met two German-Americans, a husband and wife team who were editors of a journal named *Dimensions*. Some of the essays in *Dimensions* portrayed Germany as a country slowly healing, even after three generations since World War II, from a history of genocide that had traumatised both the perpetrators and the victims. As part of the global post-colonial experience, I understood how the Caribbean, Africa, Asia and other so-called developing places had repeated the genocidal patterns of Europe and America. Perhaps one should not say 'repeated': the Third World hasn't so much repeated anyone's brutality as manifested its own. This was what David Rudder realised when he said in his song "Heaven"[90] that "Heaven" was not in South Africa or Rwanda or Kigali. That is, diasporans need to stop romanticising ancestral spaces which concealed the same horror as elsewhere.

By treating the Caribbean delegates as specimens of transitionality, the Conference lost an opportunity for openness and unmasking and probing the insecurities that faced Europe now that the tribes were on the move, and a multiethnic cosmopolitan future seemed to threaten the placidity of the herrenvolk.

I didn't say all of this of course. Dumbness and restraint were proper masks to wear in the circumstances. But I did wonder if something more would have been gained at that plenary session if all had been encouraged to stop 'othering' each other and lay our collective human vulnerability on the table. For if, as one of the slogans on the conference poster proclaimed, "there is no periphery, there is no longer any centre", then why weren't we all collectively occupying this same centreless, peripheriless space? Why weren't we taking the discourse much further than we could take it, given the Conference's structuring of differences, rather than of what we in common and in fact shared?

Notebook #13: 12th May, 2000
The Drummond Symposium took place on May 6th 2000. I returned from the "Transitional Identities" Conference on May 2nd, 2000, to find student research papers, a handful of emails and a package from Clinton Hutton with valuable material and six hours of tapes. I mentioned before the difficulty of writing anything of worth about wordless songs. Well, I played each song and tried to say in words what was going on with the music. I integrated my observations with data gained from Clinton's interviews with Sister Mary Ignatius,* Matron of Alpha Boys' School where Drummond spent several years, and members of the Skatalites (particularly Dizzy Moore*) who knew the entire history of that iconic band, and Ernest (Ernie) Ranglin* "a master jazz guitarist and pioneer in popular Jamaican music." [Clinton Hutton, Letter of 19th April, 2000.]

From the fifteen songs that Clinton sent, I gained the impression of a work-a-day Drummond of the dance halls, imposing his voice on the sentimental music of the day or retiring into the background after brief 8-bar solos. There were also those more impressive and more carefully developed compositions, where the rest of the band withheld their voices so that Drummond's voice could dominate, usually at the song's centre, but on occasion from beginning to end. Drummond's trombone dominated, including and containing all the other instruments. Normally, in brass 'combos' such as saxophone quartets, the soprano or alto saxophone is dominant in stating the melody. In the Skatalites, Drummond reversed the order of things. The other horns accompanied him (as in a New Orleans band such as The Dirty Dozen,* where the leading and dominant voice was that of the baritone saxophone). The weight of Drummond's trombone, resting on top of the chorus of underlying horns, gave the music its characteristically melancholy tone even when the melody was a sentimental one.[xxii]

---

xxii. See "Valley Prince" or "Farther East".

In my Symposium paper, which I entitled "This Broken Music" (deriving my name from Anthony McNeill's poem "For the D, Don"),[93] I noted that the task that lay before all categories of presenters, whether they were academics like Kamau Brathwaite, Clinton Hutton and myself, or people who knew Drummond well or people like Johnny "Dizzy" Moore who had played with the Skatalites, or the current Alpha Boys' Band, who were slated to render a musical tribute – the task that confronted all performers was to try to assess the weight of a life, the depth of a spirit, what Tony McNeill had called this "heaviest spirit of sound".

From early, as all who knew him testified, Drummond had been a person of few words, a man of silences, a soul withdrawn. Yet his vocation demanded that he located himself among people – the band, the audience – that he should through his voice, the trombone, "speak his melancholy power to the distances..."[xxiii] The trombone could howl in the middle of some sentimental curve of song. Drummond had a habit of leaning, just that little bit longer, just that little bit more heavily, on a note, and in doing so he'd define what that moment meant, giving it meaning, point. The music was his language, all commentators agreed, his means of talking to the world.

For Drummond, the challenge was to play his feelings and in this way reach out to the world around him. For Drummond's audience the challenge was to describe the feelings, often ambiguous, that Drummond's music aroused in them. For the critic/commentator, the task was even more difficult: to say *why* the music made him or her feel what he or she felt, and to say how Drummond achieved the 'sound' that he did.

Zoltan Kodaly wrote this of Hungarian folk melodies of which he was an avid collector:

"Like their language, the music of the Hungarians is... terse and lapidary, forming... masterpieces that are small but weighty. Some tunes of a few notes have withstood the tempests of centuries."[xxiv]

Terse, "small but weighty" are some of the words that spring to mind when one thinks of or listens to Drummond's music. I think of his compositions and his solo statements within each composition, as foundation stones for a structure that those who have succeeded him have been steadily building. As foundation stones they will outlast the tempests of centuries. All the signs and sounds proclaim it.

---

xxiii. See Anonymous (Gordon Rohlehr) "White Fridays in Trinidad", *Savacou* 3/4, March, 1971.
xxiv. Ates Orga, Album notes to Zoltan Kodaly – 1967, *Music for Cello*, Naxos, 8,553160, 1996, p. 4.

Task #1 – What to make of Drummond's life from the few details one has been given?

Task #1 I perceived as the work of the historian and ethnomusicologist. That work had been going on fitfully for many decades and in the case of Drummond would involve collecting and piecing together Drummond's biography. I did not think that we in the Caribbean had been sufficiently diligent in the area of biography. I shared Kamau Brathwaite's anxiety in this respect. In the Caribbean we recognised basic immutable facts: people lived and died, their lives an obscure journey between the twin darknesses of pre-birth and post-death. Drummond lived, illuminated the gloom of his being and ours with his sound, then died, some people said, under suspicious circumstances in a madhouse that has steadily emerged in Jamaican and other West Indian poetry as a metaphor of the society itself and the existence of its citizenry.

From the narrative of Dizzy Moore one learned that the love relationship between Don and Margarita was as strange as its predictable ending was violent. Yet one learned little from any of the interviews that explained either the relationship itself or the murder that ended it in 1965. Moore described Drummond as deeply melancholic, introverted and given to extreme mood-swings. He lived too much inside his head and needed someone he could confide in.

> He didn't say much with words... and if something went wrong he might just stand there and hold the instrument and don't play a note for the rest of the night. He had mood swings.

Drummond's schizophrenic behaviour "became like part of the show." The madman as curiosity: a Caribbean trope.

Margarita, Anita Mahfood, became a follower of the band. "She loved dancing. She is one of the better-shaped dancers that I know." Like the eccentric Drummond, she attracted audiences:

> "That's why she lost her life. She went to John Smith Drive in the night and Donald forebode her to do that. And she did it anyway. Cause like he loved the trombone, she loved the dancing."

Moore described the strangeness of Margarita's violation of the class and colour codes of the society. Breaking out of the barriers set by race and class, she visited the Back o' Wall camp where the brederen wore burlap loin cloths and walked with sticks. She too was wearing burlap, but well-designed, and there was "a bunch o' people behind her... Hundreds o' people; some giggling, and wondering; this white lady..."

She had come to Moore, who at the time was a freelance almost homeless musician attracted to Rastafari doctrine and shunned by family, the Military Band where he once played, and Count Ossie, the famous cult drummer who nonetheless disapproved of dreadlocks. Moore could not afford a wife. Anita turned to Drummond who was at the time part of Count Ossie's entourage.

Drummond did not want Anita (Margarita) to dance. Moore sensed that he would kill her and warned her. She told him, "Don loves me." Moore said, "That is why he will kill you." "Woman ah Come," Anita's love song for Drummond was, Moore said, composed by Drummond, who frequently sang it before he gave it to Anita. A narcissist, he had written a praise-song for himself.

Classified as a "criminal lunatic", Drummond was confined in Bellevue Mental Asylum where there were more questions than answers about how he was treated there. Was he really allowed his trombone? What solos did he play? Were any of them recorded? Was it understood that his music had always been his main means of both reaching inside and communicating with the world outside? What really happened in Bellevue?

And why is the Don's grave unmarked? Unknown?

"as if i man did never in dis place
as if i man did never have no face."?

In 1977, an attempt was made to name the annual Jamaican Song Festival after Drummond, but some people objected to naming the competition after a man who had been convicted of murder and certified as a criminal lunatic. His name was withdrawn from the contest. People were sensitive, even as murders and mad people multiplied, about how "things Jamaican" were symbolically represented. There were objections raised against the Drummond Symposium of 2000, even though in the three decades between his death in 1969 and the Symposium in 2000, the madman or mad woman had become metaphorised into Eshu-Elegbara, the pointer of the way and teller of those truths that society would prefer to keep hidden. Sometimes, as in Leroy Calliste's "South Trumpeter",[92] the madman appears as the prophet of all dreamed apocalypses. Sometimes, as in David Rudder's "Madman's Rant", the lunatic becomes the interpreter and unmasker of social hypocrisy, political double-think and double-say.

Drummond as Legba, muse and guide through underworlds of the self, appears in Tony McNeill's "For the D, Don". Here Drummond is mythological ancestor, a guide, a sculptor of pain. McNeill doesn't want to learn Drummond's pain. He has (or had) his own pain, his own inner darkness to contend with. What he wants to learn rather in this prayer-poem is the shape that Drummond was able to give to his pain or hurt, his unhealing wound. This pain cannot be dodged. It "captures", it possesses the traveller whom it compels to make repeated night-journeys into dread city. Dread city is simultaneously Brathwaite's Kingston and James Thomson's "City of Dreadful Night",* that region of the soul, that dark area of everyone's being that most people prefer to leave alone.

Both Ernie Ranglin and Dizzy Moore referred to the jazz improvisations of Drummond and the other soloists in the Skatalites as "journeys". Ranglin also repeatedly spoke of those journeys as narratives, requiring skill, absolute mastery of medium and instrumental voice, and fidelity to the truth of one's experience. McNeill, then, wants to learn with respect to his own medium of words, the sort of mastery that Drummond displayed in his language of purest and truest sound.

> Teach me to walk through juke boxes
> & shadow that broken music
> whose irradiant stop is light.[93]

Drummond is muse and guide; McNeill wants to "shadow that broken music" in the sense of sticking closely to its contours of sound; in the sense, too, of recognising his own work as the shadowy imitation, the echo of a cry of pain and a fissuring that has already been sounded by Drummond's horn. It is, I said, the *shape* that concerns him, and the journey through noise towards the silence and darkness in and through which shaping becomes possible. So that at the terminus of the music's sound, or at its stops, the pauses, the interstices between its howlings, light, illumination, epiphany radiates.

The metaphors here are psycho-religious. The imagery of Psalm 23, of various prayers, hymns, long-lost liturgies, inform the poem's quest. e.g. "Yea though I walk through the Valley of the Shadow of Death…." Or "Be thou my guardian and my guide": perennial funeral service hits. But this invocation is more like African ancestor reverence, and it also belongs to the European literary tradition of Dante, Virgil, Milton and Conrad, where the artist seeks guidance from the spirit of an earlier ancestor in order to explore the dark places of his own being.

> guide, through those mournfullest journeys

> I back into harbour Spirit.

Those who have never sinned or fallen short of the glory, whose eyes are clear of motes or beams, have objected bitterly to this elevation, this apotheosis of the criminal and the lunatic; this transfiguration of the madman into muse, spirit guide and teacher. McNeill signals such transfiguration by rendering "Spirit" with a capital "S". The Drummond he invokes has become translated, transmuted.

Yet, the Drummond McNeill invokes resides only in the "broken music" that he left as heritage. This Drummond has become a deathless voice of sound, has become pure poem that still speaks wordlessly to some of us, which still "captured [us] nightly into dread city," as the hurt once captured and compelled Drummond into making those quite brief (8 or 16 bars) but also quite profound journeys into the city of dreadful night that resided within himself.

One interesting feature of McNeill's poem is its sudden pluralising of the questing narrative voice.

in heavens remember we now
& show we a way in to praise
all seekers together, one-heart[94]

The quest here becomes communal. The goal is the lost power of affirmation – "a way in to praise" the lost or perhaps never truly discovered kingdom of communion... the "one-love, one-heart" ideal of Bob Marley, which Drummond, who named one of his compositions *Heavenless*, may never in fact have found, though one senses that he played both love and pain, and he killed what he loved – as Dizzy Moore divined – because love turned out to be another and more bitter dose of pain. He hated Anita's self-display before all those men on stage. But as Dizzy Moore testifies, she loved to dance as much as Drummond loved to play his trombone, and no one could stop her from doing what she was inwardly driven to do, or stop him...

The Symposium went well. It was a highly charged emotional affair, a celebration not only of Drummond, but of the now ancestral sixties generation: its pioneering, signifying sounds; its significatory idioms now being rediscovered "at the end of the small hours", by first of all a young generation of whites all over America and Europe where, as I learned from the Mainz "Transitional Identities" Conference, ska was quite popular. Young Jamaicans of the dancehall era were also in transition back towards 'conscious' sounds. The Drummond Symposium became a day of testimony, probably more intense than the Bob Marley affair of February 1999, when I delivered the keynote address.

Fortuitously, I also had to deliver the rather improvised keynote at the Drummond Symposium. Kamau Brathwaite was the speaker originally selected for the keynote. But he was – in now typical Kamau fashion – stuck in his hotel awaiting transportation. It was an insufferable situation that Kamau immediately understood/translated as one of *Dis*respect. Nearly all the work of organisation had fallen on Clinton Hutton's willing, enthusiastic but inadequate shoulders. Important things like subsistence and recompense weren't in place. While the rhetoric of national self-discovery via Drummond's iconic voice ran high, the tedious nitty gritty of simple recompense was nonexistent – as in Barbados with the Central Bank address.

Kamau and I were both caught in the packed agenda of the Symposium. I have recovered his address which followed mine. Mine, as illustrated above, had been almost deliriously composed after listening to and partially transcribing 6 hours of taped conversation, during a week of travelling back into and back out of remote Nacogdoches. I thought it worked well as an introduction to the day's proceeding. The high point of the Symposium for me was Dean Fraser's and Delfayo Marsalis's teaming up with the survivors of the old Skatalites:– Brevett on the bass, Knibbs powerful on drums and Dizzy Moore on trumpet – to link contemporary New Orleans with Jamaican 1960's Back O' Wall. Marsalis, leaning heavily on the note in his vershan of "Eastern Standard Time", evoked a sigh of recognition from the back-in-times audience of geriatrics, because it showed how ska, rooted in rhythm n blues, mento and Ras, had 'given back' to its New Orleans source. Kamau's thesis about the interlinked conversation that has always been taking place between the performance cultures of African diasporans, was in full evidence at the Drummond Symposium.

The following is a transcription of what I could recover of Brathwaite's 'tidalectic' address, delivered at the Don Drummond Symposium on May 6th, 2000 at UWI, Mona, Jamaica. Material in square brackets are either my additions and paraphrases or are my guesses where the tape is indistinct.

I want to say good morning and to say how happy, proud and pleased I am to attend this conference on such an important icon as Don Drummond, and then I want to take up an image that [emerged] out of Gordon Rohlehr's keynote address: the concept of the sacred insanity, not only of the artist, but of the marginal Caribbean person who has to create a life, love and a living from the margins of society where all of us have been destituted by history…

Don Drummond's music has always given me a hint of this incandescence, this sacred insanity. I arrived in Jamaica in 1963 when Don Drummond and the Skatalites and Don himself were moving towards [the summit of their career] and their music affected me in a subtle way. My concept of the music [of the African Diaspora, unfocused during my early years in the Caribbean and my student years in England] changed when I went to Ghana where thunderous things happened, wonderful things happened that began to play an important part in my experience, in my own life. But it was not until I returned to the Caribbean that I arrived at a better understanding of the true nature of the drum in the modern world, in the [context] of modernity.

My experience in Africa was very much [that of] the traditional drum, the Atumpan, and it was not until I came to Jamaica that I came to realise how the African has to reinvent himself and herself, using the sources that have come from the Africans in Africa. So when I got to Jamaica, I realised the magical quality of what the music was doing. The music was remembering the past, but at the same time, it was inventing the future, inventing, predicting a future. This is important, because slavery has deposited upon us the notion that there is no future; that we were a people who had been brought into the Caribbean [and were now disconnected from any sense of ancestry]. [NB: blank in tape. End of side A.]

Don Drummond's slide trombone, the very instrument itself, began to give this sense that the people are moving [outward in consciousness and yearning] toward the horizon, and back again to their [homebase] in the Caribbean. My poetry began to reflect this... [back-and-forth oscillation that KB would name 'tidalectics' The poems that appeared in *Third World Poems* and *Black + Blues* all depart from what was happening in the rest of Brathwaite, who previously had been narrating slavery in small, short, broken and "coffled" lines of enchainment, but after Drummond began to write lines that expanded outward towards the margin of the page, an imagined horizon. [This is GR's paraphrase of a difficult passage in the taped narrative.]

So I have to pay tribute to Don Drummond, and to express a solidarity [with] all the artists who have [acknowledged] how his music and his presence have inspired their work and struggle. In addition to the poem by Tony McNeill which Gordon Rohlehr read, the first thing that struck me at the death of Drummond [in 1969] was Bongo Jerry's "Tribute to Don Drummond"[95] published in *Abeng* – that remarkable piece about "Don de Lion". It captures the rhythm of Don Drummond. But he says so much about what Drummond meant. Jerry says that Don Drummond's music has the effect of ganja. Now, that is a remarkable [observation]. Think of the imagination, the fusion that he had to create to get that image: "Don Drummond's music has the effect of ganja."

Then we had Mervyn Morris's "Valley Prince". Morris says:

> ...plenty people
> want me blow it straight.
> But straight is not the way...
> Oonu gimme back mih trombone, man:
> is time to blow me mind[96]

Moving towards the context of 'sacred insanity'... And then we have Tony McNeill, "Saint Ras".[97] Here the man is trying to cross a road [perilous with traffic]. All of these things are what Drummond is saying. Later we have Jean Breeze's "Madwoman Chant" [i.e. "Riddim Ravings"].[98] And Erna Brodber begins... Finally, there is a remarkable book by Kwame Dawes, *Natural Mysticism*,[99] in which he talks about the influence of Reggae on his poetry and on the aesthetic of the Caribbean. He talks about those poems I've mentioned, the nature of Drummond's trombone and the effect it had on him as a young boy growing up here in Jamaica.

I note that Clinton Hutton is working... on his book on Drummond. That brings me to the second point I want to make: the need for an 'ital' intellectual. We don't really believe that we have intellectuals, you know. We are 'emotional'. But we could not have survived and created anything in the Caribbean unless there was a very strong intellectual component. We cannot separate the 'intellectual' from the 'emotional'. We have the 'little' intellectual tradition of the 'folk', the 'sufferers', the people who have had to create because they had nothing else to do. Creation becomes the salvation of the sufferer.

I draw your attention to Ken Post's *Strike the Iron*[100] and his books about the rebellion of 1937-38. Post's work contains a lot of material that we have not really gone into carefully, because we have been more interested in the political statements that he has been making. But that rebellion, as Post shows, was a manifestation of people's struggle, determination and achievement.

Then there is M.G. Smith's *Dark Puritan*.[101] M.G. Smith was an anthropologist and an artist. He interviews this 'simple' person in Grenada and publishes the complexity of his life, and he records this in the person's words, which is very important when you are dealing with the little tradition. Because the great tradition uses the Standard English Dictionary language. The little tradition requires that we record what is said, because how the word is said, the inflexion, is as important as the word itself.

Two members of this Symposium are looking at rebellion and revolution as [manifestations] of the little tradition, issues from below. Coming from above you get the teaching, the overall statement, the bombast, the orchestra. From below, you get the small group, you get the Skatalites.

The other place where you find a record of the intellectual history and achievement of the little tradition is the people's churches, ignored out of embarrassment, out of ignorance. I'm thinking of Santeria and other such religions that have not yet been codified in any serious way, and therefore remain marginalised. Because they remain marginalised, we have the experience of people like Don Drummond, whose achievement is vitiated by the structure in which they are trying to perform. The artist, the person of consciousness and imagination, arrives at a block, a stubborn obstacle that is almost impossible to surmount. In real life it happened to Bedward,* in fiction the experience is there in *Brother Man*;[102] it is there in A *Quality of Violence*.[103]

You have a situation where a person is born into a very shallow environment. I suggest that the people who have to write the intellectual history of the little tradition have to deal with this. And of course, the people of the little tradition are the ones who are the foremost in writing their history and dealing with it in all the ways that they can. First of all, we have birth and the circumstances of that birth, the burden and the environment of it. In the case of Drummond, we know the town where he was born, but do we know anything about the circumstances of the birth and the nourishment?

We know that the mother is there and she provides the nourishment. The father is not present, and the mother is in fact responsible for getting him into Alpha Approved School at the age of nine, because she says she cannot cope with the wayward boy. Now the mother, these submerged mothers of our culture, they come and go. The biography of 'the Mother' is still not being done. Without her we would not be here. Drummond's mother, unable to cope on her own, goes to Alpha, where her son is mothered by the institution. Alpha becomes his surrogate mother. It is fortunate that Drummond's mother is able to do this, because many of our little tradition artists have nowhere to go at all, and the result is what we have today: the man on the block; the movement into violence and instability and a certain sense of the absence of God in the society.

[What follows is Brathwaite's attempt to imagine what happens to Drummond after his mother delivers him to the sanctuary – when compared with the street – of Alpha Approved School. Alpha becomes his surrogate mother and provides the essential structure of education and training that leads to his eventual achievement as a musician. But there is what Brathwaite perceives as a "terrible contradiction", because an institution, with the best of intentions, cannot provide the love or inspiration that a still alienated , introverted and probably narcissistic youth needs.]

This creates all sorts of problems, especially when you ('the artist') come to the Crossroads. At the moment of the Crossroads the artist is moving straight into an enigma, which in Drummond's case assumes the form of Margarita Mahfood, the dancer. She provides him, for a while, with a love that seems to be a substitute for the mother-love that he lost at the age of nine and the surrogate love of Alpha that he had to leave behind as he grew into manhood.

At the crisis of the Crossroads one is faced by the visage of the enigma in the cracked mirror. You look at yourself and see the enigma. You do not see yourself. You see the enigma you are in love with: Margarita. You are in love with whoever moves in at that time. You wish to create a different sense of [?] rather than the eternal one in which you're living." [At the high point of the crisis, the protagonist, a narcissist repelled by his own half-cracked image, smashes the mirror and kills both the enigma and, it seems, his own sanity. Yet for Drummond, this is a moment of liberation. He gives himself up to the police "because he's more free, more at peace."]

After this reading, Brathwaite returns to his first assertion: the need for Caribbean societies to understand and accommodate their own "sacred insanity".

In many societies, the so-called 'mad person' is a prophet of that society. He or she is accepted as a part of the society, not necessarily living cheek by jowl. Sometimes they have to live on the outskirts. In the suburbs, or in a tree. But the point is, they are an essential part of the society, and that is what we have to try to understand. And therefore, as I conclude, it is time, it is overtime that we develop a Caribbean psychiatry to deal with this notion of 'sacred insanity.'

We need also to develop a Caribbean pharmacopoeia, to go back to the herbal medicine of the ancestors, because it is that whole area that deals with insanity, so-called insanity, and which heals those contradictions. It is only the 'balm' that, growing out of the knowledge of the earth, can heal contradiction. Therefore we need to know a lot more about Santeria, about Vodun, about hounforts, tonnelles, all of these things. We know the names. In the next conference such as this, we will have people from that area to sit with us and talk.

Most of this loudly-applauded address seemed not to be directly related to Drummond, but to various Brathwaitean concerns – the shattered mirror, the enigmatic mother/ surrogate mother/ distracted, psychically paralysed son/ sacrificial lover – that he appended to the figure of Drummond as he became transformed into a national racial icon, legend, saint and victim. Kamau served as shaman and *okyeame* at this ordination ceremony. Drummond, either as ghost or flesh-and-blood man, did not and could not represent all the things he was made to represent in Kamau's address. Like Coleman 'Hawk' Hawkins of Kamau's post-9/11 poem "Hawk"/ *Ark*,[104] Drummond had become a Brathwaite metaphor.

Letter #119 of 12ᵗʰ May, 2000 was written by me and emailed to Anthony Phillips, historian of UWI, Cave Hill Barbados. Kamau Brathwaite had turned 70 on 11ᵗʰ May, 2000 and Phillips had organised a day of tributes in which I had not participated. I had just returned to Nacogdoches after the Drummond Symposium and was due to leave again on the 15ᵗʰ May for my journey back to the political turmoil of Trinidad and Tobago. My letter of apology, addressed to KB and carbon copied to Phillips ran:

Hail Kamau,

Drummond's music and heaviest spirit of sound drove both the imminence and the eminence of your Seventieth clean out of my head, or I'd have wished you 'happy birthday' since last week at Mona. It's great to know that you are still creating, and that this milestone finds you at home among marl, sunsong, aquamarine and casuarinas. Stay well; keep writing, and I'll keep reading your wordworks.

Gordon

Notebook #13: Wednesday, 06th December, 2000: Kamaufest
The celebration of Kamau's 70th took place between Friday, December 8th, 5:30 p.m. – 8:00 p.m., and Saturday, December 9th, 9"00 a.m. – 6:00 p.m. at New York University. The occasion was hosted by the Department of Comparative Literature, the Reed Foundation, the Humanities Council, the Center for African Studies & Institute for African-American Affairs, the College of Arts and Science, the Faculty of Arts & Science, the Graduate School of Arts and Science, the Center for Latin American and Caribbean Studies and the Program in Creative Writing.

So many hosts pointed to not just a transitionality, but a variety, a complexity of identities, growing out of the web of relationships – social, cultural, political, economic – that existed between the two Americas (N & S), the archipelago of islands in between them, and the isthmus that linked them together. Kamau was simultaneously located and dislocated in many places and situations. And he wasn't so easy to find either. I tried to contact him. First his phone was busy; then I got his answering machine with its "Don't know if this thing is working… but." I left a message as commanded and phoned Elaine Savory. There was someone trying to get me while I was speaking to Elaine. I suspected that this was Kamau whom I again tried to contact at the same number as before. A woman's voice said that no Kamau was living there.

It was very cold outside. I had to meet Tim Reiss for lunch at midday (Wednesday, 06th December, 2000). Reiss was about my age, I guessed, or younger. He was slim, bright-eyed, easy to talk to and eager to talk. He'd brought Zweli-Bansi Sibiya, a young Zulu whose poem or praise song would open the ceremony on Friday evening. Tim said that the book of essays (*For the Geography of a Soul*),[105] which was being printed in Eritrea, wasn't finished: a confusion of fonts, a tangle of vershans, a something of something.

Tim then recounted his attempts to get Walcott, who now lived in Greenwich Village, to speak at the celebration. First, Walcott, whom Tim contacted from Berkeley California where Tim really lives and to where he commutes fortnightly, was too busy to listen. He was, in fact, about to leave for St Lucia, and he suggested that Tim should contact him there. Tim rang him next day and explained that the occasion was to honour Kamau in his seventieth year. Walcott's rejoinder was that he too was seventy and that no one was honouring him. He could envisage participating in a joint honouring event, in which he and Kamau could/would both utter words of honour, praise, blessing, or better still, trade poetic aesthetic punches at each other [NB my words, not Tim's or Derek's]. But he wasn't going to participate otherwise.

Tim also drew a blank when he later contacted Derek about attending anyway, just for the occasion, the community of goodwill, of artist support-ing artist, (Kamau's much dreamed-of fellowship that he still hoped existed beneath old rivalries and sour antagonisms of reality). No, said Derek. Why was no one honouring him? Why no big effort or book of tribute essays? There were things happening on Derek's behalf, I knew, but these had started too late for Walcott's seventieth and would have to wait for his seventy-fifth. Incentive, I guessed, for Walcott to survive up until then. His twin brother Roderick had been one of the victims of this Zero year.

On Thursday, 07th December, after wandering around Manhattan's "great anthill" (John Donne), I at last contacted Kamau on the phone. He had asked me to bring copies of some of my books and arranged for his secretary Isis Costa to collect them. This did not happen. Isis and I stood shivering at opposite ends of the same narrow street. Kamau arranged for me to meet Bronwyn Mills, a graduate student of his, who was researching Calypso Rose. He told me about a performance of Salif Keita* due to take place at 6:30 p.m… But I had had enough of outside and prepared to chill out (ha ha) in my room on the fourteenth floor of a building close to the New York Stock Exchange and Chase Manhattan and Trump Towers, ignoring, reading and sleeping through the press and pangs of hunger.

Kamau's 70th birthday conference/celebrations featured a grand array of scholars from several different part of the globe: historians Hilary Beckles* and Tony Phillips* from UWI, Cave Hill; Margaret Gill,* poet and Carib-bean Studies lecturer at Cave Hill, a close friend of Kamau's and a 'believer' in his ideas; Rhonda Cobham,* Trinidadian/Barbadian, brilliant UWI Mona graduate, now Professor of literature at Amherst; Elaine Savory, British, indigenised Barbadian, UWI, Cave Hill lecturer in literature, now Professor at the New School, NYU; Mervyn Morris, Professor of Litera-ture at UWI, Mona, a colleague that Brathwaite too frequently numbered among "the Establishment". Pam Mordecai,* poet, writer of short stories, UWI Mona, Jamaica, a close and sensitive reader of Kamau's poetry; Professor Mervyn Alleyne,* Linguistics, and a major theorist on African continuities in Diasporan speech; Lasana Sekou,* poet activist and pub-lisher from St. Martin [he'd become Kamau's publisher in this new era, see *Words Need Love Too*; as well as of Amiri Baraka's highly controversial *Somebody Blew up America*].

Other publishers present were Kassahun Checole of Africa World Press, Chris Funkhauser of We Press, Ian Randle of Ian Randle Publishers, Jamaica and Helen Tartar and Saitosh Daniel of Stanford University Press. Organiser in Chief of the event was Tim Reiss. As with the 1994 Neustadt honouring ceremony, this Kamaufest was closed by the Consul General of Barbados in New York. This time the diplomat was the Honourable George S Griffith, who spoke after calypsonian Gabby's performance on Saturday night (December 09th).

Ngugi wa Thiongo, Silvio Torres Sailliant (organiser of the 1992 Symposium of Queen's Community College), Manthia Diawara,* Jacqueline Bishop* and Patricia Penn Hilden* also attended. I delivered one of the keynote addresses. It was entitled "Yes, Words Need Love Too". It was followed by Rhonda Cobham's "I and I: Epitaphs for the Self" a major statement on how writers construct and continuously reconstruct identities and late in their careers write the 'epitaphs' by which they would prefer future generations to read their work and lives. Rhonda Cobham's paper – later expanded to become a book – would be dismissed by Kamau in his latter days as "disrespectful".

Mervyn Morris reminisced on Brathwaite's Mona days, still a delicate topic, but one that Morris, who had often been the target of Kamau's anger, probably felt he ought to discuss in public; to give his side and balance the equation. He felt that it was safe to do this now that Brathwaite seemed to have established firm new roots in an applauding metropole. Kamau, however, acclaim or no acclaim, was still a deeply insecure individual in a city that he had always feared as being "so vast/its ears have ceased to know/ a simple human sound" [*The Arrivants*, 54]. This perception, reinforced by those of all the exiled Caribbean writers – Naipaul, Salkey, Lamming, Patterson – deepened when the World Trade Center, only a mile away from Kamau's Lower Manhattan apartment, was plane-bombed on September 11th 2001.

The first piece of GR/KB correspondence I can now find that mentions 9/11 was Letter #120, Sunday, January 21, 2002, which was a rather long time not to have said anything about such a momentous happening. On contemplation I've realized that 9/11 occurred only fifteen days before my father's death on Wednesday, 26th September, 2001, and that my thoughts were in meditation on the meaning of my father's, my family's and my own residence on earth. [See Gordon Rohlehr, Chapter Three, *Musings, Mazes, Muses, Margins: a memoir* (Leeds: Peepal Tree Press Ltd, 2020), 89-99]. 9/11 indeed, shrank into the stress and anger caused by the increased security that became the "new norm" at airports throughout the world, and I had, since the 1990s, become something of a frequent flyer.

Culture II, Jan 9th-12th, 2002
Culture II, a three-day mega-conference staged in honour of Kamau Brathwaite, featured three generations of scholars, poets, fellow historians and enthusiasts, all of whom had been touched by the multiple facets of his illuminating pioneer work. The conference began with annunciations of drums and the youthful intensity of the UWI Dance Society who, in their offering "Poetry and Motion", danced a medley of KB's poetry, spines twisted tight around the *poteau mitan of* "Negus", read by their own youthful *okyeame* whose voice tapered into Kamau's

resonant voice, dubbed from the Argo recording of *Islands*.

Since the seventies, "Negus" had been vilified by Ken Ramchand's "Pit is pot" parody and mocked by Walcott's "It, it, it is not a good poem."[108] Yet it had not only survived scathe and scorn, but had triumphantly emerged, as the dancers, huddled in their cramped Middle Passage space, body curving to body, restored the proper intensity to the poem's prayer of awakening, its ceremony of the reopening of the time-portal and corridor between Mona and Onyame.

The dignitary who delivered the Invocation was Kofi Anyidoho, a fifty-five year old Ghanaian poet, who held a B.A. Honours degree in English and Linguistics from the University of Ghana, Legon, an M.A. in Folklore from Indiana University, Bloomington, and a PhD in Comparative Literature at the University of Texas at Austin. Anyidoho had taught at primary, secondary and university levels, and had been Professor of Literature in the English Department, Legon, and acting Director of the School for the Performing Arts. His major academic publications included *The Pan-African Idea in Literatures in the Black World* (Accra: Ghana Universities Press, 1989); *Transcending Boundaries: the Diaspora Experience in African Heritage Literatures* (Evanston: Northwestern University Press, 1995) and "Poetry as Dramatic Performance" in Tejumola Olaniyan and Ato Quayson, *African Literature: an Anthology of Criticism and Theory*.

Anyidoho knew both Brathwaite the man and his poetry. In his closing address, Brathwaite referred to Anyidoho as the person who had "sent me an invitation way back in 1986/1987 when I was really sucking salt." Anyidoho at the time was at the Du Bois Institute in Accra.

One couldn't imagine a person more suited to be guest-speaker at what was turning out to be a ceremony of investiture of Kamau as shaman and okyeame. Anyidoho, however, was a last-minute substitute for Wole Soyinka who had been called upon to officiate at the funeral of his friend, the recently assassinated Chief Justice of Nigeria. Referring to himself as an antelope who had been forced to walk in the footsteps of an elephant, Anyidoho began and ended his address with invocations. His opening invocation was a praisesong to Kamau, establishing his identity as ancestor and vessel holding the clear water of the creative word and as pathfinder for the Diasporan's journey back to the land of his ancestors. His final invocation sent Kamau forward into the future where, as wordbearer, he would illuminate and inspire other warriors, bringers and bell-ringers of light.

Anyidoho's address focused on *Masks*, Brathwaite's poem of return, mourning and atonement, the middle passage of *The Arrivants*. Anyidoho was preoccupied with the paradox of disjuncture and reconnection, the ambiguity of erasure and memory, banished language, traumatized consciousness and yet ever-renewed and invincible song. Between his address and his later reading of poems, he envisioned Diasporan Africans as both irretrievably lost and miraculously alive in their own space. What Diasporans had lost could only be atoned for by a recovery of the word. Diasporan man must try to learn just one of Africa's two thousand or so languages; just one, and the estrangement would disappear. A hopeful dream.

Yet Anyidoho also understood, and freely admitted, that the Diaspora had forged its own styles and sensibilities, its own sounds and rhythms which he, an African steeped in the education of both Africa and the Western Atlantic, only partially understood. Linkages, reconnections, the reopening of overgrown, obliterated pathways, the navigation of ancient rivers flowing backwards to Olodumare, that is, Kamau's lifelong undertaking, would remain as challenge.

Two days and over one hundred conference papers, nine plenaries commandeered by battalions of distinguished senior and youthful scholars, separated Kamau's near-ecstatic closing address from Anyidoho's invocations. My little tape-recorder captured most of what KB said, but also lost a great deal of his voice through the asides, jokes, jibes, frequently loud applause that smothered the endings of sentences. Kamau asked me for a copy of the tape. What follows here is the essence of what I retrieved, accompanied by my running commentary on KB's not always coherent performance of what he called "Golokwati".

Golokwati

Thank you so much. I have here two chairs which are empty. These two chairs represent the ancestors. We tend to forget them sometimes... But on this evening we have to try to remember them. I also have to remind you that this is... a continuum of the slave plantation; and the fate of those slaves, as far as I know, has never been appeased.

I don't think that the University... that we have ever had a ceremony that deals with the recognition of their presence and the appeasement of their torture and therefore the redemption of their souls. I'm not going to be able to begin it now, because my function is to thank you and to read a few poems in between the thanks. But everything that I will do is in recognition of the ancestors, my ancestors, your ancestors..."
[KB reads a poem that I can't identify.]

We're going to take this very slowly. Just relax. This is poetry. This is poetry. This is where we [leave the space?] of everyday life and we enter a kind of spiral, a kind of flute music which you have to be part of... So when the blessings of the poem come upon thee, it creates light, lights, spirit... metaphorical life of what swims below the water of the page... These are the blessings and the gifts that we set out with on this journey... unstable ground, ungrounded firmament, water of spirit all around me, tongues of blue birds of fire in the air.

The poem is composed from all this story, all this glory, all this terror; bread, salt, water. Golokwati, Golokwati, Golokwati.

The poem also teaches you about itself, about yourself. It tells you what you know you didn't know you know.

Mkissi is what happens when the spirit moves and moves to you and moves you: electricity of the storm of love transforming you...
[End of side B, Tape #13 Loss of ten seconds of voice]

[Side A Tape #no 14]

He's a crippled loa with a stick, at the Crossroads: Ogun's father, the stone that the builder refuse.
Legba, Legba, Legba.
The stick of Legba is the snake.
The stick of Legba is a doorway, a future you must choose, a future you must choose. [Echo of the last words of George Lamming's *Natives of My Person*]
The stick of Legba is a crossing, dark shipwreck and coast of memory. The [death?] of limbo Legba is forever... [??]

[KB reads "Caliban" from *Islands*, down to "Limbo". Loud applause.]

Golokwati is what we are celebrating this week, Golokwati, a Golokwati. That's how I see it. That's how I'd like you to see it. It is interesting how, as a people coming out of the holocaust, as people whose memories are fairly intact, but whose ability to [nominate/numinate??] and divine has been so shattered that we have not for a long time been trying to find our own words for our experiences... And it took me a long time, a long time to come to the stage where I felt confident to name things according to how I understand them. And I call things like this "Golokwati". I call poetry readings where now I talk and read and [shudder??] and shout out, a kind of sacred shadow, overcoming or overpowering, overarching each generation, nation... When two people begin to speak to each other creatively in a debate interpenetrating their thoughts, things like that...

Now people are more comfortable because I begin to understand that having made the thing, I begin to profess it; and as I profess it I want to defend it; and as I defend it, I come to love it; and as I love it I come to share it. And so everyone, certainly I, feel more comfortable. I feel more confident. I feel more in of the universe of which I am a part. So that "Golokwati", what we are having here today, is a village and this and this halfway baobab tree. In the quotation I have brought here with me, the traveller from the deserts of the North on his way to the Coast, passes at the age of 70 at the small village of Golokwati – which means just that – the place where you may rest a while in the middle of the journey. The Elders of this village say that when you are blessed, you will find at the height of your castdown & weariness, in the secret centre of its welcome, the ancient baobab tree where there are gourds (or gods) bearing the coolest water for yr limbs and glances, the sweetest water for yr thirst, its green leaves filtering horizons. Under this tree, the elders

say, glistens the blind eye of the griot that will tell this story.
    [Kamau Brathwaite, *Golokwati 2000*, Savacou North, Dept of Comparative Literature, NYU, 2000/2001]

Brathwaite quotes most of this, but interpolates significant observations of his own: that the traveller from the North to the Coast is travelling from "savannah through forest; from inland to the coast; from freedom to the barracoons and castles of Atlantic slavery; and the imagined reverse journey, that is the journey of the returning Diasporan, from Atlantic to Ashanti, from unfreedom back to freedom". Brathwaite concludes, "You see, you have to imagine that we are under the baobab tree."

From all of this, anyone following Kamau's extraordinary presentation at "Culture II", might have justifiably concluded that "Golokwati", so insistently imposed on the audience as an appropriate name for the conference itself, was, like many of KB's metaphors, ambiguous. Ancestral Golokwati was indeed a place where trails met and intersected, a place of crossroads ruled by the crippled Legba, keeper of directions and an invoked presence in Kamau's address. But conversations under the baobob tree most likely included commercial bargaining over the purchase and sale of slaves. Slaves captured from among the Savannah dwellers to the North and already traumatized, as Brathwaite so poignantly depicts in *Masks*, were unlikely to be less so as they encountered the noises, dangers and imagined demons of, first, the forest and next the barracoons of places like Elmina, their last stop before the Middle Passage and its ultimate desecration of body and soul. Yet Kamau insisted throughout his address that his audience should call the Conference a "Golokwati", and his audience largely and loudly complied.

Brathwaite next remarked that during his thirty years on the Mona Campus there had been little meaningful connection between the Campus and the community.

> We could not say that we were contributing anything from top to bottom. Unless there is this connection, this corridor between power and the... [KB's voice drowned out by loud applause, so that the ending of his sentence is inaudible]
>   Rex [Nettleford] has started to change that with these conferences which we hope will become annual affairs. Unless we have this Golokwati in which we gather as regularly as possible, we don't become accustomed to talking to each other. [There will continue to be] this fear to touch each other, this hesitation, this refusal to look each other in the eye. We tend to bad talk the other person so much...
>   And there was Roy Augier,* my nemesis. He controlled the system of the historiography... But just as I have been on my journey towards

Golokwati, so has Roy Augier. At the beginning of the Library Exhibition, he did the most remarkable comprehensive renaissance analysis of my work I have ever heard. So I have to thank Roy Augier.

He thanked Augier and the Library staff for mounting and launching the exhibition and "the great warmth and cheer" with which everything was done. He next commended the Akwaaba Drummers and the UWI Dancers for their hearty and energetic performance and the sense of joy, emancipation and liberation that they conveyed. "Akwaaba", Kamau reminded his congregation, meant "welcome" in Akan/Twi. The choice of that name for their drum orchestra was a clear indication that Kamau's *Masks* had become an iconic text and word-source in the Diaspora's quest for memory. For the Akwaaba Drummers and the UWI Dancers, Brathwaite then read from *Masks*: "Takoradi was hot," retracing the sad journey of the returning Diasporan African as he re-encounters Golokwati on his soul-shattering journey back to Kumasi. The audience applauded loudly when Brathwaite asked the poem's deepest question about the Diasporan's failure to connect with Africa: "Whose ancestor am I?" Kamau then liberally praised the choreographer for converting "the voices of the poetry into the rhythm of the voices of her choreography."

His next station in this journey was *Trench Town Rock*, "a document that many of you maybe don't even know. Remember that title. Get it up on the Internet, because it is an important aspect of what we're trying to say." The dancers had been able to convey, in a command of space that was really quite remarkable, the terror that Kamau had experienced on that night of the killings at Marley Manors. He then read "Negus", the drum-poem with which the UWI Dancers had opened the conference.

Was Kamau's intense performance meant to bring closure to the conference's circle of sound, or was he reclaiming his own voiced performance of that once controversial poem from the UWI Dancers' danced performance of it? Maybe he was refusing to be upstaged by his own poem differently rendered. There was deafening applause at the end of his passionate performance.

His next topic was "tidalectics", but he failed to clarify the concept. Sensing this, he shifted his attention to Kofi Anyidoho, the guest speaker-cum-shaman or okyeame, who had spoken the words of invocation. He thanked and complimented Anyidoho for taking Wole Soyinka's place:

Wole Soyinka, we remember him too. We are sorry to hear of the tragedy of the assassination of his friend, the Minister of Justice in Nigeria. But we think of Wole as both 'Lion' and 'Jewel': and that is why Kofi thought that he was following in the footsteps, not of the elephant, but of the lion. But Wole had to return to Nigeria; and you realise that he has been the chief mourner, not only of his particular friend, but he has been the chief mourner for many of us for many long years. He has become the chief mourner for much of the Third World. And it is our disaster that a person of his magnificence, a person of his calibre, has had to spend so much of his energy mourning our losses, mourning our breakdowns and our [?] bloodlines, when he could have been writing more lines. So we send our love to him and hope that he will eventually and soon be able to return to the Caribbean and take part in a Golokwati such as this one. And so for him and for Kofi Anyidoho: "Kingston in the Kingdom of This World."[107]

KB ends the poem "awaiting, oh my little children" to emphasise that he has been waiting and is still waiting on future generations to do something unspecified. In an earlier performance when the poem was dedicated to Kwame Nkrumah and the leaders of the Third World (Worcester, 1981 or 1983), he had ended the poem "awaiting your recognition."

KB then closes this phase of his extensive benediction by restating his Golokwati theme: "What Golokwati allows you to do halfway down the journey… is to meet old friends, make plenty new ones and then move on refreshed and hopefully stronger than before." KB heartily thanked the history Department, UWI, Mona for overseeing the publication of two books, one an anthology of poems and the other a collection of essays entitled *Considering Creole*.[108] He, however, curiously used this segment of his address to talk about his Video style and his difficulty in finding publishers sufficiently courageous or radical to entertain his experimentation with Sycorax/Video. KB had bitterly documented his travails in his recently self-published monograph, *Golokwati, 2000* (Savacou Publications, Mona Jamaica, & Savacou North, Dept. of Comparative Literature, NYU, NY, NY, 2000, 2001).

In the face of such rejection of his words, ideas and style, he showered praise and thanks on his students, both the older ones from his Mona days and his more recent acolytes at the Graduate School of NYU, a number of whom had presented papers at the Conference. These acolytes had collectively reassured him that he had not toiled in vain. Kamau blessed them abundantly: "To my students I can only say thanks. But also thank God that this happening can happen. You're harvesting the bread of years upon the waters." He in turn was overjoyed that: "people have written things which have strengthened my recognition that what one does has made sense."

Culture II left KB with a sense of having both transmitted to and received from his congregation energy and light. He cited the example of a woman who came and sat next to him before her "astonishing" presentation. "This is what she said when she came back. She said, "I was so nervous that I had to sit beside you to get strength." (Loud applause). I too am getting the strength. The strength is osmosis; the strength I got, I received from her lecture, is going to last me all week, if not beyond."

KB ended his 90 minute presentation with a new poem, unnamed at the Conference, but subsequently published as "Guanahani" in *Born to Slow Horses* (Wesleyan University Press, 2005, p. 7). This poem, reminiscent at times of Derek Walcott's "The Gulf", portrayed Brathwaite's panoramic dream-journey and homecoming to the Caribbean. Too enormous for analysis here, "Guanahani" begins in fog and gloom, but ends in sunlight, singing and a deluge of applause.

Letter #120: GR – KB, Sunday, January 21st, 2002
It began:

> Hi Kamau,
>
> Received both *Ancestors* and *Geography* weeks ago. Will write to say what I think about both when I get the space; though my initial reaction is that they are both monumental. I would have preferred more of *X-Self*, especially the New World sequences which established the nature of the hybrid personality that emerged as a result of the collision of Africa and Europe and Aztec. In the light of the current catastrophe, I've been thinking of the prophetic vision of history in *The Arrivants* and *Ancestors*. I've also been stunned by the dreadful ironies of "righteous rage". I'll jot my thoughts down soon. How have you been doing? Where were you when Xango/Caliban/ Taliban rode in with the Sheriff?
>
> Gordon

Kamau's almost immediate reply to my email was Letter 120A of Sunday, January 21, 2002, 10:52 a.m. There was a reference to the death by accident of Mark, Beverley's son, in 120A. Most of the 120A, however, assumed a "business-as-usual" or a "life-goes-on" tone, which one recognized as the tone Kamau had adopted immediately after Doris's death. KB was now trying to finish *MR* (i.e. his *Magical Realism* text), but the manuscript continued to grow, especially his

> sequences on the concept & conseQ of "CATASTROPHE." So I said that I'd thank you for sending the SPARROW[109] by sending you a surprise MR (there's also a GOLOKWATI in the works – that is ready; but was waiting to take that to the printer along w/MR. Have also produced a CD burn of ARRIVANTS – all coming yr way soon soon soon.
>
> agree w/you about X/S – pulled some of that back because of developments in RWANDA & MISSA SOLEMNIS…[110]

So KB was early in 2002 writing at full blast – *Magical Realism*, *Golokwati*, CD of *Arrivants*. Availing himself of the readily accessible resources for self-publishing in New York, he also invested heavily in advertising his name and image. Each new text displayed on its "also by" page, a veritable CV of his earlier publications and achievements. He seemed to have willingly cut out or cut up *X/Self*, because he intended to use the excised sections in *RWANDA* and *MISSA SOLEMNIS*. The title *MISSA SOLEMNIS* – signalling his bearing towards grandeur, mourning and a premonition of the end – also indicated a reconciliation with European high culture that he had once dismissed (see e.g. *Carifesta 72 Journal*) as Afro-Saxon "suckin-up". Late Beethoven providing the name for one of Kamau's millennial poems, was like Pushkin and Alexander Dumas being co-opted by the ageing C.L.R. James as African ancestors and transmitters of a line of Black creative imagination right into contemporary times. Late CLR had learned to incorporate "Black Power" into his extraordinarily wide schema of revolutionary theoretics.[111]

Letter 120B: KB – GR, Sunday, January 21st, 2002, 11:38 a.m.
In this second letter which I have read as a postscript to the first, KB suggested a 'connection' between the macrocosmic 9/11 catastrophe and the microcosmic private tragedy of his stepson's – Beverley's son – Mark's death by accident in Jamaica.

> as I kno you will understand, We all coming from the one original DNA. One wants so badly to get the feel of how the Iraquis cope, how the Palestinians deal w/death & destruction evvaday evvaday evvaday and until the TRANSPONDERS begin workin...

Private death by accident and public cataclysm, engineered as an act of jihadic retribution, became central concerns of Brathwaite's long elegiac sequence of poems, *Born to Slow Horses* (2006) and *ARK* (2004). These poems contain the wide empathy (cf John Donne's "No man is an island" and "do not ask to know for whom the bell tolls") that Brathwaite, who in *X/Self* and elsewhere dreamed Apocalyptic retribution, now seemed to want to feel. But, beneath the empathy, these poems asked the hard question of whether one is more likely to feel the personal tragedy, the death of a member of one's family, than the cosmic one beamed to the viewer as an image of breaking news. And is there something very wrong about this? Does KB feel guilty of both his inability to enter the private space and silence of Beverley's grieving and his lack of the wide world-sorrow that 9/11 seemed to require: that terrible sense of inadequacy, of compassion grown tired and run dry?

Letter #122 from KB to Paula Ellis, copied by her husband, Paul Ellis to Betty Rohlehr. (The original letter from KB was dated, Saturday, April 20th, 2002, 5:00 p.m. The copy was sent on Monday, April 22nd, 2002, 9:55 p.m.)

Paula Ellis was an M.Phil student of mine who in 2000 completed her dissertation on "Nation-building in the Poetry and Essays of Kamau Brathwaite". She was one of two 'mature' students of that era, the other being Althea Kaminjolo, a Trinidadian nurse who had lived in Zimbabwe (?) Kenya (?) and was married to a Kenyan professor who was teaching at UWI, St. Augustine. Althea Kaminjolo's thesis was on "Kamau Brathwaite in the Context of Post-colonial Discourse." It had also been successfully submitted in 2000. Both of these had been part of the "UWI wuk" I'd taken up with me to Nacogdoches.

Paula Ellis had, at the request of KB, presented Kamau with a copy of her thesis when he returned to Jamaica in January 2002 to attend *Culture II*. Kamau commended Paula for her scholarship, organization and the way she stuck to her vision, "refusing to be distracted even deterred by the numerous negative arguments that like piranha seem to surround and follow my work."

She dealt full on with negative arguments, he wrote.

> It cd not have been easy for you to have undertaken this work in such a cloudy climate and if it was not for Gordon Rohlehr as yr supervisor, I wonder if you wd. have survived – tho I feel you are a tough one!

Returning to his old grouse against the English Department at Mona, he imagined that she might not have been permitted to proceed at Mona. He claimed that several students, starting from the level of the long (7000 word maximum) Caribbean Studies essay, had "told me stories of roadblock and curfew in my part of town." He encouraged her to publish and noted that "things on KB are so scarce ['scare' in text] that they are/become precious."

Apart from the praise he gives GR as Paula's supervisor, KB was locked into the antipathy he had always felt for the Mona English Department: i.e. that despite the fact that he had resigned from UWI eleven years previously and seemed to have flourished in exile, little attention was being/had been paid to his work. This complaint was simply untrue, when one considered both the many excellent papers that presenters from the Mona Campus had read at *Culture II*, and the fact that 16 pages (450 – 466) of Tim Reiss's *For the Geography of a Soul* listed essays and books about KB's work. Excluding related or ancillary material, those sixteen pages contained about 350 articles. But KB never forgot anyone who, in his opinion, had crossed any of his many paths: never, not up until his dying day. This means that he took the praise-songs and the numerous commendations for granted, while worrying away at the perceived slights, insults, or simple differences of opinion.

Letter #123: KB – GR, Tuesday, March 12ᵗʰ, 2002, 3:40 a.m.

This letter was sent from New York University. Kamau thanked me for attending the *Culture II* Conference and asked me for a tape of the final session. He described "Golokwati", the expanded lecture/address that he had recently completed. First he summarised the earlier stages of his travels and travails, antecedents of and introductions to: "Golokwati"; this new meeting or intersection of the trailways of his nomadism.

> Golokwati is the third Middle Passage from this 'ground zero' of the soul & spirit to the glimpsing & reincarnation of the lwa Oya in the mid 90s ('Xango at the Summer Solstice'), the oasis of Cowpastor, the miracle of Dream Chad, sweet spirit water in the desert, and the gradual recognition of the outlines of what the narrative now calls Redemption – the stop at this Golokwati and the nature of the new work – the mkissi, the dreamstories, the sycorax video-style, and perhaps, above all, how this new work (e.g. Words need love too <2000> and the just completed Mountain (poems connected w/the Jamaica 2002 Golokwati)[112] says what it enacts in the 'fragmented spaceship dreamstorie', 'Défilée Agoue,'[113] 'Namesetoura,'[114] and (still to be published) KB's 9/11 Middle Passage poem which in a strange unexpected way sums up all the various routes/roots of all of us who read this work, making our various ways to or from our own births/disasters/ golo-kwatis, Hawk's last Body & Soul.

Well, insofar as one could decipher Kamau's coded orisha-possessed language, this was the entire map of KB's travelling soul; the places where he had already made landfall, the place where he was now, and the places where he hoped to be at his final 'arrivance'.

Letter #124: GR – KB, Thursday, 28ᵗʰ June, 2002

This was a letter about muddled arrangements for travel and accommodation to a Conference on the Commonwealth inspired by Queen Elizabeth's 80ᵗʰ Birthday. Kamau and I had both been invited to participate in this "International Caribbean Conference & Exhibition" whose stated aim was to measure the contribution of the West Indian migrant community to the Commonwealth. Funding for the Conference/ Seminar that was due to take place on July 12, 2002, was being provided by agencies that viewed it simultaneously as part of the celebrations of the Queen's Diamond Jubilee and of the Commonwealth's five or more decades of existence. The Conference, therefore, had to be made to seem to be related to these broad British nationalist concerns. Yet, organized by the Caribbean-run TCS Tutorial College,[115] this

"International Caribbean Conference and Exhibition" sought to explore the situation of the Black (mainly African diasporan) migrant community after fifty years in England.

Kamau, replying almost immediately to my query about travel arrangements said in *Letter #125, Thursday, 28th June, 2002,* that he had, as usual, his own alternate agenda and itinerary.*

> My position is that long before they come up, am I invited by Sussex to receive an Hon Doc; so am going over for a 2 weeks fling: Wales (17) to see my sister Joan get (hopefully) her Ph.D in Libraries & the Info Age; 18 reading w/Grace, John & James Berry @ Sussex; 19 My Hon Doc; 22 Geo Padmore (i recall you there) last year; tho I don't kno if you hear that John was recently in hospital again, recurring what Sarah calls 'unstable angina' 24 shadda at Af. Centre, back out 30th July via Bajan to 15 Aug.[116]

The "International Caribbean Conference & Exhibition" on 12th July, was just another semi-colon in this itinerary; the two most significant events of which were to be KB's being awarded an Honorary Doctorate by the same University that had in 1968 awarded him the real one, and Joan Brathwaite's doctorate in Wales.

Part of Kamau's mission, whenever he visited the UK, had always been to search for signs that CAM still existed, despite all indications that the organisation that he had known in the 1960s had disappeared. Most of its original members had either returned to the Caribbean or migrated to the USA. Other potential artists, scholars, publishers, cultural or political activists, were involved in other causes. The Grenadian folk singer, broadcaster and educator, Alex Pascall,* a man who, like Kamau, had compiled his own private archive on the Empire Windrush generation of Caribbean migrants into Great Britain, spoke ruefully of the atomized state of the migrant intelligentsia, and their inability to come to any consensus about the best means of signifying their cultural presence in the land of their adoption. His own suggestion when funding was offered had been to build a twenty million pound millennium cultural centre, a permanent institute or museum, together with a library, and concert hall. The Millennium Centre would be dedicated to Caribbean history, culture, performance and business. Pascall's idea was scuttled by the divided Caribbean elite who quarrelled among themselves even as they tried to expropriate the idea and the project. [Conversation between Gordon Rohlehr and Alex Pascall, Sunday, 08 April, 2001].

In the end, nothing happened with Pascall's big idea. Sponsorship was instead offered to lesser schemes, such as the "International Caribbean Conference & Exhibition" held the next year at the Wembley Plaza Hotel. That Conference suggested that there was no single West Indian or Black community in Britain, but several groups, divided by class, place of origin, ethnicity, race, ideological persuasion and mutual ignorance of the history of their own collective struggle and residence in a still strange and at times hostile land. This atomized state meant that there had emerged no collective position. The "Black" diasporan community of the new Millennium, was weak and was aware of having been marginalized and ignored. The Caribbean diasporan community had remained the hustling, survivalist thing that it had been in the Caribbean. And the first law of survivalism has always been, *moi-meme*; myself; individualism.

Survival had demanded flexibility, shape-shifting, the ability to fit the self into any situation. This meant that no coherent 'game plan' had emerged among Black diasporans. One did whatever was necessary, and quite different and even opposite things might be necessary in different circumstances. While some, even many, might perform brilliantly under these circumstances, the group, as a whole, never seemed to be getting anywhere. Educationally ghettoized, the West Indian community was provided with curricula that reflected nothing of their history. They moved and grew up in a void. The real objective of the conference, then, became how to plot out strategies for dealing with this phenomenon of void and this reality of transitional identity.

The organization of the Conference fell on too few shoulders. Funding came late. Tickets, travel and hotel arrangements, everything came late. There was great confusion about who was paying for what. The whole affair was for me an adventure into vagueness and stress. Complaining to Kamau in *Letter #126: GR – KB, Thursday, July 04th, 2002* about my bewilderment over the arrangements for my participation in the upcoming Caribbean Conference, I ended my letter: "Have faith. Float in your own space, sail in your own sea and in your own ship. All will be well." These sentiments evoked a reply from Kamau in *Letter #127, KB – GR, Saturday, 06th July, 2002*:

> The wrong kind of critic(s) wd. say that this is GR's ZEN; others wd try make out a case ref GUYANA and there's certainly an element here, still unXplore (d). But is high time somebody begins to Xplore the itself/ word/world of GR.

I thought this an odd response to the clichés of my advice. Why did Kamau find these words special or unusual? GR's ZEN? Did he sense that I was talking about or to myself? That these words were about my journey and related to how I had dealt and was dealing with Guyagony?[117] He implied that there was an element about me that had remained 'unexplored' and that it was time that 'somebody' began to explore the word and world of GR.

My question was: Why hadn't KB, who was certainly the person most acquainted over 35 years with my wordworks, attempted this Xploration? My answer was that KB was too deeply engrossed in himself and in the resonant trauma of his own journey to explore anyone else's; except he could relate the other's journey to, and incorporate the other's trauma into his own. [cf. "I am becoming my own poem for Mikey Smith"]. Maybe he couldn't do that with my writing. He had once said of my review of *Islands* that: "You writin so sweet pun my work dese days I almost fraid to read it (you) in case I get *influence*" [*Letter #20, KB – GR, 2nd October, 1970*]. He was, in spite of this fear, ever eager for me to reveal and share my reactions to his words.

In other words, KB was, or had become, too involved in his own journey to appreciate the travels and travails of another fellow-traveller. While he had once claimed egolessness as his ideal and praxis, the Ego was certainly the arena where his most intense battles were being fought. Kamau never attempted any serious exploration of the "itself word/world/ of GR" who without either hope or faith has been floating in his own space and sailing in his own ship and on his own sea, quite unassured of St. Juliana of Norwich's affirmation, repeated resignedly by T.S. Eliot, that all things will be well. "All manner of thing shall be well."

From Hawk to Ark

As we have seen, Kamau in his new map of his life's journeyings [*Letter #123, KB – GR, Tuesday, March 12th, 2002*], defined *ARK* as a special summing up of "all the various routes/roots" not only of his own journeys but of the travels of the African Diasporan tribe. *ARK* was KB's response in poetry, song, dance, performance to 9/11. In Letter #128, GR – KB, Wednesday, December 11th, 2002, I wrote, among other things, about the bitter controversy that had arisen among academics in the USA (especially New Jersey, where Amiri Baraka was Poet Laureate) over Baraka's lacerating reaction to 9/11, "Somebody Blew up America".[118] I wrote:

> I only just read about the Baraka Laureate controversy. I think he's rubbed a terrible amount of historical indictment in their faces; as they should have expected he would; and they can't bear it. But this is precisely what rap, hip hop, Gil Scott-Heron,* the Last Poets,* Shepp,* Trane,* all the *dies irie* voices of the nameless devastated – marcus, malcolm, martin, mandela – have been saying. 9/11 is "de flame dem from on high dem" in its darkest descent and it has illuminated the names of the nameless dead, and enumerated all the crimes of the builders of Babylon [throughout all ages]. So there has been the physical attack on the twin towers, followed by the laceration of language and laughter in poems such as Baraka's: [songs of rage and retribution] that have begun to dismantle the towers

of Prospero's history.

Could my note about these interlinked voices of indictment, these Isaiahs, Ezekiels and Daniels of the apocalypse, have partially inspired Brathwaite's *ARK*?

ARK, three years in composition, resembled *Shar*.[119] *Shar* was a response to the trial by flood and landslide that lay at the vestibule of Kamau's decentred exit from Jamaica, while *ARK* was KB's response to the trial by fire and the "snowflakes" of dust and ashes, that marked his equally traumatic exit from New York and return, not to 'home' but to the final harrowing of Cowpastor, Barbados. *ARK* was released almost simultaneously by *Savacou* Publications, Mona, Kingston 7, Jamaica, and by *Savacou* North, Department of Comparative Literature, New York University, 2004. The Jamaican edition acknowledges Beverley Brathwaite, while the New York edition acknowledges Isis Barra Costa, Kamau's Secretary/typist/Administrative Assistant.

My copy came with an accompanying letter, dated "Saturday now Sundee February 19/20, 2005 (i.e. on my 63rd birthday). In the letter KB thanked me for my phone-call and news of a new publication (probably *A Scuffling of Islands*) as well as Lexicon's reprint of 'one of the earlier books (probably *Pathfinder*). He in turn was sending two copies of *ARK* and one of 'Namsetoura' from *Hambone 17*. He spoke of:

> the cruel ineffective no-support saga of trying to save Cow Pasture (oil pipelines already laying down) the whole last green space now bein use as DUMP. all the cow(s) gone. the duncks turnin back/turnin black & sour aready: COW PASTOR it-self about to be surround in by a out-manoeuvring road. so that me don't even get no likkle COMPENSATION.

> An this (dis) was the place. the moment – when & whe i that i wd at last (?) settle down since IT. since Meroë, since Akkad. since Chad. since Mexican. re. Org the archive(s). set up a Bussa Institute of word & sound ….. fade-way at lass into the serengetti sunset.

> So hey we go again …. la lutta …. la lutta …. the pain
> …. but for how long how long
> …. betrayal(s)

This was KB's first disclosure to me of the conversion of COWPASTURE to DIS; the replacement of rural pasture land – bleak to start with – to a DUMP. This time he was confronted by 'progress', development, the tourism imperative, engineering the landslide, inspiring new hibiscus, oleander and bougainvillea landscapers. There wasn't going to be any easy retirement, any homecoming (except Walcott's "homecoming without home").[120]

ARK was published four years after 9/11. It took its first epigraph from Dawad Philip,* a 'Trinbagonian' poet resident in New York:

I can still hear
Hammer after hammer
The mortal city fall.

Its second epigraph is taken from a poem written by one of Kamau's graduate students at NYU.

that which now builds its world in the midst of its inconstant undoing.

Its third epigraph is taken from a scrawl on the Great Wall of China: "what can our children learn in the desolation." He also indicates that he wants to sing about the courage of "*firefighters in those other cities*, those who dig w/their fingers into the rumble of their death." New York, he reminds insular America, isn't the only city that has been reduced to ash and rubble. Only Americans think that the whole world is American and all the murder that the USA in its greatness has inflicted on the rest of us is just "collateral damage".

There is a dedication for Coleman Hawkins and Dream Chad (Beverley Brathwaite) "and for all the bird tulips of the loving world." Then there is a description/outline of the history of the poem whose first reading took place at the Brecht Forum NY in April 2002 at a celebration of the journal *XCP*. The first printed version appeared in *The Literary Review* 46: February 2003. Then a revised and extended *Hawk* now renamed *ARK* was due to appear in *Born to Slow Horses* (Wesleyan University Press, 2004).

We soon recognise that this introduction to the poem proper is a video of dramatis personae: musicians whose fragments of sound will augment its central theme-song: Coleman Hawkins' *Body and Soul*, last performed in Ronnie Scott's Jazz Club, in London, 11 September, 1968: that is thirty-three years before the bombing of the Twin Towers, New York, on 9/11, 2001. Since Hawk died in 1969, the Ronnie Scott performance was probably his last. Brathwaite divined that this coincidence was an omen, a spirit message sent from Hawk to the new millennium world of Manhattan's glitz, illusion and globalised commercial predation.

The World Trade Towers of 9/11 will in the poem be:

grounded on Hawk's 'Body & Soul' interacting w/among others, Duke
Trane Rollins Eliot Césaire *raga adowa fado flamenco* Rimbaud Rilke Billie*
& Nina* (both 'Strange Fruit') *ghazal* Tosh ('Fools Die') Thomas Tomkins*
gawwali & glorias like Mozart Rachmaninoff C minor . w/postlude
Marley's 'Ises' falling shimmering & rising raiment behind the poem.

(*Ark*, xi)

Though Hawk's 'Body & Soul' is the dominant Voice, there are many others, some of them poets rather than musicians. (T.S. Eliot, Aimé Césaire, Rimbaud and Rilke). John Coltrane and Sonny Rollins are there among the saxophonists. Billie Holiday and Nina Simone with their starkly different versions of "Strange Fruit" are Muses, indicting an America where lynchers still tarnish the American Dream. But then, surprisingly, Kamau includes Mozart and Rachmaninoff in his sound track. Why? He had once (Carifesta 72) rejected as distressingly Afro-Saxon, the hybridised sounds, styles and consciousness of the emerging Caribbean bourgeoisie: e.g. the steelbands birthed in Port-of-Spain ghettos measuring their greatness by playing European classical concert music; the fakedness of many of the 'folk' offerings at Carifesta, where his highest praise was for Rex Nettleford's *Kumina* and some Haitian drumming.

Yet in *ARK*, the spirit-and sound-guides seem comfortably to contain all sorts, including Indian raga, Akan adowa, Islamic ghazal, Spanish flamenco and Jamaican reggae. *ARK* is, like Geraldine Connor's* *Carnival Messiah*, super New Age, all-inclusive, Manhattan Diasporan, swallowing everything in its world Voice. Kamau explains in his video of acknowledgement that he was trying to list

(2) the names of the belovèd dead so lamented and celebrated in the poem their *nommos* spoken in all the various nation-language accents of bereave... (*Ark*, xi)

If *Rights of Passage* began with the poet's mission to write out of the taut surfaces of things

I sing
I shout
I groan
I dream
about

["Prelude" from *The Arrivants*, p.4]

ARK endeavours to in-gather all categories and dimensions of the global human Voice, to sing, shout, groan and ultimately dream in chorus *against* the righteous rage, the sacrificial waste of the *Dies Irae*, the summit of violence pitted against the material kingdom of this world.

Next there are symbols: a six-pointed wheel or star, black spokes and a white centre (p. XII); and twin shapes (XIII) that, computer-produced, render the Twin Towers as Haitian marassa. Maya Deren, the Russian-born American ethnologist of *The Divine Horsemen* who startled the 'civilised' world of the Western academe by becoming via spirit possession an inductee and participant of the vodun cult she had begun observing, writes that

> The worship of the Marassa, the Divine Twins, is a celebration of man's twinned nature; half matter, half metaphysical; half mortal, half immortal; half human, half divine. The concept of the Marassa contains, first, the notion of the segmentation of some original cosmic totality. In Voudoun songs, there still exists vestigial references to ancient African myths of origin.[xxv]

Brathwaite equates the Twin Towers to the Marassa, linking 'hyper-civilised' New York to Haitian/Dahomean/Akan mythology, to illustrate what he has painfully learned from 9/11: the architectural magnificence and tower-of-Babel aspiration to godhead on the one hand, and the failure of hubris and collapse of human overreaching pride on the other; the almost diabolical indifference of the powerful controllers of the towers to the human suffering in which the towers are planted. The towers are presented throughout the poem as dichotomy.

More hopefully, the towers as Marassa signify the possibility of uniting opposites. KB's Marassa appear as children holding hands above the space between the Twin Towers. This dream is countered by Kamau's lived reality after the bombing, living in his Washington Square apartment "inside/ this dusk(y) afternoon" like a caged dog, "our teeth snarl/snapp-ing even at halpless angels in this new dust(y) garden of the earth's delights."

How does 'Hawk', spirit of ferocity, omen of revenge, voice of indictment and retribution, transmute into *Ark*, capsule and vessel of survival after the long blind drifting voyage of "old negro, Noah?" This is the daunting task that Kamau sets himself in the poem: the task of journeying through and then beyond catastrophe: the essential journey of diasporan Africans. Brathwaite's poem contains all the Black triumphalism of Baraka's "Somebody Blew up America" but seeks to journey beyond this gloating "served-them-right" catharsis that so enraged white America.

'Hawk' (Coleman Hawkins) arrives in London in autumn: both the time of the year and the autumn of his life. The poem will oscillate between 9/11/1968 and 9/11/2001 as the narrator, a Tiresias figure, constantly bridges two times and spaces, thirty-three years apart. This sort of thing is probably easier to render in film, than words, and Kamau, as we saw in his video-style stream of acknowledgements, is very much interested in the poem as video. Hawk's first notes,

...whisp

---

xxv. Maya Deren, *The Divine Horsemen: The Living Gods of Haiti*, London, New York, Thames & Hudson, 1953, 38.

ering of something like the death
of all the certainties we'd known (*Ark*, 4)

are typical of the tendency he shared with Ben Webster* to breathe
soundless air into the saxophone, as if, he was gasping for breath, or
pushing his last oxygen into the sound. The music brings people together.
Hawk is shaman, preserver, redeemer, a high priest in a world of death
and sepulchres.

Music becomes "muse-ic" as Hawk's resurrected breath opens the
consciousness of his audience to the possibility of rage and empowerment.
(One doubts that any rendition of an old standard such as "Body and Soul"
could release long suppressed dreams of Black Rebellion.) In 1968, Coltrane,
Shepp, Dolphy,* Charlie Mingus, Roland Kirk* and Pharoah Sanders* were
some of the high priests of the rebellion of that decade: though, as we've
observed, Kamau has transformed Hawk into a representative of the
communal Voice of the time. It was a moment when Africa, India and Latin
America were simultaneously contributing to the "exploding dimensions
of song" in African American Jazz. One thinks of Hugh Masekela,*
Abdullah Ibrahim,* Salif Keita,* Randy Weston,* Mongo Santamaria,*
Chano Pozo;* the Cuban trumpeter Sandoval,* whose earliest efforts were
inspired by Santeria; Yuseef Latif,* a multi-instrumentalist, who as composer and performer simultaneously embraced and challenged Euro-
American notions of sound; and foremost among white Americans who
explored the murky depths of the City was Canadian-born Gil Evans* with
Las Vegas Tango and *Time of the Barracudas*.

Hawk, fat and scant of breath, arrives in London at a dire time, when
Selvon's Moses (in *Moses Migrating* (1983) is on the brink of departure and
Salkey's hip-strutting jive talkers are immersed in their "escape to an
autumn pavement",[121] while Naipaul's Kripalsingh of *The Mimic Men* is in
the process of losing dimension, of being flattened out by the City to which,
already and irremediably ruined, he had fled for refuge from his "tainted
encircling sea." Lamming's Teeton in *Water with Berries* is, as C.L.R. James
divined, in dire trouble and about to sever ties with the Old Dowager by
equally futile acts of murder and arson, while the Commandant has lost his
charts and his way.[122]

Kamau, remembering Hawk's recovery of both breath and solidity fixes
his glance on

the thin
and hollow image of the Hawk

alone inside the spot
-light slowly filling out his shadow at the micro
-pole . the first limp

step. first first-step. first
-set legba notes of confidence. push
-ing aside the silence for the man to walk again on
cool

laconic water. (p. 7)

He recognizes Hawk as the crippled Legba regaining his sense of direction, "remembering becoming whole & powerful again" (p. 8). Jazz music, regains the Nile and a tremendous spirit of bounty, fertility

w/a glad.ness we now know is stolen from our eyes by too

much inattention. drag & droop & dampness

And we, the scattered and terrible as Roach and Carter had begun to term us[xxvi] begin to ask "who has stolen the vision from my eyes?" and conclude that we ourselves have not paid attention to, or sufficiently celebrated the joy we've always borne within our eyes even in the face of our long-suffering. And we have thus succumbed to "drag & droop of dampness."

"Don't let the Devil make you lose your joy," has been one of the deepest and most enduring foundational texts of the African American Holiness Church. Salim Washington views this 'joy' as the power to endure and transcend the history of oppression that has been the lot of Black people. This joy-in-spite-of, this joy-beyond-all-horror was the climax, meaning and message of John Coltrane's *A Love Supreme* and the posthumously released "Joy", and is something like the 'gladness' that Kamau's collective of musicians, Hawk, Trane, Sanders, Rollins, Simone, Aretha, Satchmo, Miles, Mingus, have envoiced against the workings of "the Devil". (See Salim Washington, "Don't Let the Devil (Make You) Lose Your Joy": A Look at Late Coltrane" in Leonard L Brown, editor, *John Coltrane & Black America's Quest for Freedom: Spirituality and the Music*).

At this point in the journey towards vision, the omen of the late sixties and seventies fulfils itself, but not in a clarification of self-knowledge, certainly not in any reconciliation with those who have always been working to steal the gladness from our eyes, but in the hardening of our wish for retribution to fall on our enemies – preferably via the deeds of our hands. A transfigured Hawk returns thirty-three years later.

---

xxvi. See Roach, "Littering Earth's Centre" and Carter, "I Come from the Nigger Yard".

"rising himself again in sound towards the silver cross of an approaching jet." (p. 9)

The jet as a silver cross, becomes a Xtian missile of the Apocalypse in the hands of Islamic pilots who know how to fly and where, though not how to land. (Two for the Towers of World Trade predation; one for the White House, one for the Pentagon). The mission of these pilots is to fulfil "the full white mosque and omen of the moon." (9)

These Islamic pilots are not Diasporan Africans, though elsewhere Kamau in *X/Self* has written about "my companions of the curved cross", but it is they who have created the moment for which African Diasporans sometimes pray in their Xtian churches. *Dies Irae* is a hymn that can be found even in Anglican and Methodist hymn books. Brathwaite depicts the 9/11 holocaust as emblematic of all explosions, both man-made and divine. In "Wings of a Dove" the Apocalypse will be engineered by both "de flame dem from on high dem" and the rage-filled uprising of "de poor dem." Here, volcanic holocausts such as the explosion of Stromboli or Vesuvius or Aetna are placed in the same category as the jihadist retaliation for America's destruction in 1990 of Iraq in the Mother of All Wars.

"Man-make madness" (p. 6) is how the narrator, as yet unidentified, describes all wars, whether performed as acts of aggressive predation or acts of retributive aggression. The narrator lists some of the most infamous of such acts: Spanish conquistadors smashing the cenotes of Mexico, reducing a lake to a desert; Hiroshima, Nagasaki, Bhopal, Viet Nam:

and our life looking back
salt. as in Bhuj. in Grenada. Guernica. Amritsar. Tadjitzkhan

the shaggard sulphur-stricken cities of the plains
of Aetna. Pelée. ab Napoli. Krakatao.
the young window-widow baby-mothers of the prostitutes .

looking back looking back as in Bosnia. the Sudan. Chernobyl
(p. 14)

Maybe "man-make madness" naturally leads to mad reasoning. Catastrophes of nature and mad man-made ones are beyond comprehension, intermixed; meet meld and melt in New York's paradise of entertainment and hard bargaining. Ku Klux Klan Christianity in Birmingham Alabama, Germans in Namibia, the Herero, juxtaposed to the assassination of JFK, Pol Pot, King Leopold's Great Pyramid of Skulls (Mark Twain's *King Leopold's Soliloquy*, cited in *X/Self*.) This Bookman's archive of the dead and dying sweeps on, image after shattering image. One isn't allowed to pause; to unriddle this tangle of allusions.

Yet at this point the poem turns as KB interpolates the testimony of the wife of an American firefighter. He's used this technique before, in "Pixie" (See *Ancestors*; see *Trench Town Rock*). It seems that the interpolations of these voices help restore a sense of everyday realism to the narrative, and to warn the narrator that he is no more or less than the ordinary Voice of one diminished, like John Donne, by all this dying, hearing the bell toll. What follows is prayer:

> so let us even at this time
>
> remember the poor & the helpless
> the cold the hungry & the blown . les damnés de la terre
>
> the sick in mind & body . them that will bear
> the floor in flames the broken fence of mourning on their faces
> the lame the lonely the unnamed unloving the unleash(ed).
>
> (p.22)

KB's 'congregation' & his 'nation' are all those listed above, the doomed, the damned, the afflicted and those who in spite of all overcome. He cries out in wonder at where he has arrived

> ...following the foot -
> steps of my own self. my own self. the distress
>
> of my own rivers of this flesh
> *who feels it knows it Lord!*
> my own ash my own alph my own borders of outcry .
>
> how yu mek me sing these strange mesongs in a strange land.
> so far from music sex and saxophone (p. 17-18)

Here he acknowledges that his now long deep cyclic journey back into his lamented ruins (my own ash) and his beginnings (my own alph) has led him outside himself towards and into a contemplation of the universal distress of les damnés, who have fallen under ruins wrought by God and man; who have endured Judgement without apparent redemption.

Journeys around oneself become in turn entries into Self that are both deeply narcissistic and widely compassionate. KB at the end of the poem, is uncertain about its meaning

> and i still do not know why dis riddim is happenin happenin
> happenin happeninn
> what dis poem will say what it mean when it done
> when it come to the time of it oracle circle &

> placard an i muss face the music
> before you an read it aloud & alone

ARK ends with a message of peace and a holding of hands, as congregations in Anglican and Roman Catholic churches have been doing for some decades just before the Eucharist or nearing the end of funerals.

Kamau's movement from the genocidal theatre of all the destructive wars in colonial history to the troubled placidity of hand-clasping kumbaya campfire choruses masked a progression in consciousness and spirituality that he himself mistrusted. He mistrusted most how he and his scepticism over America's constant mantra about its being the most democratic, the greatest and most just country in the world, would be viewed by the very corporations and foundations that had funded and facilitated his post-UWI years at NYU.

As pneumonia, constant travelling and a shuttling between New York and Barbados made him seem less of an asset than NYU had reckoned he, with his constantly self-publicised CV of achievement, would have been, there began to be voices recommending his retirement and he began to talk about losing precious documents pertaining to his research and teaching: a steady "cultural lynching" that was taking place in his very home, the NYU apartment on Washington Square.

Was this simply the dementia of an exhausted, brain-weary old man? Was it the machinery of US Intelligence extending its baleful purview to this enigmatic scholar from one of its tourist outposts? Perhaps it was both: Brathwaite's dementia and the strategy of the invisible powers-that-be to exploit that dementia to the point where Kamau would willingly leave that place and retire for good at Cowpastor or wherever. Kamau was vulnerable and had since Doris's death been displaying his vulnerability in all sorts of ways. He was easy to hurt, though he was fierce in retaliation and stubborn in standing his ground.

One of the cracks in his armour had long been his fear of being surveilled. Since October 1984 [see *Letter #95, KB – GR, 22ⁿᵈ October, 1984*] he had been talking about the failure to get his "Bio-Bibliography of Caribbean Poetry" published by G.K. Hall in Boston, and his difficulties to find publishers for "Roots" and "White Power in Jamaica" as part of a single planned attack on 'our' (i.e. 'his') movement. To this he added the 'invasion' of his classes at Mona by US students:

> The destruction of our Movement goes on apace; mining the waters of our minds okay? The US Embassy people are ensconced in my class: a big operation with Augier attending the staff meeting to help ensure a voice for the SUBVERSION.

> I am told that they have been admitted not as Embassy persons, but as 'ordinary' individual students. They sit in i lectures with that push away

of the pen from i ideas and that stare away which lets all know of the
GULF

Nobody at our staff-meeting perceived a threat: except another US plant;
on the *staff* no less! She said that she wd be unhappy about teaching
under such circumstances: they all conducted under a mood of fait accompli:
what Sylvia Wynter wd. call *compliance*; some others complicity.

It was appropriately, 1984, year of Orwell's futuristic anti-utopic novel,
and KB who, at the ACLALS conference of 1971, had expressed suspicion
of the motives of certain US delegates, was here spinning a conspiracy
theory about the complicity of the UWI 'Establishment' with the US
Embassy, Big Brother, in surveilling his classes. It is clear that his suspicion
of being surveilled simply grew and grew; no more so than when after
he resigned/retired from UWI to take up a tenured position at the New
School, NYU, he had willingly placed himself under the microscope
of 'Big Brother'. Routine surveillance would become 'cultural lynching',
as he aged and began to lose control of his vast agenda and his multiplying
perspectives that could not, or could no longer be accommodated under
the original umbrella of Creole négritude.

Thus in 2002 and for several years after, he was anxious about my
response to *ARK*, which for all sorts of reasons I had not read in any depth.
I published three major collections of essays – *A Scuffling of Islands* (2004),
Transgression, Transition, Transformation (2007) and *Ancestories* (2010), all of
which, particularly the last text, were concerned with Kamau's work. These
books brought closure to my own academic career.

My close reading of *ARK* was constantly postponed, even after Kamau
sent me a CD of his performance of it. Then I bought a CD/DVD player
that could play many things that the expensive but now superannuated
Carver was rejecting as "No Disc". So was I at last able to hear Kamau's
reading of *ARK* and the conversation that followed. This performance took
place in London, around August 2005, where Kamau launched *Born to Slow
Horses*, a book of poems that had won the Griffin Poetry Prize. It was
published by Wesleyan University Press in Connecticut. "Hawk", not yet
named *ARK* was located between some older poems and other more recent
ones.

As I noted in *Notebook #15, Thursday, 16th January, 2006*, p. 205, Brathwaite
first read excerpts from *Islands* (1969, *The Arrivants*, 1973), "Shepherd",
"The Cracked Mother", now renamed "Iwa". "Days & Nights" from *Mother
Poem* and "Donna" from *X/Self* had also been relocated in *Born to Slow
Horses*. I wondered (as Michael Dash had wondered at the launching of *Jah
Music* and *The Visibility Trigger*), why Kamau had continued this habit of
recycling old poems and rereading them in the context of new and radically
different compositions. *Born to Slow Horses* was, after all, contemporary;

nearly two decades after the *Zea Mexican Diary* chronicled the trauma of the mid-eighties and guarded the vestibule of a new and more complicated phase of Kamau's life and vision. After *ZMD*, there had been *Dream Stories* (1994) and the *Magical Realism* texts, (*MR* I and II) and there had been *ARK* ("Hawk").

My half-answer this time to the riddle of Kamau's recycling of old poems and juxtaposition of old and new perceptions was that "The Cracked Mother", "Donna" and "Days and Nights" were now being presented as preludes to or omens of "Namesetoura", a new poem that envoices the undead, unburied, 'angering' spirit of the landscape. In *Mother Poem*, she was called "Sycorax", "black Sycorax, my mother." In *Islands* she was the unnamed Carib mother who, speaking for all the mothers who had in Africa or the New World been robbed and stripped of their children, who watched, in helpless rage and eventual madness, Columbus and the Catholic Church seize and devour her children.

So, the Cracked Mother evolved into first, Sycorax, then Namesetoura, a Muse that Brathwaite believed still lived and was manifesting herself at Cowpastor or its environs. She was his version of the Roman Catholic Black Madonna; she had become Muse, Warner Woman, aggrieved, defiled, despoiled flesh of landscape, dishonoured and unburied. Sycorax/Namesetoura, like Tom in *Rights of Passage*, remains "unflamed", uncremated and unburied. Kamau is concerned in *Born to Slow Horses* with death, mourning, funeral rites, late efforts at remembering or amnesia and a finality of disconnection. What happens, he asks, when a whole society – the new world of the post-Columbian Caribbean – has not been in a position to bury their dead, in the sense of knowing, acknowledging, and laying to rest their shattered ancestors?

Born to Slow Horses, KB's attempt to imagine an answer to this overwhelming question, is about the "still-vexed Bermudas" of Sycorax and Caliban, plagued by Columbus's recurrent arrival and the continuously catastrophic birth of the New World. The recycling of the confessional monologue of the Cracked Mother is Brathwaite's attempt to determine the impact of Columbus's arrival on the mind/consciousness, Anima of both African and Carib mothers/Muses.

At the August 2005, London reading, Brathwaite identified the journal of Mary Prince[123] – in particular the moment when Mary, 12, and her sisters were separated from their mother and each other – as a paradigm of the recurrent historical situation of severance, loss and anguish that is reborn whenever mothers lose their children or children their mothers.

Brathwaite tells of how his present wife, Beverley, lost her only son, Mark, who died in an accident in Jamaica in 2000. Brathwaite tries to understand her inner devastation, but is not allowed to enter into the inner chamber of mourning. How is she coping? *Is* she coping? What's taking place inside there? These questions are splinters of the larger one: How did (do) Africans mourn their dead? Have any of the ancient ancestral rituals survived beneath or beyond "Amazing Grace" (that marvellous slave trader's song) or "It Is Well with My Soul", that great statement of faith and hope in the face of deepest turmoil and loss?

Kamau writes this long poem, imagining the interiors of grief, in which he endeavours to read his wife's internal anguish from her external actions. Beverley becomes Mary Prince's mother, struck dumb at the loss of her daughters, or Sycorax, or Namesetoura – the formerly silent now enraged Muse of Severance. Beverley, transformed into Muse – a fate she could not have welcomed – metamorphoses into Orpheus after the twenty-first day of mourning and descends to the underworld to reencounter and reborn her son.

This, however, does not happen. Death is final and the cyclic movement of life through death and towards reincarnation does not happen in this poem. *Mother Poem* and *Sun Poem* both ended with the rebirth of Sycorax and the new Sun. But this does not happen in more recent death journeys. Kamau, who beneath his concern for Beverley, is also making his own orphic quest for the still-sought, still-missed Zea Mexican, may have learned from these orphic night journeys that mourning ends only when one at last recognises and becomes resigned to the truth that the beloved will not revisit the sad kingdom of this world.

Kamau is not sure, however, that Beverley, folded in silence, has become reconciled to anything. Her mourning, which he cannot enter, seems to have grown more intense after five years. In his own situation, Kamau spent months in despair that his beloved had not returned in dream or sign or haze of harmattan or endless blue and curve of sky. How has it really been after fifteen years? Do rituals of mourning ever lead to healing, catharsis, calm of mind?

I did not share these reflections with Kamau, or respond to his enquiries about *ARK*. I wrote my reflections on that poem in October 2020, after Kamau's death. He did, however, send *Letter 131, 15th March, 2005; revised Good Friday, 23rd March, 2005*. This letter, sent via Tim Reiss, was forwarded on Sunday, March 27th, 2005. I was a recipient, along with at least 200 others. It was the familiar Kamau appeal for help and it was entitled:

The lass days of KB and Cow Pastor Vandal: My Emmerton 2005[124]

The letter dealt with "(un)developments in my life i thot you shd kno." It was the same old story: isolation, physical and moral, this time at home. Kamau had refused to move when Progress had said he should. Progress had proceeded to bulldoze the trees – even the bearded fig tree which Kamau regarded as a shrine of ancient African and Amerindian spirits. Kamau's dream of retiring at Cowpastor was the same dream he had nurtured in the now ruined Irish Town home.

I had hoped, when we found this place, to found my nation here – my maroon town, resistance palenque. Bring in my archives from their shattered world – shattered in Jamaica since the Gilbert Hurricane of 1988 – an archive stretching back now almost 100 years and covering from Bay Street/Brown's Beach. Harrison College days, thru Cambridge, Ghana, SL [St Lucia], 30 years at Mona, the Caribbean Artists Movement (London) *Bim*, BBC Caribbean Voices, *Savacou*, Carifesta, paintings, sculpture (inc early postcolonial W Afr. early Rastafarian, Colly, Timothy Callender, Broodhagen, jazz records, tape recordings from almost ancient Ghana, from nearly every Caribbean voice of say or song.

.... And all this is a lament – the loss & dislocation of so much of this in Gilbert (see *SHAR*; see Herron's 'SAVING THE WORD' hear *ARK* – these are our documents for our last our lost millennium –and still more loss from worm and Ivan (2004) and a terrible break-in (5 March 05) VANDALL INVASION of our hopes and consciousness.

He then restates his dream:

to in-gather the scatta archives (Ja & NYC) here, try to heal them and from this wound of miracle, set up a BUSSA CENTRE for us all.

The centre would include a library, a conference room, performance spaces outdoor, chalets for writers, artists.

that kind of possible dream, because we had the dream we had the space we had the means – destroyed by my own Govt – w/out DISCUSSION – and digging us down and STRANGLING the holy past & constellation flute & future of this place – the egrets gone because the cattle gone. the woo doves mourn. I itch from deconstruction cement dust.

As with his various letters of indictment of the 1980s he proclaims that

my micro case here is the macro case of us all. The little done unto mwe, is the burden down upon us all upon us all.

And he laments:

It will be a shame if I hear the people saying AFTER I GONE that *Kamau muse to talk about these things **an no one lissen*** not a body do a ting trapped – BUT SURELY NOT FOR EVER – in our Metal Mental Slavery.

Images of the desert and the harmattan arise naturally out of this scenario.

my eyes are full of grit and helpless scars, as if I am the last person in the world, the lost poet, really, in the world.

It is the imagery of the "Prelude" to *Rights of Passage* or "Volta", here personalized, with no space separating poet from persona, Kamau from his masks of dislocated nummo, travelling okyeame voice.

I walked out there towards the cloud of dust – the grit – my tears = and my heart as if rebelled inside me, fit to burst w/grief & loss & helplessness & pain.

He also, ominously, considers Edgar Mittelholzer's fiery exit:

I cannot even die here now. no strength to even burn myself upon this pasture as I want to do. As I still may. Because my beloveds. whe else is there to go, to try to build again at 75?

Kamau lived on for another fifteen years, shuttling precariously between New York and Cowpastor, where he died in 2020.

I haven't found any letters between 2005 and 2007, though there may have been. Our conversations were by phone during those years in which I neared retirement. I invited both George Lamming and Kamau to the three phenomenal tribute days of my retirement. George couldn't come and Kamau, after dancing around the idea, didn't come. I was disappointed. In *Letter #131, KB – GR, 5/6 November, 2007,* Kamau apologized for not coming. He said that he had dreamt "lass night" – (the letter was addressed Washington Square West and dated 5/6 November, 2007)

that i blow up my own house at Cowpastor w/a nuclear device i was Xperimenting with. when i duck down behine the foundation wall of the kitchen, in the space juss before you come to Namsetoura Groove, i hear a pilot flying into the airport saying that he had pick up a minor major Xplosion in the area and when i look up, me doan see the house at all – not even as pile of dust or a scorch black hole – only the blue sky and the breeze.

In one of the *Dream Stories* ("Dream Chad") he had dreamt that the house in Irish Town was afire and that the looters were pillaging the ruins. It turned out that the house would be confronted by hurricane, torrential rains and landslide, as well as looters. Both fire and water are agencies of apocalyptic destruction and the IT nightmare that drove KB out of Jamaica remained deeply entrapped in his consciousness throughout the New York years, merging in *ARK* with the 9/11 death by fire of the Twin Towers and all that macrocosmic ruin symbolised.

What followed this dream of his blowing up Cowpastor was the strange apology for his failure to attend the celebrations of my retirement. The dream of this final Cowpastor catastrophe which he says was his own fault and which enacted his living fantasy of self-immolation by fire, was connected to his failure to turn up at my celebrations

> which indicates how unsuccessful i continue not being able to make it to yr justice celebration and hearing the disappointment in yr voice when i phone you. They say that evvathing happen for a reason but this i one will never get over. We come too far together thru the seasons not to have been there.

<Kamau>

He should, indeed, have been there. His apology doesn't really say why he failed to come after saying that he would try to come, if not for the opening rites of passage, for the second and third days. We waited for two hours at the airport only to discover that his name was not on the list of BWIA passengers. My diary notes of Thursday, 11th October, 2007 [*Notebook #16*] describe both the celebrations and Kamau's failure to attend.

> It was, as Lord Jim might have said, immense;[125] last week's celebration of Rohlehr. An intense ritual in several acts. A ritual of recognition, praise, and severance. A ritual that was so enormous that to awaken from it has been to enter into a new world, a new phase of life, rather, in a world that is very much the same as ever it was. Professor, the thing was stunning.

> Jean's [Jean Antoine-Dunne's] documentary video confined itself to my Guyanese background & my relationship to the poetry of Martin Carter and the novels of Wilson Harris [mainly *The Guyana Quartet*]; though my work on Brathwaite has been more comprehensive. Brathwaite himself did not come. Seemed to be ill; though this sort of thing is quite normal for Brathwaite [See, e.g. the honouring ceremony for Harris and the Symposium and Conference on Poetry and Music that followed, Liège, Belgium, Friday, 30th March, 2001 and Sunday, 1st - Wednesday, 4th April, 2001].

> Sorry neither he nor [Lamming] could make it. George said from the start that he couldn't. But Kamau was coming then not coming, then coming one day late, then not coming at all.

> Well, he missed a great show.

Transgression, Transition, Transformation was completed and available on the opening day of the celebrations. Rawle Gibbons and Michael "Philo" Phillips had completed the transference from tape into CDs of my 26-lecture series of the early 1970s, *From Atilla to the Seventies*.[126] So there was a great deal of Rohlehr stuff available. I had prepared a package for Kamau, which I would have presented to him at the celebration.

Letter #132 – KB @ NYU, edu – GR, Thursday, 3rd January, 2008
This was seven weeks after Letter #131, 5-6 November, 2007. Kamau wanted help in his effort to contact Merle Hodge* and also wanted to know of my response to his gift pack of *ARK* (the recorded performance) and his document "of the STOLENS and my [i.e. his] attendant ruminations on RACE at the end." He complained about not hearing from me.

> The breakdown of our correspondence has really hurt me. so much has been happening since we lass meet here at NYC for the K70 ting (and indeed long before that) and even then we didn't have the kind of TIME together we ought to be having. is something wrong? have i offended or disappointed in some way? if so, i pray that 2008 will find bridges – and pl help me also reach Merle.
>
> <Kamau>

He had indeed sent two CDs of *ARK* about which he had enquired on December 04, 2007 i.e. four weeks after he failed to attend my retirement celebrations. I replied on December 05th, 2007 that I hadn't listened to them as yet, and that I was "surprised" that three years had passed between the originally written "Hawk" and the performed *ARK* of 2007. In *Letter #133, GR – KB, Thursday, 21 February, 2008, 10:53 p.m.*, I replied to Kamau's letter of January 3rd. I explained that

> Here in the Carry Beyond, as the Rastas used to term this place, we are caught up in an incredible rush of changing events, governments and scenarios. At present it is the Guyana massacres,[127] which echo some of those that have been happening all the time in Trinidad and Jamaica with their horrendous murder rates that run into nearly 400 per annum in Trini and over 2000 p.a. in Jamdung. I said years ago [1993] that we were caught up in a culture of terminality, and nothing has happened since 1993 when I first said it, or indeed, since 1987 with "Trophy and Catastrophe" when the keyword I used was "atrocity" to make me change this perception of terminality. You yourself articulated the concept of "Dis" on which I have commented in my as yet unpublished Ms on *Ancestors* that I will name *Ancestories*.

You seem to think that our time of communication/friendship has been dis/connected; but that is only illusion brought about by your extreme situation(s) in Jamaica, Barbados and now New York. If after Doris's death I had suggested that you get out of Jamaica, I'd now suggest that you clear out of New York where the plunder(ing) of your archives is calculated to propel you to the edge of terrible darkness. What you have described is as unimaginable as what has been happening in the wider theatre/arena/cockpit of the Caribbean. But I don't know how one fights that sort of thing, and I personally would have left that terrible place. In your case, though, Barbados too has become another ex/tension of DIS, one that is so small and cramped and stifling that I doubt your return there would solve much. It would, however, be better than the New York you describe.

I said that I don't think we have ever severed connection because I remain connected to your work. Having done the only full-length responses so far to *The Arrivants* and *Black + Blues*, I have for some years been working on the autobiographical *Mother Poem* and *Sun Poem* and have completed typing the Ms of *Mother Poem* and [have in hand] a still-to-be typed handwritten Ms of [my reading of] *Sun Poem*. I also published in my last collection of essays, (*Transgression, Transition, Transformation: Essays on Caribbean Culture*) a revised version of "Dream Journeys", a response to all of the *Dream Stories*; probably, again, the only full and coherent response to a significant Brathwaite text.

Since we haven't been meeting in the same places over the last six or seven years, our 'connection' has to be with each other's work and ideas, and I think that I have not only done my part in this respect, but invested considerable cash in getting my work published. There hasn't been much (any) help, and there are no prizes or awards to be won for what I do. But say what? I know that I am in a terminal place and don't really expect the grace of help or encouragement. I have worked out of a state of what in "4th Traveller" you call i/sol/ence. That's the way it is, has been, and will continue to be…

Having not attended my retirement celebrations, you haven't yet received your copy of *Transgression, Transition, Transformation*. I am afraid to send it to New York for your archive plunderer to plunder.

Letter # 134, KB-GR, Saturday May 10th, 2008, 2.14 pm
Sent on the edge of Kamau's 78th birthday, this letter did not address what I had asserted in *Letter #133* of 21st February. He reiterated his complaint about the disappearance of about 700 items from his Washington Square apartment in New York.

only last night when about to start work on the page proofs of Love Axe/l for Peepal Tree Press in the UK, find Vol. One of my 4-vol tss

[typescripts] GONE – stolen clean out of its box. Now I have no way
of cking these proofs!!!

This obsession with the notion that both his major research project
and his mental and spiritual being were under attack grew more intense
as he mourned the death of one of his comrades in the struggle to
record and validate the authentic expression of Caribbean folk. In
Letter#135 KB-GR, undated but written in May, 2008 and entitled,
"Kamau Brathwaite/ On a Season of Passages: Wordsworth McAndrew*
1936-2008" Kamau reflected on the life and work of a "nativist", a great
pioneer and activist poet of our time. First he strikes the KB keynote,
prominent and dominant since the nineties:

> Culture is how we commune. How we 'make' it. What we make of it:
> the collective life of the community of the living an those who had lived
> & loved that community, now Ancestors.
>
> For enslaved & colonized people – we salvaged littorals – this 'culture'
> is v/fragile, very contested, cruelly contradictory; above all it has a Sisyphean
> nightmare quality – we constantly tryin to reach eureika & solution.
> We constantly fail and fall back.

What follows is a biography of McAndrew's life and a list of his
achievements as poet, amateur anthropologist, collector, preserver,
folklorist, who, threatened by Burnham, left (i.e. fled) Guyana with
his archives stored in a "growing mountain of boxes." Brathwaite
concluded:

> If this pricelessness is lost, it will be because our culture has not yet
> reached the stage of being able to recognize itself, to treasure & respect
> itself; to see itself in the mirror of ourselves for what we are. And there
> was no support system in place – **first to keep him home!** – or/ then
> to help him under the hurdle, into the transconsciousness limbo that
> all travaillers have to face.

Unnumbered Letter – KB – GR, Saturday, 31st May, 2008

Great Gordon,

Thanks for the sending and let's hope it will remain. As soon as you
see it you say *That's a Gordon.*

So much in one big-hebby-volume. Look in vain, tho, for the usual
lett that's been like histories of our times, sensibility; and no autograph
neetha. The absence hits ya, let me tell you. This long beach we walk.
The middle-passage sea. The enigmatic stele. Can't thank you enough
for pp. 446-447. *X/S* (2) has to begin from there, Jah helping, but not

before Jah Willing. I can underfro these middle-passages.

< Kamau >

Here's the recurrent phenomenon! Kamau receives this big-hebby-volume with gratitude, but is devastated by the absence of a covering letter or an autograph (though *Transgression* contained the only full-scale response to *Dream Stories*, the chronicle of Kamau's phase of disconnection from Mona, loss of a sense of community, critique of post-colonial miasma and the trials of independence. *Transgression* was dedicated to George Lamming who had turned 80 in 2007 and John La Rose who had died in 2006. Did Kamau feel that *his* name should be included in that dedication? Evidently he did. *Transgression* included, apart from the above mentioned "Dream Journeys", the Sir Winston Scott memorial lecture on Lamming and Brathwaite where full tribute is paid to both of these 'ancestor' writers and pathfinders. Apart from those essays, there were other references to KB (e.g. "Folk Research: Fossil or Living Bone" and a whole sequence of the final essay, "Where Is Here". What further acknowledgement did KB require?

Letter #138: KB – GR, 4th June, 2008

All Praises, all Praises, Okyeame, as I continue into TTT. Has anyone attempted to REVIEW this yet?

The answer was No. It didn't occur to KB that he should attempt a review. I put this down to the narcissistic blindness that had become more powerful as Kamau aged. Eighty, the time when things begin to take advantage over one and often hide themselves away from one when one most needs them, is also the age when all one's journeys become not only journeys around but journeys into oneself. Kamau was on the edge of eighty.

Letter #141, September 19th, 2009, was sent to me by Esther Phillips, who wrote on behalf of the committee of *BIM*, requesting a tribute to KB for *BIM*'s November 2010 publication. *BIM* was honouring KB with a special (Bajan) edition. I can't remember whether or not I sent the tribute. Trinidad and Tobago were engrossed in the political turmoil that eventually inspired Patrick Manning to call elections in midterm 2010. I was trying to publish *Ancestories* at the same time as both parties were besieging printers for pamphlets, brochures and all the visual paraphernalia of antagonistic political campaigning. *Ancestories* and the poetry it was exploring had to stand in line behind bad and bizarre politics. The CLICO debacle in which that huge trans-Caribbean financial company, extending itself into the international arena of big-time predation, had collapsed, had since January

2009 either made me into an extremely gloomy person or had opened up portals and potholes into a pessimism that had always nestled at the centre of my void. Half of my earnings had been invested in CLICO.

All these factors, including the Mediterranean cruise that Betty and I made in mid-2010 could have influenced whether or not I wrote the *BIM* tribute. I did note in my *notebook #16, Thursday, 20th May, 2010*, p. 252 – that is nine days after Kamau's 80th birthday, that:

> Kamau's 80th wasn't any big thing among the historians, though the Barbados Museum has dedicated an art exhibition to him. The exhibition isn't *about* Kamau, but at least it recognises his existence. It will run till the 30th of May.

> Of what relevance really is intellect or sensibility when confronted with the neutering effect of amnesia? the sleep of all forgetting? No point his words or worse, my words about his words: *Ancestors, Ancestories* equally pointless... They will both be submerged in the noise of events: 'politics. rain, unrest' according to Derek Walcott.

Notebook #16: 23rd May, 2010, 8:00 a.m.

> Taxi-ing on BW414, headed (I, not B-Wee) to the CSA [Caribbean Studies Association] Conference in Barbados. This time, the dead man is Rex Nettleford, who expired late last year, the day before his 78th birthday. I will reshape the UNESCO/Seychelles address, excerpting its discussion of 'Crossroads' societies, a concept that Nettleford had since Bogota 1978 and beyond in an essay about the Caribbean Archipelago, been instrumental in articulating.

Notebook #16: Wednesday, 9th June, 2010, 10:35 a.m.

> I received/saw/held/touched the first copy of *Ancestories* yesterday morning. Ken Jaikaransingh's brother brought it around 11:00 a.m. Binding and cover magnificent. Exterior margins too narrow, needing ½ inch more space. Alignment of some pairs of pages slightly out. But on the whole, the thing looks well at this time when Kamau, eighty, is apparently forgotten. Bless it and the hands, especially Betty's, but Jessie's too, that prepared it, shaped it. Bless the eyes, mainly mine, that read and reread it. Amen. Bless it and send it on its way.

Notebook #16: Thursday, 08th July, 2010, p. 312
While still on Mediterranean cruise.

> Heard from Kamau who received his two copies of *Ancestories*. Full of iises. Glad he liked it. [NB: Book dedicated to "Kamau entering 80."

No quarrel about that.]

Notebook #16: Tuesday, 13ᵗʰ July, 2010, 2:05 a.m., p. 322

Betty and I returned to New York from our Mediterranean cruise on Saturday, 10ᵗʰ or Sunday 11ᵗʰ, 2010 .... We are now nestling on the 26ᵗʰ floor of the Hilton Garden Inn, West 35ᵗʰ St., Manhattan, from whence we survey a surrounding forest of tall structures.

I've seen these giants so many times and yet they never cease to amaze. Which world is greater? The ancient world of stone and marble, column, pediment and carved statue, or this world of behemoth sailing ship, airbus, computer megastore, skyscraper, cathedral of the Virgin Macy? Will future generations gawk at the magnificence of our ruins the same way we tire ourselves gawking at lost-now-bankrupt-Greece, ruined Italy still ruled by the sullen gaze of Vesuvius? the ever-threatening Aetna?

Notebook #16: Tuesday, 13ᵗʰ July, 2010, 2.05 a.m.

Visited Kamau and Beverley at 4:00 p.m. [i.e. on Monday, 12ᵗʰ July, 2010]. The first thing I noticed was the half-light, half-darkness of the place; far too small for KB's extensive archives. Kamau looks well enough, though his small hands seemed frail and resigned when I shook them.

I heard (again) the strange story of his plundered archives. He's caught in "Ananse's, once Onyame's trap of doom" [*The Arrivants*, p. 119]. Barbados has simply negated him. The "developers" are still after his land and seem to be hoping that he will soon expire, and that the impediment to progress and new age landscaping he represents, will be [gone with the wind].

The "Round House" isn't recognised as the home of his youth, but as a "national monument" because of its age and shape and of some bones that excavators have discovered at the site. Yet they invite his youngest sister, Joan, to screw on the brass plaque declaring the house a "national monument" on May 11ᵗʰ 2010, Kamau's 80ᵗʰ birthday, oddly acknowledging that part of the importance of the site is due to his having grown up there; yet not really recognising the man at all. There's nothing on the screwed-up plaque that mentions his name.[128]

Notebook #16: 14ᵗʰ July, 2010, 3:30 a.m.

We caught the subway to 49ᵗʰ and 7ᵗʰ Ave., found the Eugene O'Neill Theatre where the year before (2009), demolished by shrimp and the antidote Piriton, I had slept through most of the doings of the green-faced Shrek. We bought tickets for *Fela!* Kamau had declined our offer to purchase tickets for himself and Beverley. It was our last day in New York.

Throughout the show I kept hearing Rudder's praise-song for Fela and "Afrikaan Beat". I saw all sorts of things: Nettleford's choreography, T & T's Carnival, Orisha movements – and heard a range of jazz references. *Fela!* seemed to be an ingathering of songs, rhythms, styles, that constantly rooted innovation in tradition.

I remembered that long-ago time when I used to imagine Trane's horn riding the riddim of Andrew Beddoe's* Orisha drums. Well, something like that is happening in *Fela:* [something that Kamau would certainly have appreciated]; the in-gathering of the 'scatta-scatta' tribes.[129]

On June 4th, 2010, Caldwell Taylor, a former Grenadian diplomat, published in *Big Drum Nation* a tribute to Kamau. Entitled "Beat Eighty Drums for Kamau" the tribute accurately traced Kamau's long and varied career:

"In half-century of fierce intellectual exertions Kamau has been at once poet, philosopher, playwright, literary critic and theorist, surveyor of the Caribbean spirit (in space and time) teacher, student of Caribbean history and discoverer and tiller of the abandoned acres of our 'inner plantations'."

Tracing KB's journey through Harrison College, Pembroke College Cambridge, Ghana, CAM and Kenya, where he received the name /title of 'Kamau' (which meant 'the silent warrior') Taylor ended the tribute thus:

"The Silent Warrior is the finest interpreter of the semiotics of our collective stress; he is the epicist of our unspeakable trauma. In his heart there beats the trembling fears of trammelled cargoes; in his fisted stanzas there exists the strategic silences that coax nation and nation languages out of this fragmented submarine existence."[130]

Letter #143: Monday, September 13th, 2010, was from Elaine Savory who, like Kamau, worked at the New School, NYU. She regretted the delay in publication of her collection of essays on how various scholars taught Brathwaite's poetry. She had received my essay since Tuesday, July 10th, 2007, but had been under considerable stress: a husband ailing with kidney cancer; a recently deceased stepdaughter; the task of completing the "huge bibliography", to prepare which she had sought and received a special grant; and the necessity she felt to "soldier on" and "get this done for KB, for us, for our field."

Kamau, Elaine wrote, was on the verge of publishing *Elegguas* (Wesleyan Press, 2010). She hoped I would write an essay/review on this collection of poems. What the publication of *Elegguas* indicated was the real difficulty in keeping pace with Kamau. He was always moving on, even when he tried to remain firmly rooted in past perceptions, already published poems or essays. He was continuously updating himself, building his monument block by block, new concepts growing out of the older ancestorial past. So Elaine, with a batch of essays and an already huge bibliography, had after three years of effort begun to feel that her still unpublished anthology was becoming "outmoded".

It is the problem of this era, the way the ever-changing present seems to render the past irrelevant and, as a consequence, the dislocation of the reader for whom the question becomes not merely "where is here?" but "what is now?" Kamau, towards his last two decades, faced challenges of keeping up and making sense of both his past and the unknown imminence of his future. In his final decade he manifested two tendencies. He frequently wrote/spoke of his perpetually diminishing and plundered archives, and blindly (literally and metaphorically) clung to the ever-expanding and unmanageable *L/X*, which would, like Elaine's anthology, remain unpublished. How did an individual or a generation keep pace with Time and Change and the now kaleidoscopic notions of relevance?

It was at this juncture, between the waning of Kamau's generation (and mine) and the emergence of a still inchoate but rootless and brilliant new one, that Andrew Armstrong of UWI Cave Hill invited me on 4th February, 2011, to participate in a "Kamau Workshop" at which I had to deliver the keynote address on Friday, 25th February. The theme of the workshop was "Kamau Brathwaite and Inter-Cultural Dialogue." KB was at the time still in New York. He wrote [*Letter #145: KB – GR, 10th February, 2011*] thanking me for agreeing to deliver the keynote address in honour (still) of his eightieth.

> Dear Gordon, Juss hear that you will keynote at a CH symposium my 80th. Thank you cyan done the honour. Have decided send you three poems from *End Poem Poems*,[131] which is where I am now (but which as a collection might nvr see the light of day – certainly not mine! Natch i wish too that you wd inc MR/MR in yr assess of Kamau on the sudden unexpected verge, but I guess you don't reach that double volume yet! Nobody has!
>
> <Kamau>

Letter #146: GR – KB, 17th February, 2011
I replied immediately to Kamau's mysterious, cryptically whispered letter:

> Hello Kamau,
>
> I have received the e-mail with the *End Poem Poems*. At first glimpse they

sound dread. What's really happening in the ice-box up there? Glaucoma? What else? I have been reading *MR*, though I haven't decided what shape my talk will assume. Stay alive; there are too many of us just dying: Rex, Barry Chevannes,* Ralph Carnegie,* Boots,* Sir Ellis Clarke* of T & T, erstwhile President and almost the last of the world's great Afro-Saxons; David Thompson,* 45 years younger than Sir Ellis; calypsonian Conqueror,* knocked down crossing the road on the way to perform in the tent. He was 75. Calypsonian Striker,* Monarch of 1958 and 1959. He was 81. Keith Smith,* journalist from Laventille; he was 64.

And there are odders, most of them great people: two pan men killed in separate incidents of drive-by shootings! Desperadoes, the greatest steelband, forced to run from its panyard home in Laventille and practice in the city out of fear of the violence and constant gunplay in the hills. Unimaginable, but true. The whole place imploding, the centre both unfindable, despite VS Nightfall's[132] quest, and unholdable as Yeats recognized nearly 100 years ago. So stay alive and get out of the ice-box up there, even if it means returning to the quarrel with coral.

I noted that Earl Lovelace had published *Is Just a Movie*, Alvin Thompson an impressive pictorial history about slavery and its aftermath;[133] and that Curwen Best had been appointed Professor. Life was goin on, I concluded, at almost the same rate as death.

I queried why he had in one of the *End Poem Poems* attributed *Waiting for Godot* to Genet, rather than Beckett. Was this tale-telling memory lapse or was it deliberate?

UNESCO, I wrote, saving the most cheerful news for last, had just published the papers from its 2007 Seychelles conference on "Small Islands as Crossroads." I had attended that conference and had a paper in the publication entitled, "Caribbean Culture in the Face of Globalisation."[134] So, I concluded, life goes on: adding the words muttered by Beckett's Malone: "Call this going, call this on."

This exchange of letters – *KB – GR, 16th February, 2011 and GR – KB, 17th February, 2011* was prophetic and ominous. It spotlighted

(1) KB's (hinted at) glaucoma, that cloud or scale that prohibits vision.

(2) KB's sense that he was dying.

(3) KB's desire to be read and for his readers/audience to be kept up to date on his recent writings. E.g. MR I and MR II. He had moved, had always been moving on across new frontiers, even as he clung to and was always incorporating past concerns and achievements in his presentation of each new poem or vision. He was forever updating pasts while probing the

undiscovered darknesses of futures that were uncertain except for the ever-looming reality of personal extinction.

Letter #146 could not have been comforting or reassuring to KB. It defined GR's as yet unnamed persona of "Bookman", observer and archivist of the dead and dying. Note the list of the new dead I so casually unreel to make KB aware of the company in which he (and indeed I) were travelling towards the end times. *Solamen miseris socios habuisse doloris*.[135] The wretched are consoled by the fact that there are companions equally wretched. KB, caught up in the specialness of his own passage, could hardly derive comfort from the good news that there were others who had recently passed: i.e. it was the entire generation that was dying out. Hard, blank, inevitable, inescapable stone.

I also provided a few examples of the current implosion taking place in T & T, which resembled the kingdoms of *DIS* that KB knew well in Kingston and Manhattan and had himself chronicled in his Kingston Poems, *Trench Town Rock* and *ARK*. There was little cause for rejoicing anywhere, it seemed.

There was also my image of KB dying in the "ice-box". It would hover in my consciousness as an image of the utterest isolation, even when Kamau had finally (late September 2011) quit New York for the friendlier oven and cage of cramped Cowpastor, choking under the dust and grit of the landscapers and developers. Cold hell, hot hell were his twin towers, the marassa of a single desolation.

Letter #148: KB to Harclyde Walcott and Beloveds, 30th September, 2011, 9:40 a.m.

This was a long letter that details his departure from New York and his rediscovery of *DIS* in Barbados. He speaks of being ashamed and in agony that the deterioration of his body has made it impossible for him to function "personally, socially culturally":

> it mek me SHAME SHAME SHAME – for me myself - .... to be so tripped destroyed to such a *grave* that i can no longer contrib personally socially culturally/and it *hurts*, as you can imag, as you will see writ *so acute* all over the agony of my txt.

The debility of old age has brought not only "agony" but "shame" "to be so *tripped* destroyed to such a *grave*." "Tripped" – feet entrammelled in mid-stride, so that one stumbles in one's journey. "Destroyed" needs no explanation. This is not just Barbados, Jamaica or New York, but Time itself, functioning as agent of Change, or Change functioning as agent of

Time: "Onyame's now Ananse's trap of doom." "Grave" says that KB saw himself as being already a dead and buried man/a corpse. He would frequently and melodramatically refer to himself as such!!

He then returned to his familiar mantra of "cultural lynching" which began late in 2004 and involved the disappearance of "more and more books, manuscripts, work in progress, teaching material – my spiritual possessions – disappearing from the shelves & boxes." Complaints to "the Authorities/the 'authors' of my being there" led to a change of locks and the installation of a door to protect the room in which most of the archives were stored. Brathwaite also installs cameras. They make no difference. 4000 items disappear. Friends, colleagues, the Authorities, the Press, along with *"Caribbean /Caribbeanist/Third World/Post-colonialist Journals – e.g. BIM, Poui, Wasafiri, Caribbean Writer, SX, JCL, JCL(S), Transition, Sargasso, Callaloo"* showed no interest in Kamau's predicament

He ended up in hospital in August 2008 diagnosed with trauma, though none of the doctors seemed able to determine what was really wrong with KB, whose self-diagnosis hinged on the question:

> how does one scope w/the vagabond spiritual loss of one's heritage & achievement and have that loss scoffed & laughed at & ignored?

The results of either (or both) Kamau's dementia or/and his having become the target of attack by 'unidentifiable' Security forces, were:

(1) weight loss from 180 to 150 lbs
(2) sleeplessness
(3) incipient blindness
(4) weakness and withering of limbs
(5) inability

> to accept any of the many invitations from all parts of th(e) world to celebrate my 81 b/day in May 2011. Indeed i can't go/get out anywhere .... A man whose life love & livelihood have been taken from him.

How does KB's description of himself as one who has been "scoffed & laughed at & ignored" square with his contrasting portrait of himself as a man who has been invited to attend honouring functions from all parts of the world to celebrate his 81st birthday? The two pictures, Kamau as mocked, scorned derelict and Kamau as revered celebrated icon, can't be reconciled. Kamau, as his debility grew and his ability to traverse the world lessened, showed less interest in those who sang praise-songs in his honour, and more in those forces and agencies, human and divine, that had worked together to terminate his narrative.

NYU pressured KB to return on grounds of age, suggesting that his resignation and return to Barbados might be the best solution to Cultural Lynching. Had the University, as Kamau suspected, enabled surveillance and the "lynching" to get rid of KB who had become an embarrassment? Was Kamau's position that 9/11 was karmic retribution for America's long record of intrusion and depredation in the Middle East, the real reason for the pressure that had been imposed on him? Whatever was the true nature of this 'conspiracy', Kamau was emancipated from his bondage at NYU and sent back to Barbados on Emancipation Day, August 1st, 2011, in a wheelchair. I had seen a few of the great men of Kamau's time – Walcott, Naipaul, Ramphal to name three of the greatest, and Lamming, to name a fourth – on wheelchairs. Brathwaite was ashamed of his.

The rest of the letter was a description of Cowpastor as a wilderness. The Government remained "in negative limbo" about whether KB and the handful of neighbours who had resisted relocation, would still be forced to move. Brathwaite despaired for the future of his dream; a Bussa-Namesetoura Cultural Centre. Gloomily, he prophesied, as he had been doing since his final days in Jamaica

w/out protection (thorns of resistance – palenQue – of yr boundaries and for yr possessions" & soul – all yr gains & discoveries & reclamations & dreams of «freedom /independence will come to nought; and w/out allies, <whatever you may have evolved as yr culture will be filtered faltered infiltrated stolen from poison spat upon & destroyed w/-out even the vestige of record or qual or eQual or quail to «mark that you tried that you Xisted that you made a contribution. As if some strange penitential retribution – certainly somebody's vengeance !you.

The final section of this letter was a reshaped version of ideas articulated since "Missile and Capsule", now relocated in Kamau's final(?) vision of history. Kamau located his New York experience in what he saw as its wider context: the co-opting or destruction of the alter/Native Revolutionary Voice by the "missilistic", "xenophobic" Western metropole. Among the listed voices of the Black World Revolutionaries (among which he located his own small voice were:

Gandhi Garvey Fanon Robeson Césaire Malcolm Stokely MLK Lumumba Mandela Nkrumah Che Fidel the Viet Cong.

There are no commas between these names/voices because, ultimately, they were all contributors to the chorus of resistance to Western imperialism.

There was, however, little room for a "silent warrior" [the meaning of the name 'Kamau'] between the crush of antagonists. There was also the inescapable paradox that the imperialistic West offered the blandishments of funded support for the arts, scholarships, opportunities, easily (?) available publishers, editors and reviewers, while Home offered none of these things. The price demanded by the West was conformity, silent surrender, and an abandonment of potentially 'subversive' ideas, concepts and metaphors of self-definition. Kamau's final notes about "metropolitan anxiety/xenophobia" – although couched in his own terms such as 'ounfa' (hounfort) and 'palenQue' and rendered in his cryptic style, were deadly accurate, as today's scenario in Trump's America and Britain's 'Brexit', makes clear.

★

What then did KB, stretched between DIS and DIS, the twin hills of ice and fire do during his final decade?

(1) He wrote four books of poetry.

(2) He continued archival work on *L/X*.

(3) He raged against physical decay, the closing of his time's cycle, "the dying of the light" (Dylan Thomas).

We kept in touch via emails and occasional phone calls. The books of poetry mapping his anticipated death journey and the extended discourses such as *Barabajan Poems*, *Golokwati*, *ConVersations* and *MRI* and *MRII*, I still need to read closely. The *L/X* (*Love Axe/l*) tome expanded but remained incomplete. He was reluctant to let it go. It was the stone that rooted him to earth, containing past, present and future, though all had begun to slip through the fissures of his mind.

Physical 'decay' manifested itself in his increasing tendency to forget even such a thing as where he had written the line "nairobi's male elephants uncurl their trumpets to heaven", which comes at the opening of *Islands*. He wanted me to tell him where to find it. He'd also lost – or couldn't find – the first three *Savacou* editions. On 17th February, 2013, he wrote requesting a copy of his "Poetry of the Negative Yes" and a Xerox of Martin Carter's *Poems of Affinity*. He couldn't find many things because he hadn't, even after two years of having returned to Cowpastor, unpacked many of the boxes. "THERE IS NO RUSH HERE to UNPACK my things so most lie in storage limbo – if, as i say they survive at all."

He worried about the health of my wife and the passage of my mother at age 101. He realised that he'd never met her and said that he wanted to know her name, and quote the letter I'd written to him as part of ORIKI III. My letter [#149, GR – KB, Wednesday, 28th August, 2013] went thus:

Hi Kamau

Thanks for your letter and the sentiments. Mom was 101 plus eight months. She retained a fair amount of coherence up to a few weeks before her passing, when she stopped talking and was unable or unwilling to get up from her bed. During her last years she dwelt more in the past than in the present and imagined that she had been to places like Australia and India [Once, crossing the interior bridge that linked Guyana to Brazil, she had ended her journey in the vicinity of the Taj Mahal]. She had lived a remarkable life that embraced two World Wars and all that had happened in Guyana and the Caribbean since the 1920s right into the present chaos. She was concerned with what she saw as retrogression among Black people, the women in particular, and deeply lamented the downward journey of the race.

She was tough, stoical, mostly undemonstrative of her feelings, but capable of a kind of rage, unforgivingly judgemental, plain-speaking and matriarchal. Yet she was remembered as kind, charitable, a great imaginative teacher, honest, responsible and concerned. Her passing marks the end of several eras.

Betty is doing fine and I am trying (not too hard) to rouse myself from lethargy and what Conrad called "the immense indifference of things." What's going on at Cowpastor?

Between July/August of 2013 and January 2017 my notebooks were preoccupied with the chaos of things in T & T. There was hardly any mention of KB, though there was the Bookman's industrious chronicling of scores of deaths, including those of Norman Girvan,* Nelson Mandela, Gabriel Garcia Marquez,* Stuart Hall* and Keith Laurence.* On Sunday, 03rd May, 2015, I noted in Notebook #18 that Bocas had dedicated its festival to Derek Walcott who had been 85 in January. They also attempted to reanimate the old Walcott versus Brathwaite scuffle and dedicated one whole hour to Kamau. It was like a reversal of Kamaufest which Walcott had refused to attend because, he said, nobody was celebrating him, although, like Brathwaite, he too was seventy years old in 2000. No *Pathfinder* or *Ancestories* was on display at Bocas 2015. None was requested of me. The Brathwaite hour was a mere afterthought, an addendumb to the real business of the day.

Notebook #19: Friday, 04th November, 2016, p. 133
I was in Barbados to speak at the launch of Aaron Kamugisha's and Yanique Hume's 750-page tome on *Caribbean Popular Culture*. The single day I spent in Barbados did not leave me enough time to visit Kamau who, in any case, seemed not to want to be visited or 'seen'. I gathered that he had been reclusive for the five years since his return from New York. His mind was still active and fairly sharp, but at 86 his movement

was severely impaired. We talked on the phone for well over an hour.

Notebook #19: Wednesday, 22nd March, 2017
Derek Walcott died on Friday, 17th March, 2017 at age 87. 2017 was also the 50th Anniversary of *Rights of Passage*. An Italian, one Ms Grazzoni, wrote me seeking permission to quote/electrify/do a video of "Black/ground Music to *Rights of Passage*." She is translating West Indian poetry into Italian. I gave her my permission, though I've never seen her video or heard from her since.

Notebook #19: Thursday, 30th November, 2017, pp. 295-298
I've been rereading *Ancestories*,[136] a text which almost no one else has read, but which is about history, trauma, as inter-generational bequest; the options of rebellion, withdrawal into silence, surrender, implosion, explosion, atonement; confession or evasion of guilt; "inversion" as an upturning or a turning inside-out – inversion and evasion – Harris's Donne,[137] Kamau's Prospero and Caliban.

Then there is the issue of 'gender' which has to be located in the contexts of history and trauma. Gender is about negotiation between women and men, both of whom are located in their little-eases [cramped medieval cages] of fixed roles, expectations, stereotypes. What are the unsigned contracts between men and women? What do they expect of themselves and of each other? What do they deliver? How are 'power' and 'maistrie' negotiated between them in contexts of survivalism? What fidelities/infidelities are necessary/inevitable as men and women *confront* each other?

Does "love" ever enter into these pragmatic negotiations? Or is "love" just another counter (like sex) in the game that is always going on – "the battle of the sexes" – most of which may be invisible, deadly, unrelenting beneath tedious or placid everyday surfaces?

Ancestories is also concerned with the question of atonement or reparation between nations: an overwhelming one. I don't think atonement/reconciliation will ever truly take place, however one might clamour for "a level playing field" between the powerful and the powerless. The powerless will never be allowed to play the same game, or by the same rules, as the powerful, who make the rules and own the ground on which the game is being played.

(Indeed, it is only in sports that occasionally the playing field *seems* almost to be level). But in finance, trade, the economics of existence? It is a different story, a different ball-game altogether). The only thing that one can argue for is fairness in the negotiated deals between global imperialism and those who live, as Charlie Mingus recognized, "beneath the underdog." But when have such negotiations ever been "free" and fair and free from fear?"

Letter #150: KB – Aaron Kamugisha/Copy to GR, 6th January, 2017
"Update on the 3rd Annual Kamau Brathwaite Lecture"

KB said he wanted to make two points without sounding churlish or childish.

(1) This is the THIRD kb lecture, but only the first one has been on KB 5/his work. is the Series simply in NAME only?

(2) I note the emphasis on FAMILY tho i don't kno why. Surely these eVents are not clan based. in any case, my WIFE has not been specially invited nor seated.[138]

I couldn't tell why Kamau contacted me, though I saw his mistrust of being honoured and his feeling that his wife had been ostracized <u>by</u>(?) or that she didn't/couldn't fit into Academe (?). How was she located in the Round House or seated at the Round Table?

Letter #151: KB – GR, 9th February, 2017
KB was answering GR – KB, November 26th, 2016

(1) He noted Fidel Castro's death.

(2) He thanked me for "the visit even if on the phone" and "the gift of books and papers."

The 'gift of books' must have been *My Whole Life Is Calypso*[139] and the unpublished ms, "Musings, Mazes, Muses, Margins",[140] a semi-autobiographical collation of narratives, dream stories and meditations that were simultaneously obscure and illuminating.

My reply to Letter #151 was:

The Kamugisha launch went well. The collection of essays is a massive 760 pages. Aaron reads beyond social sciences and history. I even heard him quoting poetry, which is unusual in most of our scholars. There seems to be more focus and direction in Cave Hill at the moment than at St. Augustine.

Kamau replied:

> Dear Gordon, Despite yr work, will this ever cease? these unfair relentless attacks? mine (or is the work really so bad??) I still remember among others the early Ramchands and MM's "Niggers, Niggers Everywhere,"[141] and Baugh's "Travelogue with a Difference"[142] and Dash[143] and the woman from Australia. MM (again) at the NYU KB Conf and now Rhonda Cobham, esp her segment on KB5 (she calls it EKB) in her Epitaphs for the Self. Isn't it Carnival time in Trini?

This was a strange reply to my letter about the Kamugisha/Hume book launch. I had spoken about my work not being read or propagated to such an extent that a writer could emerge two decades later and receive both sponsorship and kudos for research on cricket that I had already done and broadcast throughout the Caribbean two decades before. But Kamau wasn't tuned into my grouse, but into his own undead and undying hurt of the 1970s. He never transcended those times. Instead of transcension or movement beyond the dead past, he had added Rhonda Cobham's *Epitaphs for the Self* to his list of unforgivable sins.

On March 27th 2017, I wrote Kamau updating my recent activities and stating my disagreement with his disparagement of Cobham's work. My letter went:

> Hope you got my comments on Derek made in an interview on 17/3/ 17 on the afternoon of his death. Thanks for your eulogy. [Kamau had circulated, not so much a eulogy as a commentary on Walcott's funeral which had been transmitted on television.]
>
> Sorry I haven't (yet?) been able to publish "Perfected Fables Now", a collection of essays on writers and calypsonians of the 1950's-2020 period. I know it isn't 2020 yet, but what I am dealing with are writers, singers and performing artists of the transition from colonialism to neo-colonialism, via the broken road of independence. Having been ravaged by CLICO, and lacking (and not seriously seeking) a sponsor of any sort, and not earning any income, I have no money to publish what I have already said in scattered places [and little will] to start any new endeavours.
>
> I have, nonetheless, completed "Musings, Mazes, Muses, Margins", a collection of pseudo-autobiographical narratives that include dream-narratives, which I've been writing since the eighties and which have been further catalyzed by my reading of your *Dream Stories*. "Musings" also contains addresses, reveries, satirical broodings from all sorts of edges, margins, boundaries; and there are fragments of doggerel verse from time to time. I had a sort of fun putting the text together, though Betty is against my publishing what she reads as a mad production of a man with multiple personality disorder, whose other books are not selling and take up too much space in the house. I may still produce fifty or so

for special (and, of course, limited) distribution.

I'll deal with Rhonda Cobham's "I & I" when I can. I am sure she meant no 'disrespect' to anyone. She worked on the text for at least fifteen years of trying to compare the magnitudes of three enormous minds. Like me, she has a sense of the relentless closure of an era, and the complexities that emerge within identities over seven decades of exploration of the explosive and imploding societies of our Archipelago. We need to give her thanks, because there are relatively few persons, academics or otherwise, who have bothered to pay close attention to what our writers have been doing. I myself, write out of a deafening silence, and it is tiring, as you well know.

Stay well and walk good, metaphorically, since physical movement has become difficult.

Gordon.

Letter #152: KB – GR, 11th December, 2017
"Como te va? Gordon"

Kamau had seen my name on a list of invitees/attendees of the Derek Walcott Nobel Laureate moment in St. Lucia and wanted to know, what had happened during Laureate Week. I hadn't been invited. I however replied:

Letter #153: GR – KB, 11ᵗʰ December, 2017, 10:03 a.m.

Hi Kamau,

No I wasn't in St. Lucia for post-laureate devotions. Where you may have seen my name would have been among the list of contributors to a collection of essays dedicated (or livicated) to Monseigneur (Paba) Patrick Anthony on the occasion of his seventieth birthday. I know Paba quite well. He was partially trained in the 1970s at the Seminary here up Mount St. Benedict. He also wrote a doctoral thesis on Derek Walcott. He was one of a group of young priests/seminarians who were deeply involved in an exploration of the interface and intersection of Xtianity and ancestral African and other indigenous cultures, modes of perception, consciousness etc. These priests were moved by the then emerging "Liberation Theology." The Black Power insurrection in Trinidad was traumatic, in that it forced the Catholic Church to look at itself and the role that it had played as 'the plantation system at prayer'; a role that involved maintenance of the race and colour discrimination that had been part of the foundation stones of plantation and post-colonial society.

In St Lucia the establishment of the Folklore Research Centre was part of the Church's initiative in promoting Liberation Theology. It was also crucial to the construction or promotion of cultural nationalism in St. Lucia, and thus umbilically connected to the foundational efforts of Harold Simmons,* Dunstan St. Omer* and the Walcott twins, Derek and Roderick. My inaugural address, "Folk Research, Fossil or Living Bone" was given in 1993 at the request of Paba; hence its republication in the anthology that is now dedicated to him. I haven't yet received my copy, but will in time.

I have, however, written "Endsong for Derek Walcott" at the request of Opal Palmer Adisa who is editor of *Interviewing the Caribbean* emanating from the Mona Campus. She seemed to want something chatty that would be based on stories of my personal encounter with Walcott. The problem was that there were relatively few such encounters, though there were many that I have had over five decades with Walcott's poetry, plays and phenomenal journalism. There have also been my 'conversations' with the ideas and arguments of graduate students, and the manuscript of Pat Ismond, who asked me to comment on the draft of her *Abandoning Dead Metaphors*.

My "Endsong" was built around two or three encounters, which began with the undergrad (1963-1964) "Facing our Past" and my reading of the poem "In a Green Night", and ended with the obsession that I share with Walcott with sunlight on expanses of water. I didn't want to re-open the fierce controversies that were going on in the seventies and beyond. There are things to acknowledge and praise beyond the deep quarrels of the past. Walcott's death is only one of the indices of the death of our entire generation, and it confronts us with the issue of what our residence on earth has meant. "Endsong" was/is a sort of overture to this larger discourse. I don't think, however, that Paba, Robert Lee, Vladimir Lucien and the St. Lucia posse know about "Endsong" yet.

As to whether your work has been setting the market here alight? I'd say "No." Nor has mine. It hasn't been easy to get people to buy, read and discuss anything. One writes out of, in, and increasingly towards a void. That seems to be how it is.

#154: KB – GR, 26th January, 2018, 4:29 p.m.

Am trying to find out why Kamagusha (sic) here has not? yet invited you to speak the Annual Kb5 Lecture at C.H. Of the 4 so far (the 4th coming up early Feb.), only ONE has been on the subject! ah-so the ole storie goes.[144]

To which I replied [*Letter #155: GR – KB*] that maybe there were: (1) No funds or (2) C.H. [Cave Hill] could be tired of hearing my voice, or (3) It was part of the inevitable oblivion that already surrounds my generation (and Kamau's). I listed among the new dead, John Campbell,* a UWI St. Augustine historian who had inherited my office. John was only 42 and was a Pan-Africanist whom Kamau would have liked. Also just dead was Hugh Masakela* (77). I ended my letter:

Is de pestilence man, wiping out all the beautiful ones. Stay alive as long as you can.

Letter #156: KB – GR, Date uncertain; maybe 8th March, 2018

Death of Wilson Harris, "one of my closest friends in Caribbean light & lit – makin me all the moro (sic) conscious of the few i still have left like you & other NYU's & London & the Caribbean & in my shipwreck Bajan."

I pray there will be some healing blessing in this grief.

He then produced a poem: another lament for himself:

> The Award as Sword and Token
> if you a cripple poet and can't climb-up the slip steps of the podium
> shd you be denied therefore the feather'd future and the accolade?
> All that you try-for pelt behind and lyin in the shadow
> shd yr duino elegies be left out dryin in the shade?
> wheelbarrow full of stone & broeken bricks you push on through the
>   night
> and on along these blinded mirrors' terror's splinters in which you are
>   betrayed?[145]
>
> – 8 march 2018 . for wilson harris . w/bob marley & the wailers'
> *logwood burnin thru the night*

Maybe it was the dread finality of this epitaph for himself (Rhonda Cobham wasn't wrong) that made me set about what I'd started to think of doing since January 2016, when I wrote this soliloquy in my notebook #19: Friday, January 08th, 2016, 4:45 p.m.

Words Need Love Too

(i)

"Words need love too," wrote Kamau. And I have thought, with some guilt, of the millions of words that sit despondently on my bookshelves, asking to be loved, to be read, to be mulled over, to be talked about. And I have thought about all those people who write these unloved, withered words, and felt that, perhaps, the writers of words, even more desperately than the words they write, may need, but seldom get the love they openly or secretly seek.

Martin Carter once wrote a poem hoping that

> Someone, somewhere, shall know one day
> more than I read of what I do.[146]

I recognized the need. I heard in those lines the cry of a man who, though acclaimed in every rumshop of Georgetown, wanted his words to be read and written about; sought a deeper acclamation and discourse than his strangled alcoholy city was either able or willing to give him. So I have, over five decades and counting, written at length on the work of our poets, calypsonians, novelists and even historians, imposing on my meagre public the burden of reading long, arduous things; of rolling boulder after boulder of hard words; trying to lift these, my fellow verbalists, out of their solitude, by giving to their words the love they desperately need. I have tried to clarify hard, knotted obscurities, to work through rather than around entanglements of word or metaphor.

In the case of the Afterword to Victor Questel's *Collected Poems*, that Earl Lovelace disparaged and dismissed without reading what I had written,[147] my analysis of the poems, most of it, took place in a hotel room in Miami in 2012 over a ten-day period when I took my son up there for medical attention to his eyes. I had what I seldom have at home: a blank or void of time, as Questel might have termed it; and I filled that blank with words, allowing each poem to take me on its sometimes, rambling journey: "pacing the poem, going where it was going," as Derek Walcott once wrote.

My problem was how to condense my accumulated notes into a tight, coherent "Introduction". This task of synthesis would prove more difficult than the long ramble of what was eventually published as an "Afterword". I found myself in the dilemma of William James, who once apologised to his brother, the novelist Henry James, for writing him such a long letter, explaining that he didn't have the time to write him a shorter one.

In the end, I gave up and presented the more diffuse and digressive, but probably more truthful and moving journey on which the poems had led me, than the cleaned-up, tucked-in précis of the academic essay. I gave Jeremy Poynting the option of using the first four or so pages, which were probably just the sort of thing he might have wanted.

But he magnificently and magnanimously swallowed the whole thing in an amazingly generous gulp. I give thanks. Words need love too, and 'exhaustipated' (i.e. exhausted and constipated) grey essay writers need encouragement in the little time that remains, to prevent them from simply subsiding into the dreadful tedium of "tings and times", or sinking, like Joseph Conrad's Martin Decoud into "the immense indifference of things", or listening to a voiceless dreaming soundtrack without words, imagery, or coherent narrative, in the clean greyish-white closed-in windowless space of one of my recent dreams.

(ii)

"a voiceless dreaming soundtrack without imagery." Deafness? Blindness? Maybe this is what I've been caught-up in for years and years and distances, when I lie for hours between sleep and waking, quarter-dreaming without dream-images or narratives; lost in the almost-story, the shades of not-quite-words, large wildernesses and wastings of dream-time, of shapeless space.

Simple dotishness, I fear, this wandering of spirit without dream. It devours the will to do, to move, to make, to get up and git. It is a painless state, a sort of paralysis, a numbness like the bloodless tips of my fingers and toes. Perhaps it is a foretaste of the end of things, a foreglimpse of the final, original scheme: this dreaming, dreamless quarter-dream. [Thursday, 14th January, 2016, 12:10 a.m.]

(iii)

[Tuesday, March 13th, 2018, 2:00a.m.]

Less than a week after Kamau wrote his own epitaph, lament, his defiant pressing on in the midst of failing light, of steady dying, I had this dream, a death dream, like the one just referred to of the grey-white, utterly empty, windowless room.

Dream snow in some backwoodish sort of place where we – who are we? Who am I in this or any dream? We, I say, have travelled. By what? and to where? Don't know. Can't say. Only that We are there in what may be a house, a room of a house, and these white things – not yet quite snowflakes, but growing up to be so, falling.

And I feeling how horrible it would be to die in a place like this, with no one around to call or to care or to cluster and create Christ, Church, compassion, or even mere indifference. How horrible!

And I think briefly of Wilson's death and Kamau's strange anger at awards he cannot climb the stairs or approach the podium to collect; and Robert Lee's online emailing list full of writers winning dis or dat; and all those utterly alone and dying writers in the sand, in the sun, in the sea, or shivering in these strangely falling petals of yet soft snow, not even cold as yet but getting there, soon come. And feeling as I have been for some days, months now, that I should go and see Kamau before sun-fall, sand-rise and soft snow-driff, and drizzle. I of the withered brain, still being asked, arm-twisted towards a review of this or that new text, or an eulogy on the life of him or her, something or odder of my steadily dwindling generation.

Yet none of them would buy or read *Ancestories*. Too expensive; too expansive; too much love and lyric and coral of poetry strewn along its lonely pathways, the broken ledges of coralline stone, the sand and early morning dawning, the late night of weeping and sea-moan.

So I tell myself, let me go and see George and Kamau the 'unloved', not seen for years; not, so I hear, wanting to be seed even by I and I and I, who never needed to wait for him to win yet another award to tell him thanks, to give his words the love I know they need.

Tuesday, 12th June, 2018
Thus it befell that on Tuesday, 12th June, 2018, I found myself at Plum Tree Court (where Betty once used to stay in her post-retirement time as an Educational Consultant for the Cave Hill Instructional Development Unit). Plum Tree. Quiet and clean. I was there for two days. On Day One I planned to visit George, on Day Two, Kamau. It didn't work out like that. Both George and Kamau preferred Day Two. I spent Day One working on the manuscript that became *Who Owns This Stage?* [so far unpublished].[148] Aaron took me to a fish place on the beach.

Notebook #20: Friday, 15th June, 2018, 5:25 p.m., p.112.
Two days ago, I saw and spoke to, had considerable audience with George and Kamau, Grand Old Men of Barbados. Lamming just turned 91 and Kamau 88 on 11th Mayhem. Not sure exactly how I felt about both encounters. Both men are lucid; both are physically unsound. George, who had fallen and broken hip or leg or thigh, is in an old people's home on or off Rendezvous Hill, a clean and apparently, well-run place. His white mane or crown of hair is still impressive. He remembers all sorts of things. He feels that he has "done his work": meaning that he cyan do much more as novelist, essayist or, as he termed himself, "evangelist".

His son Gordon, three decades ago did law, wrote a novel, had deep dark contemplative eyes and had inherited gestures and mannerisms of his father with whom he had not lived. He had been married, divorced, and had remarried. He had children. [He died in 2021.] George's former wife, Nina Squires, a painter, was still alive. His daughter Natasha had retired from her profession as a doctor. She too had, I recalled, written a novel that had never been published. Her three children – she lived in the US – all had Ph.Ds. I can't remember what jobs they were doing, save for the son who was an educational administrator. George mulled over his early days in Trinidad. He is still capable of delight. Laughing as he slowly departs.

Kamau: a different story. He's lost all sight in his left eye and can't drive.

He has issues, a load of them; all the issues that have preoccupied his writing over the last decade. Cowpastor is near the flight path of aeroplanes as they prepare to land. Authorities tell him that he may have to move. He defies this. I was able to see the rocky coralline terrain deprived of what little scrubby vegetation it once had. This has been his chief complaint in these last days: this violation of the Muse, the Mother, by bulldozers.

Kamau has become the poet of the bruised, lacerated body, and is preoccupied with death and transition rituals. (See the *Lazarus Poems*.[149]) He's been immersed in reinterpreting rituals of the Crossroads; the Bolom is a frequent presence. His trailways are not at all easy to follow. No one has truly traversed such shadowy terrain.

He is still locked into the experience of "Cultural Lynching" [CL in his abbreviation]. Nobody, he says, believes him. He is alone in his isolation/ insulation that I think he has chosen, though he denies this. He's still writing, stubbornly, doggedly; though there seems to be less and less in the fixed denuded landscape for his sensibility to gaze or graze on. Landscape bleak: mindscape bleaker, he trudges, blindly, doggedly, morosely forward, with his Rilkean 'Duino Elegies', his words, a barrow-load of jagged, broken stones.

I tried to persuade him to let me see the so far unpublished Ms of the *Love Axe/l* which he now refers to as *L/X* or LX. [Perhaps LX is his written answer to CL. *L/X* is crucial to my intended reading of the last 25 years of KB (that is if I survive my own steady slide into obsolescence). But Kamau seems to need to cling to the Axel in its still incomplete and ever-expanding state.[150] (Shades of the earlier Bibliography of Caribbean Poets.)

Beverley: Brave, resourceful and bright woman. She has kept Kamau alive, doing the essential, the necessary. It's a rocky drive-in to Cowpastor, perilously so. But she negotiates it as she has been negotiating Kamau for the better part of two decades.

I gave copies of the typescript of *Musings Mazes Muses Margins* (which Kamau calls the M's) to both Kamau and George. George 91, Kamau 88; Will I hear from either of them? I doubt it and I doubt I'll see Kamau again. I write these last things for myself, it seems; these half-remembered, half-invented dreams.

Notebook #21: Tuesday, 04th February, 2020, 11:07 a.m.
Aaron Kamugisha, who on Thursday, 27th September, 2019 had hosted me for breakfast at the Hilton (T&T) and invited me to conduct a seminar on Brathwaite's work with his Caribbean Studies class in February, 2020, rang to inform me that Kamau had died on Tuesday, 04th February. My written reaction to such sad news was that "Another part of my life and portal of my time has closed." I suggested to Aaron that the seminar should be cancelled. He disagreed, and I travelled to Barbados, did the

seminar as planned, and returned to Trinidad. On Thursday, 06th February, 2020, I received a phone call from Beverley Brathwaite who asked me to deliver the eulogy on February 21st, the prospective date for the Official Funeral of Edward Kamau Brathwaite. They had restored the "Edward" to its rightful place. Kamau was in no position to object.

Two of Kamau's sisters had both died in December 2019: Mary in Jamaica and Thelma in England. I suggested to Beverley that Kamau's death had completed a trilogy of Brathwaite deaths. She seemed to laugh at the idea. Beverley complained that a great deal of Kamau's work remained unpublished: L/X, for example. Adopting always Kamau's position on all issues, she didn't recognise the major problems that Brathwaite had for a long time been posing publishers: (e.g. New Directions, OUP, Peepal Tree Press and Twayne): problems such as the growing obscurity of his Sycorax style, the randomness of how he functioned, the continuous revisions of manuscripts sometimes even as they were in the process of publication. He had explained a late intervention into the proofs of the new version of *The Development of Creole Society in Jamaica*, as "improvisation."

He thought that his Sycorax style (which itself was subject to 'improvisation') was making communication easier, when it was viewed by others as making simple statement more obscure. He seemed torn by two impulses: a desire to communicate and the opposite desire to withdraw from society into a protective tortoise-shell, which was at one time Irish Town (IT) and at another Cowpastor (CP). As far as I could determine, Sycorax began after Doris's death, though in her *Mother Poem* version, Sycorax is the missing, erased, yet remembered 'Mother' figure, who in "Nametracks" tells Caliban his name (*nam*) but in such a riddling form that even if Caliban were to repeat his secret name to a spirit thief or sorcerer, the listener would be confused and unable to devour Caliban's *nam*. The problem with this, though, is that Caliban himself has to confront the riddle of his partially lost/partially found identity and be in perpetual quest for his *nam*.

The later Sycorax emerged after Doris's death when Kamau began to think of Doris as a voice trapped inside one of the early computers (the Eagle), to whose primitive hard drive she had committed much of what he had written and was writing. When Doris died Kamau had a hard time recovering a significant part of his written life from its entombment within the computer. He, however, mastered the computer to such an extent that he reset a great deal of his writing, sometimes in strange fonts, until poem or performed lecture became hieroglyph.

Publishers weren't at all patient with what they saw as wilful craziness. In reaction, Brathwaite either self-published or turned to smaller and more radical publishing houses for a kind of solace.

★ ★ ★

I agreed to deliver the eulogy and, searching for what I knew I wanted to say amidst the rubble of all that I had already written on Kamau's work, I awaited news about the structure of the 'Official funeral'. This news came on Thursday, 13th February, 2020. The funeral was carded for Friday, 21st February at St. James Street Methodist Church, Bridgetown. My eulogy, the last of nine tributes, was to be seven minutes.

I wrote nothing for a week until 2:00 a.m. of the morning of February 20th, 2020, my own 78th birthday, when I received a gift of words from nowhere – a breath, a riff, a trombone melody, a kind of singing. As Deke, my son, drove me to the airport, songs soared up in my head: Roberta Flack's "You've Lost That Loving Feeling"; the opening bars of a Brahms violin sonata or trio, bright blue minor key cadenza; then a phrase from the slow movement of one of his string quartets. All these floated through my singing head and I was sort of happy, elated, relieved perhaps, that the eulogy was all but written and was different from nearly all the others that sympathetic friends, knowing of my long friendship with Kamau, had sent me in consolation and fellowship.

My eulogy was going to be dry, like the harmattan of dust from which it was to be made, and sufficiently lyrical like the gentle wet of drizzling rainfall that, defying the drought, had tickled the smoking earth of these dog days.

I completed a version of the eulogy by 1:00 p.m., February 20th. Made me feel to cry towards the end, but I told myself not to do this. "No tears in the end." After a day of sleeping and waking, I thrice performed surgery on my too-long eulogy and prepared for the drama of the funeral. I, together with Beverley, her daughter, granddaughter, two Jamaican friends, a male and a female, travelled in a stretch limousine. The atmosphere in our cabin was night-clubbish – purple fluorescent lights, a bar with glasses, ice, water, juice, rum-punch. A real cool scene. I took a rum-punch to clear my throat, soothe my brain and pacify the worms in my belly. There had been no time for breakfast.

Our driver manoeuvred his hearselike chariot through a maze of narrow streets and a succession of traffic-jammed roundabouts. Our outriders in this Official funeral stopped traffic, cleared roads as our chauffeur negotiated his oversized hearse through whatever cracks opened up in the traffic. There were formally liveried policemen at each intersection. The coffin of the Hon. Kamau Edward Brathwaite (CHB, D Phil) preceded us on this final perilous odyssey to the grey [St. James Street] Methodist Church, where we arrived at about 7:45 a.m.

The funeral was scheduled for 10:00 a.m.: a two-hour wait – a weight of time. Joan, her grandchildren, Thelma's sons, born in London, Michael Kwesi, Kamau's tall son, married and father of a girl. I hadn't seen him in years. He was born in Ghana, grew up in Jamaica and now lived in the USA.

Beverley, Joan, with their respective clusters of family and close friends, greeted early arrivants: Michael La Rose* from London, representing the spirit of his father, John La Rose and the still breathing ghost of the Caribbean Artists' Movement; Kendel Hippolyte* and Robert Lee* from St. Lucia, Kamau's first landfall on his journey back from Ghana to the Antilles; Lasana Sekou, poet and militant publisher from St. Maarten, who had published Kamau's *Words Need Love Too* and Amiri Baraka's poem about 9/11, *Somebody Blew-up America*. There were Andy Taitt and Kamala Kempadoo, Aaron Kamugisha, Cave Hill academic, editor of *Caribbean Cultural Thought* and together with Yanique Hume, editor of *Caribbean Popular Culture: Power, Politics and Performance*, one of the great books of our era, though this is not yet recognised.

Slowly, over the two hours, the Church filled with great people: Dame Sandra Mason, Governor General of Barbados; Mia Amor Mottley, the Honourable Prime Minister; dignified oldsters, a sprinkle of youth; drummers, dancers, singers in white. There were four tributes before the service and four more during the service. Good, great, eloquent addresses; moving moments like Michael Kwesi's tearful reminiscences about his love for his father; then a powerful, well-delivered (and long) tribute from Mia Mottley that covered nearly twenty-five minutes, before my spare-ribbed thrice-edited seven-minute mumble that was entitled: *Kamau: a Travelling Soul* and went, more or less like this: [N.B. I've reinserted much of what I surgically excised in order to stay within the seven minutes that were assigned to me.]

KAMAU: A TRAVELLING SOUL

Dame Sandra Mason, Governor General of Barbados, Ms. Mia Mottley, Honourable Prime Minister of Barbados; all other eminent persons in this congregation to whom respect is due:

Mrs. Beverley Brathwaite, widow of Kamau Brathwaite, family, friends, and colleagues of Kamau, my brothers, sisters and fellow citizens of the Caribbean Archipelago, mothering Atlantic and fathering Sun:

It is a great honour to have been asked by Beverley Brathwaite to deliver this final endsong: to sound the *mmenson* to and for a great drummer of poetry, who has been my close friend for over fifty years, bridging the distance between northern and southern Caribbean islands with correspondence and phone calls of generous open-hearted sharing.

I have entitled this eulogy, "Kamau: A Travelling Soul," inspired by the compilation of essays and tributes that Tim Reiss, a close friend and colleague of Kamau's at New York University, edited and published to mark Kamau's 70th birthday almost 2 decades ago in 2001. A travelling soul, Reiss recognised (as I myself have, since *Pathfinder: Black Awakening in The Arrivants of Edward Kamau Brathwaite* (1981), needed to draw its own maps into uncharted territory, and to open trailways, many of which are today being freely traversed by new generations of academics, thinkers, dreamers and writers of many ethnicities and from far-flung places that he and his words have touched. A recent checklist of essays about Brathwaite's work has revealed almost 800 and counting.

Aesthetic cartographer, pathfinder, letter-writer, tireless archivist of the African Diaspora, a Nummo like those Dogon ancestor-spirits, who though separated from their place of origin still travel on crippled legs to fulfil a mission of bearing language, creative skills and illumination to all the nations of the earth: these are some of the masks that Kamau learned to wear over seven decades of his soul-wandering. Let us refer to his own definition of his essential role and mission:

> The constant, I would even say consistent fabric and praxis of my work, has been to connect broken islands, cracked broken words, worlds, friendships, ancestories.[151]

In fulfilling this mission as link, as connection, he sent clusters of letters to fellow travellers from whom he sought all sorts of things: documents, information, music that he couldn't otherwise obtain, feedback about his poems or theories and formulations, the love that he said a writer's words needed. Friends were seined in his constantly outflung web of words, his intricate, idiosyncratic and persistently articulated visions of a scheme of things. Was there an ulterior motive beyond and beneath those letters? Was he trying to put together a dream-team of applauding acolytes who would simultaneously proclaim and nourish his ego?

Maybe… yet that was not the whole picture. In my case, from the time we first met at the second Caribbean Artists' Movement meeting in London, late in 1966, he wanted to know everything I was doing: my research into the Calypso and Oral Traditions of the African Diaspora; my thoughts on the scenarios in Trinidad and Jamaica, those sites of comparative chaos and creativity quite similar to the urban ghettos of blues, jazz, hip-hop and what Linton Kwesi Johnson once described as "vibratin violence",[152] in which African-American migrants from the Mississippi Delta and the cotton-picking South, found and still find themselves, ensnared.

Kamau was a fair sharer, a nurturer, always willing to acquire, read and recommend for publication almost anything I wrote, whether or not it related directly to his own work. I owe to him my interest in both jazz and the literature that has been generated on Black music of Africa and the African Diaspora. He monitored my moods, which he gleaned from my letters and notebook observations about what, after the 1970 and 1990 explosions in Trinidad, I had begun to refer to as "the culture of terminality". He prompted me, a born and morose pessimist, to speak out from my labyrinth of solitude and despondent silence.

Homecoming, return, one of Kamau's recurrent themes as travelling soul, was an ambiguous experience. The typical Kamau protagonist circles back to a home-grown strange. A deep nostalgia for things and landscapes as they used to be pervades Kamau's work, especially in the post New York University years. We often forget that he spent 30 years in Jamaica, years punctuated by constant travelling to lecture, do research or perform poetry. Those three decades were followed by two decades in New York. Both the Jamaican and the New York experiences ended in catastrophe. Brathwaite had become somewhat like his many poetic narrating voices, a traveller who builds home wherever his ships or feet take him, then has to resume travelling when, for any number of reasons, whatever he has built collapses. Travelling, as the praise-singer in *Masks* both remembered and foresaw, involved gains and losses.

For all his efforts to resuscitate the spirit of the Caribbean Artists' Movement, which in his young years he had helped form in London even as he was writing his doctoral thesis and publishing *Rights of Passage* and *Masks*, the traditions of the Black Atlantic remained traditions of discontinuity, displaying terrible crevasses between world-transfiguring creativity and negative tendencies of dystopia and anomie. Kamau continued to believe that discontinuity could be countered by community and correspondence. Violence, he desperately hoped, could be transformed into sculpture that would reflect the bruises of "all dem travellin years" even as it proclaimed the emerging militancy of all future encounters. Brathwaite assumed the role of rememberer, shaman and *okyeame*, the archivist of diasporic 'arrivance'.

In his later years, after Hurricane Gilbert, some strange experiences at New York University, and his well-chronicled difficulties at Cowpastor Barbados, he lamented the steady loss of his archived life, which he attributed to thieves and 'cultural lynchers', old spirit thieves reincarnated in new malevolent agencies. His answers to these principalities and powers was to keep on writing, rewriting and expanding an archival work that since 1963 *BIM* he had named *The Love Axe/l*. Via *The Love Axe/l* he would chop down the false records and stereotypes that had dominated and bedevilled mainland African and Black diasporic self-perception throughout history. Conversely and simultaneously, he would bequeath to future generations – if they could decipher his recondite Sycorax hieroglyphs – an axis or axle around which their consciousness could revolve, and the fragments of memory re-root and resurrect themselves into new wholeness and green beginnings.

I've learned that at the time of his passing, *L/X* as he now laconically termed *The Love Axe/l*, was nearly 800 pages. Kamau couldn't bring it to a close, even as his eyesight and body failed him, and his travelling soul, a crippled Legba and Nummo, could no longer move from his station at the mythic crossroads, or control directions, passages and destinies as Legba used to, even in his guise as Old Man, a lame and reduced Sun god.

Kamau could not release *L/X*, because it had become his final entombment, the encryptment in language and hieroglyph of everything and everyone he had encountered, loved, and even bitterly disliked over seventy years of travelling. The 'war' he had spoken about since the 1960s between 'cultural guerillas' and the colonial establishment entrenched on the Mona Campus, had not ended for him or been rendered irrelevant by Time: even though Time was each month closing the cycle of Kamau's generation, and every new day now gave evidence and dire illustration of the Great Subtraction before the Great Divide.

Kamau in his final Cowpastor collections of poems tried to travel in Ra's* and Coltrane's sunships into Orphic underground and interior spaces. He foresaw his own demise in the multiple deaths that surrounded him in happenings such as 9/11 which took place only a mile from where he lived in Manhattan. 9/11 was followed by a series of global apocalypses of fire, flood, earthquake and hurricane and domestic catastrophes, such as the deaths by accident of Beverley's son and more recently the murder of her grandson in Jamaica. Then between December 2019 and January 2020, Kamau's sisters Thelma and Mary both died. Kamau's passage then, completes a trilogy of final departures. He had always thought of arranging his work in trilogies. We can and should take comfort in the fact that Kamau's sun ships of travelling poems have always ended their subterranean or subaqueous night journeys with the horses of morning devouring darkness and sorrow and arising red, newborn out of the sea's womb, to gaze over the far horizon between Africa and a Barbados now sacralized through Kamau's imagination, as the beloved son comes home at so long last, and the Sun attains its zenith over the Round House[153] and Brown's Beach as the angelus sounds noon.

Kamau, my brother and my longtime friend, travelling soul and soldier of consciousness "may your journey now be straight going, may your road be a peaceful one" [Wake," *The Arrivants*, p. 210].

Gordon Rohlehr
20th, 21st, 25th February, 2020

Postlude: *Vale atque Ave*

After tributes, eulogy, sermon, organ-chant, drum-beat, there was the gathering in the church yard, the drive to the cemetery in open windy country, more drumming, singing, eulogising. I thought of looking for my sister Gloria's gravestone, but desisted. My movement, rusty and painful as any Legba's, hasn't been too good these days.

Thus exited Kamau amidst hymns, Orisha and Spiritual Baptist chants aimed, I guessed, at "our never-returning ancestors of old." ["Wake." *The Arrivants*, 201]. I don't know if any of the ancestors came at the drums' summons. There was to be a repast at Joan's place, but I wasn't of Joan's party. My repast was another rum-punch – an unruly fellow – who kept overspilling as we drove along in our stretched-out nightclub hearse to Beverley's homestead. I lunched at the hotel at 2:45 p.m. when, for $38 B'dos, plus gratuity, I feasted on my last supper before next morning's early departure:

"2 slabs/slaps of sweet potato pie c. 2/5ths of an inch deep, four inches long, 2½ inches woide. 2 sloices of fish, advertised on the menu as floine, but seeming otherwise to my eyes, my occuli, blurred with dust and a drizzle of tears; a scattering of forlorn lamenting broccoli;
2 glasses of water."

I survived. Just after dawn next morning, along the highway to the airport, I saw purple and red bougainvillea and pink oleanders glowing, haloed in soft sunlight. My driver smiled and nodded: "Landscapers." He said, proudly, "developers."

"Farewell, Sister Gloria. Walk good," I prayed. "Farewell, Brother Kamau. Vale, Adios Barbados."

The Return

I flew back to T & T just before the onset of the pandemic and the expiry of my passport ordered my travelling soul to take a rest. We floated through and above a thick haze of Sahara Dust. I sensed the presence of Kamau, who in 1971, long before Joseph Prospero, the atmospheric alchemist of a meteorological station in Florida, had identified the dust as being that of the harmattan: a visible though almost intangible link to all those lost crossings of the desert in ancestral Africa.[154]

I couldn't see either the wrinkled Atlantic or the shrouded Northern Range as we approached Trinidad, and I earnestly hoped that the pilot, one of our local men and an evolved taxi-driver knew where he was going and what he was doing with "the white people" plane. When he at last burst through Kamau's parting shroud of dust, I swore that he was approaching the runway too fast, like in Guyana. We landed gently before there was a bramp!! And a broomp!! – potholes or depressions on a runway that, constructed during a former political régime's reign, had not fully lost its memory of the days when it was mere gravel in Coosal's or Junior Sammy's quarries.

Ave, I sang, Welcome, Trinidad.

Daniel, Frederick, Gordon Rohlehr
Tuesday, 16th September, 2020
Thursday, 22nd October, 2020
Thursday, 19th November, 2020

ENDNOTES

Note: Biographical identification of people mentioned in the text will be found in the Index of names and Organisations.

1. First published as a pamphlet (19 pp, n.d.) by the Commonwealth Institute and commented on in Kamau Brathwaite's paper of the same name in *Caribbean Quarterly*, Vol. 14, No. 1/2, "A Survey of the Arts" (March-June 1968), 91-96.
2. See the notes on Orlando Patterson and V.S. Naipaul in the Index of Names and Organisations.
3. "Pebbles", *The Arrivants* (OUP, 1973), 196.
4. *The Islands in Between: Essays on Caribbean Literature* (London: OUP, 1968). See also Sylvia Wynter's trenchant criticism of many of the essays in the book (not Rohlehr's, which she admired) in "We Must Learn to Sit Down Together and Talk About a Little Culture" in *We Must Learn to Sit Down Together and Talk About a Little Culture: Decolonising Essays*, ed. Demetrius Eudell ([*Jamaica Journal*, 1968] Leeds: Peepal Tree Press, 2022), 88-145.
5. Soyinka's critique of negritude ("a tiger does not proclaim his tigritude, he pounces", is quoted in Janheinz Jahn, *A History of Neo African Literature* (London: Faber, 1968), 266.
6. *The Bomb* was a populist scandal sheet that had fertile territory in the corruption endemic in Trinidadian politics of the 1970s and 1980s.
7. This essay, "Caribbean Critics", appeared in both *Southern Review* Vol. 5, No. 3 (1969) and *New World Quarterly* Vol. 5, Nos. 1-2 (1969) and was collected in *Roots* (Ann Arbor: University of Michigan Press, 1993), 111-126. Whether James wrote a rejoinder cannot be ascertained.
8. This piece. "White Fridays in Trinidad" was published as a diary by Anon in *Savacou* No. 3/4, 1970-71, pp 18-24.
9. A reference to the Black Power rebellion in Trinidad in 1970 and the Morant Bay rebellion in Jamaica in 1865, where, led by the Native Baptist leader, Paul Bogle, Jamaican peasants challenged planter and colonial power and suffered a vicious pogrom of state revenge.
10. KB possibly refers to Walcott's "Dogstar", in *The Castaway* (London: Cape, 1965), 13.
11. "Harmattan Poems", *Black Orpheus* 2, No. 7 (1972), 4-12.
12. See "White Fridays in Trinidad", op cit., 23-24.
13. "Volta", (*Masks*) *The Arrivants*, 107-109.
14. And see Ivar Oxaal, *Race and Revolutionary Consciousness: An Existential Report on the 1970 Black Power Revolt in Trinidad* (Schenkman, 1971); and Raoul Pantin, *Black Power Day: A Reporter's Story* (Trinidad: Hatuey Productions, 1990).

15. KB refers to the source of the title of Lamming's novel in a line from Derek Walcott's poem "Epitaph for the Young: XII Cantos" (1949): "You in the castle of your skin / I the swineherd" and to the character of Makak, the charcoal burner, in Walcott's play *Dream on Monkey Mountain* (1967/1970).

16. One non-Caribbean critic who in part understood the significance of the ACLALS conference as signalling a moment of aesthetic break was Laurence Breiner in *An Introduction to West Indian Poetry* (Cambridge UP, 1998), 1-24.

17. This paper was never published, though, as Gordon Rohlehr notes, Ramchand quotes this parody of "Negus" in a chapter on Edward Brathwaite's *The Arrivants* in *An Introduction to the Study of West Indian Literature* (London: Nelson, 1976), one of the ten Caribbean texts Ramchand choses for serious study, as an issue to discuss whether rhythm matches sense.

18. Reprinted in *My Strangled City* ([1992] Leeds: Peepal Tree Press, 2019), 98-119.

19. Ibid., 118.

20. *My Strangled City*, 149-233.

21. *The Shape of that Hurt*, 94-125.

22. For an account of the Forbes Burnham years of PNC party paramountcy in Guyana that contextualises GR's condensed assessment, see for example Latin American Bureau, *Guyana: Fraudulent Revolution* (London: LAB, 1984); and Colin Baber and Henry B. Jeffrey, *Politics, Economics and Society* (London: Francis Pinter, 1986).

23. See *My Strangled City*, 125-126.

24. Neither of these papers appears to have been published.

25. Published as "Carifesta: Doing it Our Way", *Journal of Ethnic and Migration Studies*, Vol. 3, Issue 4, 1974, 343-348.

26. Jagan's *The West on Trial* (London: Michael Joseph, 1966) deals with the years after the 1961 elections when, with CIA support, the PNC opposition fomented what became a virtual civil war. See The Latin American Bureau publication, *Guyana: Fraudulent Revolution* for an account of the rigged elections.

27. See Andrew Salkey, *Georgetown Journal: A Caribbean Writer's Journey from London via Port of Spain to Georgetown, Guyana, 1970* (London: New Beacon, 1972).

28. By the St Lucian playwright, Roderick Walcott.

29. This paper can be read at: https://www.scribd.com/document/ 544142038/UNESCO-1978-Intergovernmental-Conference-on-Cultural-Policies-in-Latin-America-and-the-Caribbean-Bogota.

30. "University of Hunger" ([*Poems of Resistance*, 1954] *University of Hunger* (Newcastle: Bloodaxe Books, 2006), 84-85.

31. The direct quotation comes from an interview C.L.R. James gave to Ian Munro and Reinhard Sander in "Interviews with Three Caribbean Writers in Texas", *Kas-Kas*, African and Afro-American Research Institute, 1972), 31. James continues, after saying that he doesn't think that Brathwaite's poetry is "genuine and spontaneous". to say, "I may be wrong – it's just a personal opinion. Many good critics think otherwise."

32. Pat Ismond, "Walcott versus Brathwaite", *Caribbean Quarterly*: Vol. 17, No. 3-4, pp. 54-71, q. 63.

33. See for instance, "The African Presence in Caribbean Literature", *Roots* ([1970-73] University of Michigan, 1990), 190-258.

34. To add to GR's history of the fate of LX, as the eventual intended publisher, I can add these details. Its first published appearance was in instalments in *Bim* ("The Love Axe/1": Developing a Caribbean Aesthetic 1962-1974", *Bim* 61 (June 1977), 53-65; "The Love Axe/ 1": Developing a Caribbean Aesthetic 1962-1974", *Bim* 62 (December 1977), 100-106; "The Love Axe/1": Developing a Caribbean Aesthetic 1962-1974", *Bim* 63 (June 1978), 181-192.) The manuscript first sent to Peepal Tree (c. 1994) came via Anne Walmsley, no doubt as a CAM connection. We typeset this, sent this to Kamau who exploded that this was not his LX. The version we had, an expansion of the *Bim* articles, came to around 180 typeset pages. This was in c1997. What followed in c2002 was a box containing 1,400 A4 pages set Sycorax style. The problem was that this version was incomplete: missing pages, missing references, missing cross-references. There were two problems here. Firstly, at some point after I let Kamau know this, the computer on which he'd written it had packed up and he could not make the updatings needed in ways that matched the original pagination. Secondly, in the form it was in (1,400 A4 pages) the book would have been outrageously expensive to print. Unwisely, I attempted a version of KB's Sycorax style that was more economical in layout but could at least be corrected and cross-referenced and could be printed by more cost-effective means. Kamau hated it, but we agreed that a "plain-text" version was the best way ahead. This in the end came to a two-volume edition of 298+321 pages, original chapters in one volume, the notes on notes, like a coral reef, in the other (this version was in in progress 2006-2008). This version also grew from the original box of printed sheets as Kamau discovered new pieces of information. Sadly, as GR notes later in this memoir, KB, on a couple of occasions, thought that I had inserted material which he had in fact sent me, and was at first indignant about the matter, though apologetic when he was sent evidence that he had originated the new material, and it's important to say that throughout we maintained

a very amicable relationship. KB was very clear, though, that LX could not be published until he had proofed it thoroughly, but this he was unable to do because of failing sight. In 2020, Beverley Brathwaite, as his literary executor, agreed to allow publication of LX if Gordon Rohlehr wrote an introduction. Gordon was engaged in writing this memoir and I don't think he thought that LX needed an introduction and he died without writing one. LX remains in limbo despite attempts to persuade Beverley to let us go ahead with publication.

35. Published as *Wars of Respect: Nanny, Sam Sharpe and the Struggle for People's Liberation* (Kingston: API for the National Heritage Week Committee, 1977 [64pp]).

36. These were *Jamaica Poetry: A Check List: Slavery to the Present* (Kingston: Jamaica Library Service, 1979 [36pp]) and *Barbados Poetry: A Check List: Slavery to the Present* (Mona: Savacou Publications, 1979 [16pp]).

37. Published as *History of the Voice: the development of nation language in anglophone Caribbean poetry* (London: New Beacon, 1984 [87pp]).

38. *The Arrivants*, 42-45.

39. *The Arrivants*, 222-224.

40. *Black + Blues* (Cuba: Casa de las Americas, 1976), 32-34.

41. *Third World Poems* (London: Longman, 1982),

42. *Jah Music* (Kingston: Savacou, 1986), 23-26

43. "The Spoiler's Return", *The Fortunate Traveller* (London: Faber, 1982), 53-60.

44. Mutabaruka, "Sit Dung pon de Wall", *The Next Poems* (Kingston: Paul Issa, 2005), 33.

45. David Rudder, "A Madman's Rant", *No Restriction: The Concert* (1996).

46. In *My Strangled City* (Peepal Tree ed.), 234-278.

47. In *The Shape of that Hurt* (Peepal Tree ed.), 68-93.

48. Published as "The Shape of That Hurt", *The Shape of That Hurt* (Peepal Tree ed.), 156-179.

49. Michael Dash, *Journal of West Indian Literature*, Vol. 1, No. 2, 87-90.

50. *The Shape of That Hurt* (Peepal Tree Ed.), 195-226. The quoted matter from the notes does not appear in the essay as published.

51. Edward Baugh, "Edward Brathwaite as Critic: Some Preliminary Observations", *Caribbean Quarterly*, 28, Nos 1/2 (1982), 66-75.

52. Jean D'Costa, "The Poetry of Edward Brathwaite", *Jamaica Journal*, No. 3, 24-28.

53. Collected in *The Shape of That Hurt* (Peepal Tree ed.) 266-276.

54. An unpublished novel. An extract "Christine", appeared in *Bim* vol. 8, no. 32, 1961, 246-250.

55. *The Zea Mexican Diary*, 176.

56. *Trench Town Rock* (Providence: Lost Roads Publishers, 1994), 20.

57. *Trench Town Rock*, 11, 18.

58. *Trench Town Rock*, 12.
59. *TTR*, 59.
60. *TTR*, 67.
61. *TTR*, 68.
62. Kamau Brathwaite writes further about the murder of the lecturer, Cliff Lashley, in "Ghana, South, Bajan Poets," part 3, in *Barabajan Poems, 1492–1992* (Kingston: Savacou North, 1994), 80. See Ronald Cummings, "Cliff Lashley and the Radical Practice of Memory", Feb 2023, https://smallaxe.net/sxsalon/discussions/toward-native-humanism.
63. *TTR*, 67.
64. *TTR*, 68.
65. Mona: Savacou Working Paper, 1982.
66. 1982, title page "Lecture at the University of Bremen, June, 1980, Caribbean culture."
67. *World Literature Written in English*, Vol 24 No. 2, 1984, 373-383.
68. See *Missile and Capsule*, ed. Jurgen Martini, Universitat Bremen, cyclostyled, 1983, 9-54.
69. See note 34 above.
70. GR, *Pathfinder: Black Awakening in the Arrivants of Edward Kamau Brathwaite* (Trinidad: author, 1981).
71. Bridget Jones writes about Kamau Brathwaite in "'The Unity is submarine': aspects of a pan-Caribbean consciousness in the work of Kamau Brathwaite", in *The Art of Kamau Brathwaite*, ed. Stewart Brown (Wales: Seren, 1995), 86-100.
72. Derek Walcott's criticism of Carifesta is referenced in Bruce King, *Derek Walcott: A Caribbean Life* (2000), 402.
73. "The Dream of Coming in with the Rain" in *The New Aesthetic and the Meaning of Culture in the Caribbean: Proceedings of the Carifesta V Symposia August 1992*, ed. Pearl Eintou Springer (Port of Spain, Trinidad: National Carnival Commission, 1995).
74. *Ancestors* (New York: New Directions, 2001) 131-138.
75. KB's published work on MR did not come out until 2002: *Magical Realism*. Vol. 1. New York: Savacou North, 2002.; *Magical Realism*. Vol. 2. New York: Savacou North, 2002.
76. "Jazz and the West Indian Novel." *Bim* 44 (1967): 275–84.; "Jazz and the West Indian Novel." *Bim* 45 (1967): 39–51; "Jazz and the West Indian Novel", *Bim* 46 (1968): 115–26. Republished in Roots (Ann Arbour: U Michigan, 1993), 55-110.
77. "Salt", *X/Self* (Oxford: OUP, 1987), 5
78. The Neustadt International Prize is a biennial award funded by the University of Oklahoma and World Literature Today. Awardees include OctavioPaz, Max Frisch, Raja Rao, Tomas Transtromer,

Naruddin Farah, Edwidge Danticat and Ismail Kadare, several of whom were Nobel winners.

79. Mary E. Morgan, "Highway to Vision: the Sea our Nexus", *World Literature Today*, Vol. 68, No. 4, Kamau Brathwaite: 1994 Neustadt International Prize for Literature (Autumn, 1994), 663-671.

80. "Salutation", *World Literature Today*, Vol. 68, No. 4, 661-662.

81. "Kamau Brathwaite: The Voice of African Presence", *World Literature Today*, 677-682

82. Edward Brathwaite, *Odale's Choice* (London: Evans Brothers, 1967).

83. "George Lamming and Kamau Brathwaite: Nationalists, Caribbean Regionalists, Internationalists", Issue 24 of Sir Winston Scott memorial lectures, Barbados, 1999, 28pp.

84. *Barabajan Poems 1492-1992* (New York: Savacou North, 1994).

85. *ConVersations* with Nathaniel Mackey (New York: Savacou North, 1997).

86. The white swimmer, Julian Hunte's adventures are on *Barabajan Poems,* 289-296.

87. "Stone", *Middle Passages* (Newcastle: Bloodaxe Books, 1992), 49-54.

88. *Trench Town Rock*, 9-18.

89. *ConVersations*, 184-189.

90. Rudder's *"Heaven"* featured on his album *No Restriction: The Concert* (1996).

91. "For the D, Don", *Reel from "The Life Movie"* (Jamaica: Savacou, 1972), 41.

92. In Leroy Calliste and Selwyn Newton, *From 1498 to 1972: 474 Years of Pain and Suffering* (Trinidad: authors, 1972), 78-79. In *Voiceprint* (London: Longman, 1989), 93.

93. *Reel from "The Life Movie",* 41

94. Ibid.

95. Bongo Jerry, "Roll On, Sweet Don", *Abeng* 1 (17 May 1969), 16. 4.

96. Mervyn Morris, *The Pond* (London: New Beacon, 1973), 7.

97. "Saint Ras", *Reel from "The Life Movie",* 39.

98. *Riddym Ravings & Other Poems* (London: Race Today Publications, 1988), 58-59.

99. *Natural Mysticism: Towards a New Reggae Aesthetic* (Leeds: Peepal Tree Press, 1999).

100. Ken Post, *Strike the Iron: A Colony at War* 2 vols (New Jersey: Humanities Press Inc., 1981).

101.M.G. Smith, *Dark Puritan* (Jamaica: UWI Department of Extramural Studies, 1963).

102. Roger Mais, *Brother Man* (London: Cape, 1954).

103. Andrew Salkey, *A Quality of Violence* (London: Hutchinson, 1960).

104. "Hawk", *Born to Slow Horses* (Connecticut: Wesleyan University Press), 92-114; *Ark, a 9/11 continuation poem* (New York: Savacou North, 2004).

105. *For the Geography of the Soul: Emerging Perspectives on Kamau Brathwaite* (New Jersey: Africa World Press, 2001).

106. See note 17. Walcott's review of *Rights of Passage* was published in the Trinidad Sunday Guardian, 19 March, 1967 and reprinted in *Derek Walcott: The Journey man Years*, Vol. 1 (Rodopi, 2013), 222-226.

107. "Kingston in the Kingdom of this World", *Third World Poems* (London: Longman, 1983), 50-53.

108. No title corresponding to Considering Creole or an anthology of poems published by UWI Press, could be found. KB/GR were probably referring to *Questioning Creole*, first published as a special issue of *Caribbean Quarterly* in 1998, and later expanded into a book edited by Glen Richards and Verene Shepherd and published by Ian Randle Publishers in 2002. Information from Aaron Kamugisha.

109. *Gordon Rohlehr, My Whole Life is Calypso: Essays on Sparrow* (Trinidad: author, 2015).

110. "The Rwanda Poems," according to Jacob Edwards existed only as an audio recording of a 1994 performance, although the closely related cycle "Rwanda" appears in print as part 3 of "New Gods of the Middle Passages" in Brathwaite's 2001 *Kamau Monograph*. The latter is also listed as *Caribbean Quarterly*/ Kamau Monograph (2001). "The Rwanda Poems" are also section 26 of *Golokwati 2000*, 313.

  "Missa Solemnis" won first prize in the Frank Collymore Literary competition in 2006. Excerpts from this poem were performed by Sonia Williams at the Walcott Warner Theatre, UWI, Cave Hill. 2010. Extracts from the poem, in six parts, described as begun in Ghana in the 1950s, appeared in *Poui: Cave Hill Journal of Creative Writing*, No. 11, December 2011, 13, 26, 68, 73, 118, 131, 167.

111. C.L.R. James gave a talk in London in 1967 on Black Power which can be found at https://www.marxists.org/archive/james-clr/works/1967/black-power.htm.

112. *Golokwati 2000* (New York: Savacou North, 2002).

113. "Défilé Agoué" may refer to the poems "Defilee" and "Agoue" in *Words Need Love Too* (St Martin: Nehesi, 2000), 18 and 63.

114. "Namsetoura" Part 11 of *Golokwati 2000*, 248.

115. A privately run co-educational school based in Harrow, England.

116. Joan is Joan A. Brathwaite, Grace is Grace Nichols, John is John Agard, Geo Padmore is the George Padmore Centre, the archive located above New Beacon's bookshop; John is John La Rose and Sarah is Sarah White.

117. Gordon Rohlehr wrote about his "Guyagony" in "Among School Children: or What New Life Beyond the Ashes of the Past" in *Perfected Fables Now*, 236-257.

118. First published in *African American Review*; Saint Louis Vol. 37,

Iss. 2/3, (Summer 2003): 198-203 and then in *Somebody Blew Up America and Other Poems* (House of Nehesi, 2003). The poem puts the destruction of the twin towers into the context of the long history of colonial terror. It was accused by Israel-supporting organisations of being anti-semitic.

119. Kamau Brathwaite, *Shar: Hurricane Poem* (Kingston, Jamaica: Savacou, 1990), unpaginated.

120. "Homecoming: Anse La Raye", *The Gulf and Other Poems* (London: Cape, 1969), 127-129.

121. *Escape to An Autumn Pavement* (London: Hutchinson, 1960, rpr. 2009).

122. GR refers to George Lamming's novel *Natives of My Person* (London: Longman, 1972) and *Water with Berries* (London: Longman, 1971).

123. *The History of Mary Prince, a West Indian Slave, Related by Herself* (1831).

124. KB alludes to a calypso by the Mighty Gabby, "Emmerton", about being dispossessed of homeland when the singer's ancestral village on the edge of Bridgetown was bulldozed to make way for a sewage treatment plant. On the album, *'Til Now* (2000).

125. GR alludes to Lord Jim, the eponymous hero of Joseph's Conrad's novel. Jim is a man of immense girth. *Lord Jim* (1900) ends of course with its hero's death by shooting. A Freudian image for retirement?

126. At one time distributed by The Blue Editions.

127. The Guyana massacres GR refers to involved alleged complicity between members of the PPP Government, in particular the Minister for Home Affairs, Ronald Gajraj (whose visas to enter the USA and Canada in 2004 were cancelled), a career criminal drug dealer, Roger Khan (who was sentenced to 40 years imprisonment in the USA in 2009), and elements of the Guyana police force in death squads (e.g. the Phantom squad) estimated to have carried out the extra-judicial killings of between 200-400 young Black men between 2002-2006 in response a surge in crimes. See https://www.reuters.com/article/idUSTRE66I5WA/.

128. But see "Growing Up at the Round House with Our Brother Kamau" (with Thelma E. Abrams and Joan A. Brathwaite), in *Bim*, Special Issue, November 2010.

129. *Fela!* was a musical written by Bill T. Jones and Jim Lewis, based on music and lyrics and events in the life of the late Nigerian Afrobeat composer and activist Fela Anikulapo Kuti (1938-1997). It opened in 2008.

130. The tribute can be found at https://www.bigdrumnation.com/2020/02/10/beat-eighty-drums-for-kamau-caldwell-taylor/. It was reposted in February 2020.

131. Whether *End Poem Poems* were absorbed into any of KB's final collections – *Strange Fruit, Liviticus* and *The Lazarus Poems* – is unclear.

132. Borrowed from Derek Walcott's poem "The Spoiler's Return" in *The Fortunate Traveller* (1981).
133. The book Alvin O. Thompson published in 2010 was *Confronting Slavery: Breaking Through the Corridors of Silence*, but a book that better matches GR's description is *Visualizing Slavery Images and Texts* published in 2015.
134. Published in Gordon Rohlehr, *Perfected Fables Now: A Bookman Signs Off on Seven Decades* (Leeds: Peepal Tree Press, 2019), 259-274.
135. A quote from Christopher Marlowe's play *Dr Faustus* (c. 1592).
136. Gordon Rohlehr, *Ancestories* (Trinidad: Lexicon, 2010).
137. A reference of course to the character in *Palace of the Peacock*.
138. I have seen the Aaron Kamugisha side of the correspondence and it is clear both that KB's complaints were responded to and that no disrespect was intended. It seems that KB assumed that in naming the lecture series in his name, all of them would be about him – which was never the declared intention.
139. Gordon Rohlehr, *My Whole Life is Calypso: Essays on Sparrow*.
140. Gordon Rohlehr, *Musings, Mazes, Muses, Margins* (Leeds: Peepal Tree Press, 2020).
141. This is a reference to Mervyn Morris's review of *Rights of Passage*, "Niggers Everywhere" in *New World Quarterly*, vol 3 No. 4, 1967, 61-65. Whilst not uncritical, Morris describes *Rights of Passage* as "worthy of detailed examination by the highest international standards". Morris regards *Rights* as a "very public" poem, which he regards as partly its weakness, "partly its strength". KB would not have liked MM's stated preference for Walcott's poetry.
142. This references Edward Baugh's long and generally balanced review of *Masks* in *Bim*, Vol 47, July December 1968, 209-211. Baugh does indeed use the phrase "travelogue with a difference" and perhaps does not show any recognition of why the subject matter of *Masks* should have been so important to Brathwaite.
143. This references J. Michael Dash's review of *The Visibility Trigger* and *Jah Music* in *The Journal of West Indian Literature* Vol. 1, No. 2 (June, 1987), pp. 87-90.
144. GR accepted the invitation to deliver the 8th annual Kamau Brathwaite lecture, which he did virtually from Trinidad in May 2022 and was one of his final public lectures.
145. This poem does not seem to have been published anywhere.
146. Martin Carter, "Rain Falls Upward" (1966) *University of Hunger: Collected Poems and Selected Prose* ed. Gemma Robinson (Newcastle: Bloodaxe Books, 2006), 123.
147. At the launch of Questel's *Collected Poems* at the Bocas Litfest in Port of Spain in 2016, Earl Lovelace seemed unhappy that GR's

spoken statement at the launch did not appear to him sufficiently enthusiastic about the 1970 Black Power uprising.

148. It is to be published in 2025 by Peepal Tree Press.

149. (Middletown: Wesleyan University Press, 2017).

150. See note 34 above.

151. Kamau Brathwaite (1994) Neustadt Lecture: "Newstead to Neustadt". *World Literature Today* 68(4): 653–60. Quoted in *Ancestories* (2010), v.

152. The phrase ("vibratin violence is how we move") comes from LKJ's "Street 66" on *Bass Culture* (1980).

153. Where Kamau Brathwaite grew up in Barbados. See "Growing Up at the Round House with Our Brother Kamau" (with Thelma E. Abrams (d. 2019) and Joan A. Brathwaite), in *Bim*, Special Issue, November 2010 (online at https://www.bimlitfest.org/articles/growing-round-house-our-brother-kamau).

154. First published as a sleeve note to the Argo recording of *Rights of Passage* and quoted in "The African Presence in Caribbean Literature" in *Roots*, 190-191.

INDEX OF NAMES AND ORGANISATIONS

Adisa, Opal Palmer (1954-) is a Jamaican novelist, poet, academic and storyteller, currently based at UWI Mona. She lived and taught for many years in the USA. She is the author of twelve books including: *It Begins with Tears, Caribbean Passion, I Name Me Name, Until Judgement Comes* and *Painting Away Regrets*. Her poetry, essays and stories have been anthologized in over two hundred journals.

AJS, A.J. Seymour (1914-1989) was a Guyanese poet, critic and autobiographer. He was the founding creator of a modern Guyanese literature, primarily through his editorship of the long-surviving literary journal, *Kyk-over-Al* from 1945-1961. His own publications include *Over Guiana, Clouds* (1944), *Sun's in My Blood* (1945) and many smaller collections. His *Collected Poems 1937-1989* was published in 2000.

Alexander, Lorrimer. No information could be found.

Alice, see Alice Walker.

Alleyne, Mervyn (1933-2016) was a Trinidadian sociolinguist and dialectologist whose work focused on the creole languages of the Caribbean. He taught for many years at UWI Mona. His publications include *Roots of Jamaican Culture* (1988), *The Construction and Representation of Race and Ethnicity in the Caribbean and the World* (2002) and, with Arvilla Payne-Jackson, *Folk Medicine of Jamaica* (2004).

Andaiye (1942-2019) was a Guyanese writer, activist for social, political and gender rights. She was a member of the executive of the Working People's Alliance, a founding member of the women's group, Red Thread. Her essays are collected in *The Point is to Change the World: Selected Writings of Andaiye* (London: Pluto Press, 2020).

Antoine-Dunne, Jean is a filmmaker, academic, and editor who was born in Trinidad where she taught at UWI St Augustine. Now retired, she lives mostly in Ireland. She has specialised in comparative studies of Caribbean and Irish literature, with a particular focus on the work of Derek Walcott. She edited *Interlocking Basins in a Globe: Essays on Derek Walcott* (2013) and wrote *Derek Walcott's Love Affair with Film* (2017).

Anyido, Kofi – See GR's full description, p. 85.

Armstrong, Louis, Satchmo (1901-1971) was an African American jazz trumpeter and singer whose recordings between c 1925-1936 with the Hot Five, Hot Seven and later his Orchestra established him as the premier exceptional solo artist and improvisor in jazz. Thereafter, whilst his music was bypassed by new developments from Ellington's big band compositions to bebop, he sustained a career and achieved wider popularity.

Atilla the Hun (1892-1962) was Raymond Quevedo, a Trinidadian calypsonian who is written about passim in Gordon Rohlehr's *Calypso and Society in Pre-Independence Trinidad* (1990). He functioned between 1939 to the late 1940s, when he became a politician. He was the author of a book about his life, *Atilla's Kaiso: A Short History of Trinidad Calypso* (1983).

Augier, Roy (1924-) is a St Lucian historian, developer of the history curriculum in the universities and schools of the English-speaking Caribbean and was a senior administrator at the University of the West Indies. His best known book is, with Douglas Hall, Shirley Gordon, and Mary Reckord, *The Making of the West Indies* (1960). He was chairman of the drafting committee for UNESCO's *General History of the Caribbean*, and after teaching at UWI Mona was Pro-vice Chancellor at Cave Hill (Barbados).

Awoonor, Kofi (1935-2013) was a Ghanaian poet, novelist, historian, academic and diplomat who was tragically killed in a terrorist attack in Kenya. His poetry collections include *The Promise of Hope: New and Selected Poems, 1964-2013* (2014), the novel, *This Earth, My Brother* (1971) and *The African Predicament: Collected Essays* (2006). He was an advocate for Ewe culture within Ghana.

Baille, Basilius was a Surinamese drummer from the Djuka, maroon community.

Baraka, Amiri (1934-2014) was an African American poet, dramatist, critic and writer on jazz. Formerly LeRoi Jones, Baraka moved from an Afro-centric position to a Black Marxist perspective. His best known works include the novel *The System of Dante's Hell* (1965), the plays, *Dutchman* and *The Slave* (1964), and his books on jazz, *Blues People* (1964), and *Black Music* (1968). His collected poems were published as *SOS Poems 1961-2013*. His title poem in *Somebody Blew Up America & Other Poems* (2003) aroused furore with its implication that the USA got what was coming to it in 9/11 and it was charged with being anti-semitic.

Baugh, Edward, Eddie (1936-2023) was a Jamaican poet, critic, actor and academic. He was one of the founders of the post-colonial development of Caribbean literary studies, who wrote fine literary biographies of Frank Collymore and Derek Walcott. His collection of poems *Black Sand* (2013) contains a moving poem dedicated to Kamau Brathwaite, though they sometimes crossed swords at UWI, Mona.

Bechet, Sidney (1897-1959) was a jazz musician who played the soprano saxophone. He was one of the first African American jazz men to find a sympathetic home in France.

Beckford, George (1934-1990 was a Jamaican, a leading member of the New World movement and, with Lloyd Best, argued that plantation societies were not just economic units but total institutions that enmeshed all aspects of the society including its class formation, cultural patterns and racial hierarchies, and that even when Caribbean societies no longer depended on monocrop agriculture, they remained shaped by their plantation pasts. Beckford's books include *Persistent Poverty: Underdevelopment in Plantation Societies in the Third World* (1973), and *The George Beckford Papers* (2000) which shows his concern with culture as well as with economics.

Beckles, Hilary McD. (1955-) is a Barbadian historian, author of *Natural Rebels* (1989), *A History of Barbados* (2006), a historian of Caribbean cricket, and prominent articulator of the case for reparations in *Britain's Black Debt* (2013) and *How Britain Underdeveloped the Caribbean* (2021). He is currently Vice-Chancellor of UWI Cave Hill and was knighted in 2007.

Beddoe, Andrew was an Orisha drummer from John John, Trinidad who played a prominent part in the development of steelband from tamboo-bamboo to iron to tuned pans. His work is recorded on a couple of Smithsonian Folkways albums, including *Little Carib Theatre Drummers: Drums of Trinidad* (1956).

Bedward, Alexander (1859-1930) was a Jamaican revivalist preacher and prophet who attracted a mass African Jamaican following in the August Town area. His explicit call to organise as Black Jamaicans was regarded as threatening by the colonial state who had him imprisoned on the grounds of lunacy.

Bennett, Louise (1919-2006) was a Jamaican poet, folklorist, transcriber of Anancy stories, actor and performer. Her most influential book was *Jamaica Labrish* (1966) a collection of her patwa poetry written over two decades, influential because it forced other Caribbean poets into taking patwa seriously. She trained and worked in the UK as an actor between 1945-1950.

Berry, James (1924-2017) was a Jamaican poet, editor and author of fiction for younger readers. He was an active member of CAM. His anthology, *News from Babylon: The Chatto Book of Westindian-British Poetry* (1984) was the first predominantly Black British poetry anthology. Berry's own poetry collections included *Fractured Circles* (1979), *Lucy's Letters* (1982), *Hot Earth, Cold Earth* (1995) and *Windrush Songs* (2007).

Best, Curwen (1965-) is professor of Popular Culture, Literary, and Cultural Studies at the UWI, Cave Hill. He is the author of *Kamau Brathwaite and Christopher Okigbo: Art Politics and the Music of Ritual* (2009), *The Politics of Caribbean Cyberculture* (2008), *Culture @ the Cutting Edge: Tracking Caribbean Popular Music* (2005), *Roots to Popular Culture: Barbadian Aesthetics from Kamau Brathwaite to Hardcore Styles* (2001), *Barbadian Popular Music and the Politics of Caribbean Culture* (1999).

Best, Lloyd (1934-2007) was a Trinidadian economist and public intellectual, who was one of the founding members of the New World Movement, which became the Tapia House movement in Trinidad and latterly The Trinidad and Tobago Institute of the West Indies. Best's important work includes *Essays on the Theory of Plantation Economy: A Historical and Institutional Approach to Caribbean Economic Development* (2009).

Biko, Steve (1946-1977) was a Black South African activist, pan-Africanist and socialist who was murdered by the South African police. He founded the Black People's Convention arguing that Black South Africans could not depend on white liberals and had to liberate themselves.

Bishop, Jacqueline (1971-) is a Jamaican poet, novelist, artist and ceramicist resident in the USA. She is the author of the novel *The River's Song*, two collections of poems, *Fauna*, and *Snapshots from Istanbul*, an art book, *Writers Who Paint... Three Jamaican Artists*, *The Gymnast and other Positions*, short stories, essays and interviews which won the Bocas prize for non-fiction and most recently *Patchwork: Essays and Interviews in Caribbean Visual Culture*.

Bishop, Maurice (1944-1983) was the leader of the revolutionary New Jewel Movement which came to power in a coup against the dictatorial regime of Eric Gairy in 1979. Bishop himself was murdered by soldiers loyal to Bernard Coard when the New Jewel Movement split in 1983.

Bishop, Pat (1940-2011) was a Trinidadian educator, artist and musician who was best known for her work with the steelband movement and as a dynamic force in Trinidad's cultural development. Gordon Rohlehr wrote a powerful requiem for her in *Perfected Fables Now: A Bookman Signs off on Seven Decades* (pp. 174-178).

Bobb, June taught at Queens College of the City University of New York. She is the author of *Beating a Restless Drum: The Poetics of Kamau Brathwaite and Derek Walcott* (Trenton: Africa World Press, 1997).

Bogle, Paul (1822-1865) was a deacon in the Native Baptist church in the parish of St Thomas in Jamaica and an ally of the mulatto politician George William Gordon. He led a march of Black peasant farmers and others to the Courthouse in Morant Bay. After the violence that resulted, the British Governor Eyre ordered the slaughter of over five hundred Jamaican peasants, including the hanging of Bogle and Gordon.

Boots (see James Carnegie),

Brand, Dionne (1953-) is a Trinidadian poet, essayist and novelist long based in Canada. Her fiction includes *Sans Souci and Other Stories*, *In Another Place, Not Here*, *At the Full and Change of the Moon*, *What We All Long For*, *Love Enough* and *Theory*. Her collected poems *Nomenclature: New and Collected Poems* was published in 2022. Her best know work of nonfiction is *A Map to the Door of No Return: Notes to Belonging* (2001).

Brathwaite, Doris (1926-1986), known as Zea Mexican, Kamau Brathwaite's wife and steadfast support. She was the author of *EKB: His Published Prose & Poetry, 1948–1986* (1986). His grief over her death from cancer is recorded in *The Zea Mexican Diary: 7 September 1926 – 7 September 1986* (1993).

Brathwaite, Joan A. was Kamau's sister, Reference Librarian at UWI, Cave Hill and the author of *Women and the Law* (1999).

Breeze, Jean 'Binta' (1956-2021) was a Jamaican poet, actor and outstanding performer of her work. She wrote about the schizophrenia she lived with throughout her life. Her poetry collections include *Riddym Ravings and Other Poems, Spring Cleaning, The Arrival of Brighteye and Other Poems, Third World Girl: Selected Poems* and *The Verandah Poems*.

Breiner, Lawrence is an American academic who has written one of the best general studies of Anglophone Caribbean poetry, *An Introduction to West Indian Poetry* (1998) and pioneered the study of the Tobagan poet, Eric Roach, *Black Yeats: Eric Roach and the Politics of Caribbean Poetry* (2008).

Brodber, Erna (Lixie) (1940-) is a Jamaican novelist, social historian and pioneer of psychiatric anthropology. Her work traces the African heritage of Caribbean people, including the psychic damage wrought by enslavement, and the strategies individuals and communities have evolved to heal themselves. Her novels are *Jane and Louisa Will Soon Come Home* (1980), *Myal: A Novel* (1988), *Louisiana* (1994), *The Rainmaker's Mistake* (2007), *Nothing's Mat* (2014). Her nonfiction includes *Woodside, Pear Tree Grove P.O.* (2004), *The Second Generation of Freemen in Jamaica, 1907–1944* (2004), *The Continent of Black Consciousness: On the History of the African Diaspora from Slavery to the Present Day* (2003), and *Moments of Cooperation and Incorporation: African American and African Jamaican Connections, 1782-1996* (2019).

Broodhagen, Karl (1909-2002) was a Barbadian artist/sculptor best known for his statue of Bussa breaking free from the chains of enslavement.

Brown, Sterling (1901-1989) was an African American poet, editor, anthologist, folklorist and academic. He made jazz and African American speech patterns an integral part of his poetry. *The Collected Poems of Sterling Brown* was published in 1980.

Brown, Stewart (1951-) is a poet, editor, artist and critic. As a teacher in Jamaica, he edited and published a literary magazine, *Now*; co-edited *Voiceprint* with Mervyn Morris and Gordon Rohlehr; edited *The Heinemann Book of Caribbean Poetry* (with Ian McDonald), *The Oxford Book of Caribbean Short Stories, Caribbean Poetry Now, The Art of Kamau Brathwaite, All Are Involved: The Art of Martin Carter, The Bowling Was Superfine*. His own work includes his collection of poems, *Elsewhere* and *Tourist, Traveller, Troublemaker: Essays on Poetry*. He taught at the University of Birmingham for many years.

Brown, Wayne (1944-2009) was a Trinidadian poet, fiction writer, critic, columnist, yachtsman and mentor to many younger writers, who lived for much of his life in Jamaica. He was the author of fictive prose collected in *The Scent of the Past and other stories* (2011), two collections of poetry, *On the Coast* and *Voyages,* and a biography: *Edna Manley: the private years.*

Burnham, Linden Forbes S. (1923-1985) was the prime minister and president of Guyana between 1964-1980 and Executive President for life of the Republic of Guyana until his death. After the break-up of the united African/Indian PPP, he led the People's National Congress as a political party that appealed to the interests of the Afro-Guyanese. His authoritarianism, election rigging and badly managed command-state economy led to the collapse of Guyanese society and mass emigration. His one undeniable decolonising achievement was hosting the first CARIFESTA (qv).

Butler, Tubal Uriah (Buzz) (1897-1977) was a Grenadian-born Baptist preacher who was a labour leader and then politician in Trinidad and Tobago. He came to prominence in the 1937 oilfield workers strikes which resulted in rioting in which 14 people died and Butler was tried for sedition, acquitted but sentenced to two years in prison for incitement to riot and then detained for six years during the 1939-45 war. Butler formed his own political party and served in the legislative council between 1950-61.

Callender, Timothy (1946-1989) was a Barbadian artist, musician and novelist. His novels include *Martin's Bay, How Music Came to the Ainchan People* and a collection of stories, *It So Happen* and experiments in photo-novels. A writer of great promise, he allegedly became addicted to crack cocaine and died in disputed circumstances.

Calliste, Leroy was a Trinidadian poet, author with Selwyn Newton of the privately published collection, *From 1498 to 1972: 474 Years of Pain and Suffering,* Trinidad c. 1972.

Calliste, Leroy aka Black Stalin (1941-2022) was a Trinidadian calypsonian famed for his leftist, decolonising political songs. He won the Calypso Monarch competition for the first time in 1979 (with "Caribbean Man" and "Play One") and again in 1985 with "Ism Schism" and "Wait Dorothy", in 1987 with "Mr. Panmaker" and "Bun Dem" – which consigned arch colonialists from Columbus to Ronald Reagan to hell, and again in 1991 and 1995. He recorded at least 13 albums between 1979 and 2006. GR writes about him in *A Scuffling of Islands: Essays on Calypso* (2004), 79-91, 95, 339-341 and passim

Cameron, Norman E., (1903-1983) was a polymathic Guyanese mathematician, teacher, historian, dramatist, essayist, anthologist and cultural activist influenced by Garveyism. His work includes the anthology, *Guianese Poetry: 1831-1931* (1931) *The Evolution of the Negro* (1935), the plays *Three Immortals* (1953). His work is given the acknowledgement he sought in Jocelynne Loncke's *Norman E. Cameron: The Man and his Works* (Georgetown, Edgar Mittelholzer Memorial Lectures, seventh series, 1981).

Campbell, John (1966-2018) was a historian who taught at UWI, St Augustine, who specialised in contemporary Caribbean civilization and culture. He published *Beyond Massa: Sugar Management in the British Caribbean, 1770-1834* (2012).

Caribbean Artists Movement (CAM). See Anne Walmsley's comprehensive history of the movement, *The Caribbean Artists Movement, 1966–1972: A Literary and Cultural History* (New Beacon Books, 1992). Set up in London by Kamau Brathwaite, John La Rose, Louis James and Andrew Salkey to support and bring together Caribbean writers and artist in the UK and at home, CAM met in people's houses and student centres, holding conferences in 1967 and 1969. It ceased to have a significant UK focus when key members returned to the Caribbean or went to the USA and Canada. *Savacou* (qv) was described as a journal of CAM.

CARIFESTA is the Caribbean Festival of the Arts, defined as performing arts, visual arts, literature and education in culture. It is the child of CARICOM designed to enhance a sense of Caribbean unity by bringing artists from all Caribbean countries to a single host country, from across all language areas. Since 1972, when Guyana hosted the first CARIFESTA, there have been 15 Carifestas at irregular intervals, involving 10 different countries and with different degrees of national investment in the festival's success. Criticism has focused on the fact that states send favoured artists and play safe, whilst Derek Walcott lashed the hypocrisy of Caribbean states for the cynical exploitation of their artists whilst providing no consistent support for the arts unless it promotes tourism.

Carnegie, James (1938-2007), known as Jimmie and 'Boots', was a Jamaican teacher, sports journalist, historian and author of *Some Aspects of Jamaica's Politics 1918-1938* and a novel *Wages Paid* which is an inventive portrayal of power relations on sugar plantation in the period of slavery.

Carnegie, Ralph (1936-2011) was the Dean of the Faculty of Law at UWI, Mona, Jamaica, principal at UWI, Cave Hill, and credited with being a major influence on thinking about law in the postcolonial Caribbean.

Carpentier, Alejo (1904-1980), was born in Switzerland, but grew up in Cuba, his spiritual home. He was imprisoned as a leftist and exiled by the Machado dictatorship in 1927 and lived in Europe and Mexico. He returned to Cuba in the 1940s but was again exiled to Venezuela in 1945. He returned to Cuba after the 1959 revolution. As a Cuban novelist he is widely credited with the invention of marvellous realism (*lo real maravilloso*). His novels include *The Kingdom of this World* (1949), *The Lost Steps* (1953) and *Explosion in a Cathedral* (1962) and as nonfiction, *La música en Cuba* (1946).

Carter, Martin (1927-1997) was the Guyanese national poet and a major poet on any scale. Imprisoned by British imperialism after their overthrow of the elected PPP government led by Cheddi Jagan in 1953, Carter wrote *Poems of Resistance from British Guiana* (1954). After the split in the PPP and being expelled from it as an ultra-leftist, he later joined forces with Forbes Burnham's PNC and was for a time Minister of Information and Culture until he resigned in disgust over the PNC's corruption and authoritarianism, writing the line "the mouth is muzzled by the food it eats". Carter's later collections, written in an increasingly gnomic style, *Poems of Succession* (1977) and *Poems of Affinity* (1980), chart the degradation of Guyanese society in the later 1970s. *University of Hunger: Collected Poems and Selected Prose* (2006) is his testament.

Castro, Fidel (1926-2018) led the small band that overthrew the USA-backed Batista dictatorship in Cuba. He was prime minister of Cuba from 1959-1976 and president from 1976-2008. Originally a leftist Cuban nationalist, he became a more orthodox Marxist-Leninist under unrelenting attempts at subversion by the USA and necessary reliance on the Soviet Union. He was a touchstone for political identity in the Anglophone Caribbean, dividing leaderships on the right who were in the Washington orbit from people on the left who admired Cuba's cultural nationalism and its resistance to American imperialism, who were prepared to accept the elements of authoritarianism as a regrettable consequence of Cuba's besieged situation.

Césaire, Aimé (1913-2008) was a Martinican poet, playwright, politician, and writer. He was one of the founding writers and theorists of the Négritude movement. He wrote five collections of poetry including *Cahier d'un retour au pays natal* (1939), *Les armes miraculeuses* (1946), *Soleil cou-coupé* (1948), *Corps perdu* (1950), *Ferrements* (1960), *Cadastre* (1961), and *Moi, luminaire* (1980). *His plays include La Tragédie du roi Christophe (1960), Une saison au Congo and Une Tempête* (adapted from Shakespeare's play). His works of prose include *Discours sur le colonialisme* and *Lettre à Maurice Thorez*. He was close to the French Communist Party until the Soviet invasion of Hungary and the latter work is his critique of Stalinism.

Chad, or Dream Chad is Kamau Brathwaite's wife Beverley, née Reid.

Chapman, Matthew James (1796-1865), was the Barbadian author of *Barbadoes, and Other Poems* (1833) and *Jeptha's Daughter: A Dramatic Poem* (1834). He lived in England from 1827 and was a practising physician. Though there was a Matthew Chapman who built the Sunbury Estate House in 1660, the poet Chapman does not feature in the Legacies of Slavery database as a person who benefited from compensation paid for emancipated slaves.

Chevannes, Barry (1940-2010) was a Jamaican sociologist, anthropologist and activist in radical peace and social causes who taught at UWI Mona and did outreach work among the Rastafari community. He was a singer-songwriter and guitarist, whose hymns were used in churches. His books include, *Rastafari: Roots and Ideology* (1994) and the edited collection *Rastafari and Other African-Caribbean Worldviews* (1995), *Betwixt and Between – Explorations in an African-Caribbean Mindscape* (2000), and *Learning to Be a Man: Culture, Socialization and Gender Identity in Five Caribbean Communities* (2001).

Chookolingo, Patrick D. (c1922-1986) was a journalist and newspaper editor famed for introducing a populist, muckraking journalism to Trinidad in his work on the *T & T Mirror* and the scandal sheet, *The Bomb*. He had one story broadcast on *Caribbean Voices* under the name P.D. Lincott.

Cipriani, Captain A.A. (1875-1945) was a white Trinidadian of Corsican descent who following service in the British West India Reegiment in World War I, became a labour leader campaigning on behalf of the "barefoot man", and a pioneering advocate for self-government. He led the Trinidad Working Men's Association, which became the Trinidad Labour Party, and was regularly elected as Lord Mayor of Port of Spain.

Clarke, LeRoi (1938-2021) was a major African Trinidadian artist, poet and chieftain of the Orisha community. His collections of poetry include *Taste of Endless Fruit* (1972); *Douens* (1976), *Eyeing De Word – Love Poem for Ettylene* (2004), *De Distance Is Here, The El Tucuche Epic 1984-2007* (2007), and *Secret Insect of a Bird Deep in Me, Wanting to Fly* (2008).

Clarke, Sir Ellis (1917-2010) was a distinguished civil servant and diplomat who became the first President of Trinidad & Tobago when it became a republic in 1976.

CLR (James, C.L.R.) (1901-1989) was one of the most important thinkers the Caribbean has produced. Born in Trinidad, he was an early articulator of the anti-colonial mission in *The Case for West Indian Government* (1933). His novel *Minty Alley* (1936) was about the "middle-class" discovery of the Trinidadian working-class world. His study of the Haitian revolution, *The Black Jacobins* (1938) put that uprising in the context of both its folk roots and its world-historical setting of global modernity, whilst his study of cricket, *Beyond a Boundary* (1963) was a profound study of how excellence in cultural expression was and could be a life-enhancing revolutionary goal for the Caribbean. The sad irony was that when James returned to Trinidad after three decades away in Britain and the USA, he was put under house arrest by Eric Williams, the man he'd mentored, and the leftist Workers and Farmers Party which he jointly founded was swept away at the 1966 polls by the force of Black and Indian ethnic nationalisms.

Cobham, Rhonda (Cobham-Sander) (1952-) is a Trinidadian-born professor at Amherst College and one of the most perceptive critics of Caribbean writing. Her book, *I and I: Epitaphs for the Self in the Work of V.S. Naipaul, Kamau Brathwaite, and Derek Walcott* (2016) examines how these three writers attempt to consolidate their literary legacies in their later works. She has published over 30 articles and book chapters exploring a broad range of issues, from nation, history and language to gender, race and sexuality. Her work has appeared in journals such as *Small Axe, Anthurium, Caribbean Quarterly, Jamaica Journal, World Literature Written in English, PMLA, The Journal of Commonwealth Literature, The Black Scholar* and others.

Coester, Markus is a lecturer in ethno-musicology at the University of Bayreuth in Germany specialising in the study of Ghanaian Highlife music. With Wolfgang Bender he was the editor of *A Reader in African Jamaican Music, Dance and Religion* (2015).

Collier, Gordon teaches English at the Justus-Liebig-Universität Gießen. He has written widely about Caribbean literature and postcolonial writing and published *Us / Them: Translation, Transcription and Identity in Post-Colonial Literary Cultures* (1992) and edited the two volumes of *Derek Walcott: The Journey Man Years: Occasional Prose 1957-1974: Volume 1: Culture, Society, Literature and Art*; *Volume 2: Performing Arts* (Amsterdam: Rodopi, 2013).

Colly, Collymore, Frank (1893-1980) was a Barbadian poet, short story writer, actor, editor, publisher, artist, schoolteacher and mentor. His own poetry *Thirty Poems* (1944), *Beneath the Casuarinas* (1945), *Flotsam* (1948) and *Collected Poems* (1959) is part of the movement towards a contemporary Caribbean poetic voice, but probably his major contribution to Caribbean letters was his founding and sustaining of the magazine, *Bim*, from 1944 to 1975, and his encouragement of the early careers of Derek Walcott, George Lamming, Kamau Brathwaite and Austin Clarke. He also wrote a pioneering short book, *Notes for a Glossary of Words and Phrases of Barbadian Dialect*.

Coltrane, John (Trane), (1926-1967) was an African American saxophonist, playing both tenor and soprano. His recordings with Miles Davis and Thelonious Monk in the later 1950s are still classics, but it was when he put his own band together in 1959 with his album *Giant Steps* that he was recognised as one of the great innovators of jazz, pushing it away from a reliance on standards, pushing the sounds that could be made on the saxophone to the instrument's extremes, whilst still commanding a mass audience with the spiritual intensity of his album *A Love Supreme* (1965) though only more open-minded listeners followed him all the way with even more adventurous and abstract albums such as *Ascension* and *Meditations* of 1966. *Sunship* (1965, 1971) is one of the albums GR mentions.

Connor, Geraldine (1952-2011) was a British ethnomusicologist, singer and theatre director, the daughter of Trinidadian actors Edric and Pearl Connor. She was involved in British theatre of the 1970s, such as *Jesus Christ Superstar*. She went to Trinidad from 1976-84 were she taught music and was actively involved with the steelband movement. Her crowning achievement was the staging of *Carnival Messiah* (2003, 2007) a reworking of Handel's oratorio with Trinidadian stylings.

Conqueror, Mighty, Leroy Paul (1939-2011) was a Trinidadian calypsonian famous for "Trinidad Dictionary", "Woman and Money" (1962) "Dem Trinidad Yankees" and "Fresh Water Yankee". He migrated to the USA in the 1970s.

Cooper, Carolyn (1950-) is a Jamaican cultural theorist, newspaper columnist, advocate of the national use of patwa, and is the emeritus Professor of Literary and Cultural Studies at UWI Mona. She is the author of foundational books on Jamaican popular musical culture and its spread in the world: *Noises in the Blood: Orality, Gender and the 'Vulgar' Body of Jamaican Popular Culture* (1993), and *Sound Clash: Jamaican Dancehall Culture at Large* (2004). She is the editor of *Global Reggae* (2012).

Count Ossie (1926-1976), born Oswald Williams, was a Jamaican drummer, Rastafarian, musical group leader and pioneer of Rastafari rhythms in Jamaican music with the track 'O Carolina'. His group, Mystic Revelations of Rastafari produced two epochal albums, *Grounation* (1973) a mix of free-form jazz, songs, chanting and spoken groundings, and *Tales from Mozambique* (1975).

Cudjoe, Selwyn (1943-) is a Trinidadian scholar, literary theorist, historian, publisher and columnist. He taught at Wellesley College Massachusetts from 1986. His books include *Caribbean Visionary: A. R. F. Webber and the Making of the Guyanese Nation* (2011), *The Role of Resistance in Caribbean Literature* (2010), and *Beyond Boundaries: The Intellectual Tradition of Trinidad and Tobago in the Nineteenth Century* (2002) and *The Slavemaster of Trinidad: William Hardin Burnley and the Nineteenth-Century Atlantic World* (2018). He was the editor and publisher of Callaloux Press and organised the first Caribbean Women's Conference in 1988.

D'Aguiar, Fred (1960-) is a British-Guyanese poet, novelist and memoirist who has taught for most of his life in the USA. He is the author of five novels including *The Longest Memory, Dear Future, Feeding the Ghosts, Children of Paradise* and eight poetry collections including *Mama Dot, Airy Hall, British Subjects,* the verse novel *Bloodlines, Continental Shelf*, and *Letters to America*. His plays include *High Life* and *A Jamaican Airman Foresees His Death. Year of Plagues: A Memoir of 2020* is his first non-fiction book.

D'Costa, Jean (1937-) is a Jamaican novelist, literary critic and linguist. She has lived in the USA since 1980. Her best-known novels for younger readers are *Sprat Morrison* (1972) and *Escape to Last Man Peak* (1976). She has written a monograph on *Roger Mais: The Hills Were Joyful and Brother Man*, and literary/ linguistic studies with Barbara Lalla, *Language in Exile: Three Hundred Years of Jamaican Creole*, and *Voices in Exile: Jamaican Texts of the 18th and 19th Centuries* (2009), and *Caribbean Literary Discourse: Voice and Cultural Identity in the Anglophone Caribbean* (2014).

Dabydeen, David (1955-) is a Guyanese-born novelist and poet and historian of art, who has been variously a university professor, a member of the executive board of UNESCO and the Guyanese ambassador to China. His novels include *The Intended, Disappearance, The Counting House, A Harlot's Progress, Our Lady of Demerara, Johnson's Dictionary* and *Sweet Li Jie* (due in 2024). His poetry includes *Slave Song, Coolie Odyssey* and *Turner. Hogarth's Blacks* is a study of the Black figure in 18th century British art.

Damas, Léon Gontran (1912-1978) was a poet and politician who was born in Cayenne (French Guiana), settled in France and later in the USA. He was one of the theorists of Négritude and an editor of *Présence Africaine*. His poetry collections include *Pigments* (1937). *Poèmes nègres sur des airs Africains* (1948), *Graffiti* (1952), *Black-Label* (1956) and *Névralgies* (1966).

Dash, J. Michael (1948-2019) was a Trinidadian scholar who was a specialist in Haitian literature and French Caribbean writers. Dash's publications include *Edouard Glissant* (1995), *The Other America: Caribbean Literature in a New World Context* (1998), *Haiti and the United States* (1988), and *Culture and Customs of Haiti* (2001). He taught at UWI Mona, Jamaica and later at New York University.

Davis, Miles (1926-1991) was an African American jazz trumpeter and bandleader who continually re-invented himself and released epochal albums that defined whole phases of postwar American music, from bebop, West Coast 'cool', hard bop, post-bop, jazz funk and jazz rock. His essential albums include *Birth of the Cool* (1949/57), the albums with John Coltrane (*Walkin', Cookin' and Relaxin'*), the modal music of *Kind of Blue* (1959), the albums with Wayne Shorter and Herbie Hancock such as *Miles Smiles* (1967) and *Nefertiti* (1968) and the electric Miles including *Bitches Brew* (1970) and *On the Corner* (1972).

Dawes, Kwame (1962-) is a poet, novelist, short story writer, playwright, critic, academic and editor and one time singer in a reggae band. He was born in Ghana, grew up in Jamaica and has lived the bulk of his life in the USA. He is the author of over thirty books, the poetry collections including *Progeny of Air, Prophets, Jacko Jacobus, Shook Foil, Impossible Flying, Wheels*, and *Sturge Town*; the fiction *Bivouac* and *A Place to Hide*; and the influential study, *Natural Mysticism: Towards a New Reggae Aesthetic*, which Kamau Brathwaite noted with approval.

Dayan, Joan (now Colin Dayan) is a professor in humanities at Vanderbilt University. She has written on prison law and torture, Caribbean culture and literary history, as well as on Haitian poetics, Edgar Allan Poe, and the history of slavery. Her book *Haiti, History, and the Gods* (1995) is an important and influential study in bringing together fieldwork and cultural studies to the understanding of the sacred and the secular in Haitian history. She also published a translation of René Depestre's *A Rainbow for the Christian West*.

De Caires, David (1937-2008) was a Guyanese solicitor, journalist and newspaper proprietor whose *Stabroek News* (from 1986) became an important part of the struggle against the restrictions on the media and state control of information in Guyana in the 1970s and 1980s. He was involved with the New World Group in the 1960s in Guyana and the publication of *New World Fortnightly* and *New World Quarterly*.

Dent, Tom (1931-1988) was a jazz scholar, playwright, oral historian, journalist and cultural activist. He was a board member of the Jazz & Heritage Foundation and served as executive director from 1987 to 1990.

Depestre, René (1926-) is a Haitian poet and novelist and one-time Communist activist. For much of his adult life he was forced to live in exile, staying longest in post-revolutionary Cuba, but falling out with the regime and has lived in France since 1978. His best known poetry collection is *Un arc-en-ciel pour l'Occident chrétien* (*Rainbow for the Christian West*) (1967) and his novels *Le Mat de cockagne* (*Festival of the Greasy Pole*) (1979) *Hadriana dans Tous mes Rêves* (1988) (*Hadriana in All My Dreams*) are his only books translated into English.

Deren, Maya (1917-1961) was an experimental American filmmaker, born in the Ukraine, whose book, *Divine Horsemen: The Living Gods of Haiti* (1953) is a close and deeply sympathetic look at rituals of possession and of dance, one of Deren's preoccupations. She saw in voudoun a means of escape from the conventional self into community, not as a loss but as an expansion of possibility. Her film, with the same title, was released posthumously in 1977.

Diawara, Manthia (1953-) is a Malian writer, filmmaker, art historian and cultural theorist who has taught at universities in the USA since the mid-1980s. His books include *African Cinema: Politics & Culture* (1992), *In Search of Africa* (1998), and *We Won't Budge: An exile in the World* (2003). He has made many films, including on figures such as Angela Davis, Ngugi Wa Thiongo and Edouard Glissant.

Dirty Dozen, The (1977-) is an African American New Orleans brass band which has combined traditional street marching styles with contemporary funk, modern jazz and pop music. They have made at least fifteen albums, the best probably being *My Feet Can't Fail Me Now* (1984) and *Funeral for a Friend* (2004) where they go back to street basics.

Dobru (Robin Ravales) (1935-1983) was a Surinamese poet and acclaimed performer who was an important figure in the *Wie Eegie Sanie* [Our Own Thing] movement, promoting Surinamese language and culture, and advocating Surinamese independence within a united Caribbean. He ensured that Suriname participated in the first Carifesta held in Guyana in 1972. He wrote in Sranan Tongo, but also translated his poetry into English. Always on the left, for a time he became minister for culture in the Bouterse government after the 1980 coup.

Dolphy, Eric (1928-1964) was an African American jazz saxophonist (alto and tenor) bass clarinetist and flautist and composer whose premature death deprived jazz of one of its great innovators. He played with Charles Mingus and John Coltrane, and his album, *Out for Lunch* (1964) sounds as fresh and challenging as it did sixty years ago.

Drummond, Don (1932-1969) was an outstanding Jamaican jazz and ska trombonist whose work with the Skatalites still inspires and remains widely available on CD. Drummond was an iconic figure, deeply influenced by Rastafarianism and the turn to Africa, who was afflicted by mental health issues and was incarcerated in the Bellevue Asylum in Kingston after he murdered his partner, Anita Mahfood.

Ellis, Paula is a Barbadian who undertook an M.Phil on Kamau Brathwaite at UWI St Augustine. She is a poet and retired pharmacist. Her poem "A Goloquatie for Kamau" was published in *Kamau 85* online at ArtsEtc.

Evans, Gil (1912-1988) was a Canadian composer, pianist and arranger of scores for large-scale jazz bands. He was most famed for his work with Miles Davis (*Miles Ahead*, *Porgy and Bess* and *Sketches of Spain*) but also arranged the songs of Jimi Hendrix for a jazz orchestra. He came to prominence with *Birth of the Cool* recorded in 1949 but not released until 1957, and kept up with the continuing changes in jazz with the avantgarde of the 1960s and 1970s with albums like *Into the Cool* (1962).

Fido, Elaine Savory (now Savory) has published widely on Caribbean and African literatures, including *The Cambridge Introduction to Jean Rhys* (2009). She lived and worked for many years in Barbados. Her poem collection *flame tree time* was published by Sandberry Press. Recently she has published in postcolonial ecocriticism and environmental humanities. In 2021, she retired from The New School (New York) as Emeritus Professor.

Figueroa, John (1920-1999) was a Jamaican writer, poet, journalist, broadcaster, and educator. His poetry is collected in *The Chase* (1992). He was a contributor and reader in the BBC's *Caribbean Voices* and served as the first General Editor of Heinemann's *Caribbean Writers Series*. He edited two volumes of poetry drawn from the *Caribbean Voices* programme, *Dreams and Visions* (1966) and *The Blue Horizons* (1970).

Fitzpatrick, Miles (1936-2019) was a lawyer, active in leftwing politics in the 1960s and 70s as one of the Guyanese members of the New World Group. During the Burnham period, he staunchly opposed the undermining of the rule of law and a constitution that put virtually unlimited power in the President's hands. In the 1980s, he was one of the group who helped restore independent reporting through the founding of *Stabroek News*.

Flack, Roberta (1937-) is an African American singer and songwriter whose most successful period was between 1971-1985 when she had a series of hits in the r&b charts, mostly with covers. She was seen as being at the smoother end of soul.

Forbes, Curdella (1957-) is a Jamaican novelist, short story writer and academic who has taught at UWI Mona and at Howard University in the USA since 2004. Her study, *From Nation to Diaspora. Samuel Selvon, George Lamming and the Cultural Performance of Gender* (2005), sees their novels through a feminist lens. She has written for younger readers with *Songs of Silence* and *Flying with Icarus*. Her adult fiction has explored elements of the speculative and African Caribbean mythology in *A Permanent Freedom* (2008), *Ghosts* (2014) and *A Tall History of Sugar* (2018).

Francis, Donette is director for the Center for Global Black Studies and past director the American Studies Program at the University of Miami. Her research and writing investigate place, aesthetics and cultural politics in the African Diaspora. She is the author of *Fictions of Feminine Citizenship: Sexuality and the Nation in Contemporary Caribbean Literature* (2010).

Franklin, Aretha (1942-2018) was an African American singer and pianist, the Queen of Soul, with a series of outstanding albums through the 1960s and 1970s which included *I Never Loved a Man the Way I Love You* (1967), *Lady Soul* (1968), *Spirit in the Dark* (1970), *Young, Gifted and Black* (1972), *Amazing Grace* (1972).

Fraser, Dean (1957-) is a Jamaican saxophonist who has played on hundreds of reggae recordings from the late 1970s to the present. A compilation of his work can be heard on *The Very Best of Dean Fraser*.

Gabby, Mighty (Anthony Carter) (1948-) is a Barbadian calypsonian and composer for theatre who has been a consistent critic of neo-colonial government behaviour, including over favourable treatment of tourism and the Barbados government's support for the American invasion of Grenada with "Boots" one of his most celebrated songs, and "Emmerton" another. Between 1968-2010 he was a regular winner of Calypso Monarch and Crop-over titles.

Garvey, Marcus Mosiah (1887-1940) was a Jamaican writer, activist and founding figure of African/ Black race consciousness in the Caribbean and the USA. In the USA, where he migrated in 1916, his United Negro Improvement Association (UNIA) was the largest and most dynamic Black Nationalist organisation, advocating Black self-reliance, Black capitalism, separation from whites and a return to Africa. The UNIA newspaper, *The Negro World*, reached Black communities throughout the African Diaspora and Africa itself. In 1923 Garvey was convicted of mail fraud, imprisoned for two years, and then deported to Jamaica in 1927. He lived for the last five years of his life in England. He was an immense influence on the ideology of Rastafarianism.

Gaunt, Darren Scott is an Australian scholar whose book on Kamau Brathwaite, *Mother and Sun: Reading Kamau Brathwaite's Mother Poem and Sun Poem* (1999) was published by Flinders University, South Australia.

Gibbons, Rawle (1950-) is a Trinidadian playwright, theatre director, lecturer and theorist of theatre. He taught at the Centre for Creative and Festival Arts, UWI St. Augustine. His publications include *A Calypso Trilogy, No Surrender – A Biography of the Growling Tiger* (1994), and his long-awaited study, *Traditional Enactments of Trinidad: Towards a Third Theatre* (2023).

Gill, Margaret is a Barbadian critic, scholar and poet. She has curated film and visual arts shows. She teaches at UWI Cave Hill. She was twice winner of a Frank Collymore Literary Endowment Award. She self-published a poetry collection, *Machinations of a Feminist* (2021).

Gilmore, John T. is a Barbadian who taught at UWI Cave Hill before teaching at the University of Warwick since 1996. His research interests include British and Caribbean literature in the long eighteenth century in English and Latin. His publications include *The Poetics of Empire: A Study of James Grainger's The Sugar-Cane* (2000), and he was one of the editors of *The Oxford Companion to Black British History* (2007).

Girvan, Norman (1941-2014) was a radical Jamaican economist, one time Secretary General of the Association of Caribbean States and shaper of Caricom into a coherent trading bloc. He was active in the New World Movement in the 1960s and with Brian Meeks edited *The Thought of New World: The Quest for Decolonisation* (2010). His other books include *Foreign Capital and Economic Underdevelopment in Jamaica* (1971); *Aspects of the Political Economy of Race in the Caribbean and the Americas* (1975) and *Corporate Imperialism,*

Conflict and Expropriation: Essays in Transnational Corporations and Economic Nationalism in the Third World (1978).

Glissant, Edouard (1928-2011) was a Martinican poet, novelist and influential thinker on the nature of Caribbean history and culture. He criticised the racial essentialism of Négritude and argued instead for Creolité as a recognition of the region's hybridity as the source of its dynamics of change. He countered the binarism of Western self and colonised other with the idea of the opacity and unknowability of the colonised other as a place of difference. His best known book is *Poétique de la relation* (1990), translated as *Poetics of Relation* by Betsy Wing. He published 11 collections of poetry accessible through *The Collected Poems of Edouard Glissant*, trans. Jeff Humpreys (2005). His fiction includes, *La Lézarde* (1958)/ *The Ripening*, trans. Michael Dash (1985); *Le Quatrième siècle* (1964)/ *The Fourth Century*, trans. Betsy Wing (2001); *La Case du commandeur* (1981)/ *The Overseer's Cabin*, trans. Betsy Wing (2011); *Mahagony* (1987)/ *Mahagony*, trans. Betsy Wing (2021).

Gomes, Albert (Bertie) (1911-1978) was a Trinidadian politician famed for histrionic performances, a pre-independence first minister. In the 1930s he was part of the group that included A.H. Mendes, C.L.R. James, Ralph De Boissiere and others around magazines such as *Trinidad* and *The Beacon* which began to write about working class and Black Trinidad. After independence, Gomes settled in the UK and wrote a lively memoir, *Through a Maze of Colour* and a novella, *All Papa's Children*.

Gonzalez, Anson (d. 2015) was the inspiration behind an upsurge of Trinidadian writing in the 1970s and 1980s, both through his own poetry, collected as *Artefacts of Presence* (2010) and through sustaining *The New Voices* as a regularly published literary journal between 1973 and 1992, being the encourager of countless writing careers and publishing significant collections of new work by other writers, including Victor Questel and Jennifer Rahim.

Goodison, Lorna (1947-) is a Jamaican poet, short story writer, memoirist, artist and essayist. From her first collections, *Tamarind Seed* (1980) and *I am Becoming My Mother* (1986) she has been recognised as a major Caribbean poet, publishing a further thirteen collections including her *Collected Poems* in 2017. She has written three short story collections: *Baby Mother and the King of Swords* (1990), *Fool-Fool Rose Is Leaving Labour-in-Vain Savannah* (2005) and *By Love Possessed* (2012); *From Harvey River: A Memoir of My Mother and Her Island* (2007) and *Redemption Ground: Essays and Adventures* (2018). She lives in Canada.

Goveia, Elsa (1925-1980) was a Guyanese historian considered one of the founders of modern Caribbean historiography. Her books include *A Study on the Historiography of the British West Indies* (1956) and the seminal *Slave Society in the British Leeward Islands at the End of the Eighteenth Century* (1965). She was the first female Professor at the University of the West Indies.

Grainger, James (c. 1721–1766) was a Scottish doctor, translator, and author of the Georgic poem, *The Sugar Cane* (1764). He went to St Kitts in 1759 and died of a fever in 1766. Based on Virgil's Georgics and following English poems such as John Dyer's *The Fleece* and John Philips's *Cyder*, Grainger's poem, in four books, covers scenery, geography, agricultural production and the processing of sugar in the estate factory. The fourth book writes about the enslaved people ("Afric's sable progeny"), with mildly liberal sentiments but without questioning the horrors of plantation life, and elsewhere he offered hints on how to manage Negroes.

Greaves, Stanley (1923-) is a Guyanese painter, sculptor, poet and classical guitarist. As one of the region's outstanding international artists, his paintings have gone to the heart of Guyanese distinctiveness, including character archetypes, history, elections, and responses to the fiction of Edgar Mittelholzer and Wilson Harris. The range of his work is discussed in Rupert Roopnaraine's monograph, *The Primacy of the Eye: the Art of Stanley Greaves*. His poetry collections include *Horizons*, *The Poems Man* and *Haiku*. He lived in Barbados from 1987 and has lived in the USA for the past few years.

Guillén, Nicholás (1902-1989) was a major Cuban and world poet, a communist and writer about Cuban musical forms. Of mixed African-European ancestry, he described himself as "the Yoruba from Cuba", but also paid respects to both his black and white grandparents. His poetry, beginning with *Motivos de son* (1930), *Sóngoro cosongo* (1931) and *West Indies Ltd.* (1934) is a celebration of Cuban Africanness, the creativity of its musical forms, such as the *son*, and militant anti-imperialism. Until the Cuban revolution he mostly lived in exile. He was regarded as Cuba's national poet. A representative sample of his work is *Yoruba from Cuba: Selected Poems of Nicolas Guillen* (trans. Salvador Ortiz-Carboneres).

Hall, Stuart (1932-2014) was a major academic, writer, and cultural studies pioneer. He grew up in Jamaica but lived all his adult life in the UK. He was Director of the Birmingham Centre for Contemporary Cultural Studies and Professor of Sociology at the Open University. The first editor of *New Left Review*, he was also founding editor of the journal *Soundings* and author of many seminal articles and books on politics and culture. An autobiography, with Bill Schwarz, *Familiar Stranger: A Life Between Two Islands* was published in 2017.

Hamner, Robert (1941-) is an American academic who has focused on Caribbean writing and Joseph Conrad. His books include Twayne studies on *V.S. Naipaul* and *Derek Walcott*; *Joseph Conrad: Third World Perspectives*; *Critical Perspectives on Derek Walcott*; and *Epic of the Dispossessed: Derek Walcott's Omeros*.

Harris, Wilson (1921-2018) was a Guyanese novelist, poet, literary theorist, and one of the Caribbean's most original thinkers. Harris's first published novel was *Palace of the Peacock* (1969), followed by a further 23 novels with *The Ghost of Memory* (2006) as the most recent. His novels comprise a singular, challenging and uniquely individual vision of the possibilities of spiritual and cultural transcendance away from the fixed empiricism and cultural boundedness that Harris argues has been the dominant Caribbean mode of thought. He has written some of the most suggestive Caribbean criticism in *Tradition the Writer and Society* (1967), *Explorations* (1981) and the *Womb of Space* (1983), commenting on his own work, the limitations of the dominant naturalistic mode of Caribbean fiction, and the work of writers he admires such as Herman Melville.

Hawkins, Coleman (1904-1969) was an African American jazz musician and the first player to make the tenor saxophone the solo instrument it has become. He traversed the swing era and continued into the bebop and after eras by updating but not radically changing his style. With a broad, lyrical and sometimes gruff tone, he influenced almost half of all jazz saxophonists (Lester Young the other half). His solo on "Body and Soul" was a landmark recording in 1939 that heralded the start of modernist abstraction in jazz. He is of course the Hawk of Brathwaite's poem in *Born to Slow Horses* and the dedicatee of *Arc* (2004) Brathwaite's poem about 9/11.

Hearne, John (1926-1994) was a Jamaican novelist, historian, teacher, journalist and social commentator. He was the author of five novels that look at Jamaica from the perspective of a "red" man of mixed but predominantly European heritage, including *Voices under the Window* (1955), *Stranger at the Gate* (1956), *The Faces of Love* (1957), *The Autumn Equinox* (1959) and *The Land of the Living* (1961). Later there was *The Sure Salvation* (1981), set on a slave ship. In the 1980s, he moved to the right in politics and was well-known as a provocative commentator in the Jamaican press. Together with Morris Cargill, he wrote three James Bond-style thrillers under the name John Morris.

Hilden, Patricia Penn is Professor of Native American History and Comparative Ethnic Studies at the University of California, Berkeley. She has published works about gender, race, and politics, including *When Nickels Were Indians* (Smithsonian Institution Press).

Hill, "Bobby" Robert A. (1943-) is a Jamaican historian and academic who has worked mainly at universities in the USA. He is a leading scholar on Pan-Africanism and the work and writings of Marcus Garvey and the UNIA and is editor-in-chief of The Marcus Garvey and Universal Negro Improvement Association Papers. He is C.L.R. James's literary executor and edited *Walter Rodney Speaks: The Making of an African Intellectual* (1990).

Hill, Errol (1921-2003) was a Trinidadian playwright, actor, academic and historian of Caribbean theatre and carnival. He worked in England (with the BBC), at UWI in Jamaica and Trinidad, in Nigeria and in the USA from 1968 until his retirement. His plays include *The Ping-Pong, Broken Melody, Man Better Man, Wey-Wey, Strictly Matrimony, The Square Peg.* His historical works include *Trinidad Carnival: A Mandate for National Theatre* (1972), *Shakespeare in Sable: A History of Black Shakespearean Actors* (1986) and *The Jamaican Stage, 1655–1900* (1992).

Hippolyte, Kendel (1952-) is a St Lucian poet, playwright, former lecturer and director and researcher into areas of Saint Lucian and Caribbean arts and culture. His poetry has been published in journals and anthologies regionally and internationally. He has taught poetry workshops in various countries and performed at literary events within the Caribbean and beyond. His poetry collections include, *Birthright* (1997) which collects his earlier collections, *Night Vision*, *Fault Lines* (which won the OCM Bocas poetry prize), and *Wordplanting* (2019).

Hodge, Merle (1944-) is a Trinidadian novelist, teacher of writing and a literary critic. Her novels include *Crick Crack Monkey* (1970), *For the Life of Laetitia* (1993) and *One Day, One Day, Congotay* (2022). All her fiction comes out of a radical political, class and gendered sensibility. *One Day, One Day, Congotay* is her magnum historical opus of African Trinidadian life from 1890s to the 1950s, the Spiritual Baptist movement and the struggle against colonialism and for a Black identity. She was actively involved in the cultural and educational activities of the revolutionary government in Grenada until forced to flee by the USA invasion.

Holub, Miroslav (1923-1998) was a Czech poet who brought his practice as a clinical pathologist and an immunologist into the scientific vision of his poetry. He came to wider attention with the publication of an English translation, *Selected Poems* (1969) which appeared in the Penguin Modern European Poets imprint, with an introduction by Al Alvarez. The collection was much admired by poets such as Ted Hughes and Seamus Heaney.

Hume, Yanique is a scholar, dancer, choreographer in Afro-Caribbean forms, and priestess who teaches at UWI Mona. She is the co-editor of *Caribbean Cultural Thought: From Plantation to Diaspora* (2013) and *Caribbean Popular Culture: Power, Politics and Performance* (2016), *Passages and Afterworlds: Anthropological Perspectives on Death in the Caribbean* (2018), and the author of papers on performance in Haiti, Kumina and Peter Tosh.

Hurston, Zora Neale (1891-1960) was an African American novelist, short story writer, ethnographer and filmmaker who focused on folk culture in the American South, Haiti and Jamaica, where she involved herself as a participant rather than an observer. *Tell My Horse: Voodoo and Life in Haiti and Jamaica* (1938) is her account. Hugely underrated in her lifetime, her novels and short stories have been republished in recent years to renewed attention, including: *Jonah's Gourd Vine* (1934), *Their Eyes Were Watching God* (1937), *Moses, Man of the Mountain* (1939).

Hutton, Clinton is Emeritus Professor in Political Philosophy and Caribbean and African Diasporic Culture and Aesthetics at UWI, Mona whose research interests include History, Caribbean/ African diaspora culture), cosmology/ spirituality and philosophy. His books include *The Logic & Historical Significance of the Haitian Revolution & the Cosmological Roots of Haitian Freedom* (2005). *Colour for Colour Skin for Skin: Marching with the Ancestral Spirits into War Oh at Morant Bay* (2016) and he was co-editor of *Leonard Percival Howell and the Genesis of Rastafari* (2005).

Ibrahim, Abdullah (1934-) is a South African jazz pianist, formerly Dollar Brand. Between 1960 and 2020, still performing in his eighties, he has made over 75 albums. He was in exile in the USA in the apartheid years, absorbing more African elements in his music in the era of African American Black nationalism. Outstanding albums include *Ancient Africa* (1973), *Echoes from Africa* (1979), *Water from an Ancient Well* (1985) and *Yarona* (1995).

Ignatius, Sister Mary (1921-2003) was the nun who ran the Alpha Boys School in Jamaica which provided musical training for many of Jamaica's best musicians, taken in as wayward boys. Graduates included Tommy McCook, John 'Dizzy' Moore, Don Drummond and Rico Rodriguez. See Heather Augustyn and Adam Reeves, *Alpha Boys School: Cradle of Jamaican Music* (2017).

Ismond, Pat (1944-2006) was a St Lucian scholar and critic who taught at UWI St Augustine. She was a passionate enthusiast for Derek Walcott's work and wrote a well-received monograph, *Abandoning Dead Metaphors: The Caribbean Phase of Derek Walcott's Poetry* (2003). She also wrote an article "Walcott vs Brathwaite", *Caribbean Quarterly*, Vol. 17, No. 3/4 (September - December 1971), 54-71 which could be read as implying an unfortunate polarity between Euro-Walcottian light and Brathwaite and African darkness.

Jackson, George (1941-1971) was an imprisoned African American who discovered Marx, Lenin, Mao and Fanon when he began to educate himself. He was befriended by Angela Davis to whom he had sent the papers that became *Soledad Brother: The Prison Letters of George Jackson* (1970). He died in an attempt to escape from prison in 1971. A second posthumous book, *Blood in My Eye* was published in 1972. Jackson's case drew attention to the racism of the USA's justice and prison systems.

Jagan, Cheddi (1918-1997) was the first elected chief minister in British Guiana in 1953 but was in power for only 127 days before Britain invaded the colony and arrested an imprisoned Jagan and key members of his party. An avowed Marxist-Leninist who never acted outside constitutional electoral politics, whose economic policies were social democratic, Jagan, though his party won elections in 1955 and 1961, was ruthlessly undermined by the British and American governments, ironically heralding the one-party pseudo-socialist rule of Forbes Burnham and 25 years of rigged elections. After the first free elections of 1992, Jagan became President until his sudden death. He was regarded by friend and foe alike as a man of uncorruptible honesty. His autobiography, *The West on Trial* (1966) records his modest Indo-Guyanese background, growing up on a sugar estate.

Jahn, Janheinz (1918-1973) was a white German scholar who, influenced by the Négritude movement, wrote two, at the time, influential books that argued for the unity of sub-Saharan African cultures. His book *Muntu: African Culture and the Western World* (1958, trans. 1961) argued that African culture, far from being doomed to destruction or homogenization under the onslaught of the West, is evolving into a rich and independent civilization that is capable of incorporating those elements of the West that do not threaten its basic values. His *Neo-African Literature: A History of Black Writing* (1969) extends the analysis to the African diaspora, including the Caribbean. Later theorists saw Jahn's work as both essentialising and underplaying the actual diversity of African cultures.

Jaikaransingh, Ken (1951-) is a Trinidadian who has been variously a teacher, publisher and book distributor who, in his retirement, has returned to writing and published two collections of short stories, *The Mark of Cane* and *The Carnival is Over*. As the CEO of Lexicon Books, he was the courageous publisher of several of Gordon Rohlehr's books.

Jamaican National Dance Theatre was founded in 1962 by Rex Nettleford and Eddy Thomas, with Nettleford acting as its artistic director and principal choreographer. It drew on African Caribbean folk traditions and cultural themes as well as modern dance. Its stated aim was "projecting the movement patterns and customs of the island to people locally and abroad". Its earlier history is documented in Rex Nettleford and Maria LaYacona's book, *Dance Jamaica: Cultural definition and artistic discovery: The National Dance Theatre Company of Jamaica, 1962-1983* (1985).

James, Cynthia (1948-) is a Trinidadian poet, novelist and university lecturer who lives in Canada. She has published short stories, *Soothe Me Music* (1990); poetry, *Iere, My Love* (1990), *Vigil: A Long Poem* (1995), *La Vega and Other Poems* (1995) and *Watermarked* (2014). Her novels include *Bluejean* (2000), *Sapodilla Terrace* (2006) and *I Dreamt You Planting Corn and Marigolds* (2023), and a literary study *The Maroon Narrative* (2002).

James, C.L. R. See CLR.

James, Louis (1933-) is Emeritus Professor at the University of Kent, Canterbury. In the 1960s, he taught at UWI, Mona, and published widely in the fields of Victorian, Modern and Caribbean literature. His publications include *Fiction for the Working Man* (1963), *Jean Rhys* (1978), *Caribbean Literature in English* (1998). While at UWI, he also edited *Islands In Between* (1968).

Jerry, Bongo, Robin 'Jerry' Small (1948-) is a Jamaican dub poet, Rastafarian, historian and broadcaster, whose four poems in *Savacou 3 / 4* in 1971 ("Sooner or Later", "The Youth" "Mabrak" and "Black Mother") were at the heart of the debate about the language of Caribbean poetry between GR and Eric Roach. In later life he has worked as a photographer, editor of several cultural publications and radio show moderator.

Johnson, Linton Kwesi (1952-) is the Jamaican-born, Black British poet, musician, performer, essayist and political activist. LKJ's political activism with the British chapter of the Black Panthers, then the Race Today Collective went hand in hand with his dub poetry performances and albums such as *Dread Beat an' Blood* (as Poet and the Roots) (1978), *Forces of Victory* (1979), *Bass Culture* (1980), *Making History* (1983), *Tings an' Times* (1991), *More Time* (1998). His published poetry and prose include *Voices of the Living and the Dead* (1974), *Dread Beat An' Blood* (1975), *Inglan is a Bitch* (1980), *Tings An'*

Times (1991) and *Mi Revalueshanary Fren: Selected Poems* (2002; 2006). *Time Come* (2023) collects his essays on music, politics and culture.

Jones, Bridget (1935-2000) was a British academic, married to a Jamaican, who pioneered the introduction of French Caribbean literature into the curriculum of UWI, Mona and at colleges in the UK. She published widely in journals and anthologies on figures like Damas, Depestre, Clitandre, Schwarz-Bart and co-authored with Sita Dickson Littlewood *Paradoxes of French Caribbean Theatre* (1998) which is a major reference work indexing 400 plays written since 1900 in either French or Creole languages by authors from Cayenne, Guadeloupe, and Martinique.

Julien, Terrence is a Trinidadian who taught Cultural Anthropology at LaGuardia College, New York.

Kallicharan, Laxmi (1951-2002) was a Guyanese cultural activist, editor and presenter of cultural programmes of Indo-Guyanese dance and music at a time in the 1980s when Indo-Guyanese artists were struggling to have their work recognised as truly Guyanese. She edited *Shraadanjali* (1986), an anthology of Indo-Guyanese poetry. She died in a fire in 2002.

Kaminjolo, Althea is a Trinidadian who completed an MPhil on Kamau Brathwaite at UWI St Augustine and contributed a short story to *The New Voices* in 1986. She edited *Women and Development Studies: a decade of development* (Women & Development Studies, UWI. St Augustine, T&T. 1993).

Kamugisha, Aaron is a Barbadian academic and writer who specialises in intellectual history and the social, political and cultural thought of the African diaspora. His latest book is *Beyond Coloniality: Citizenship and Freedom in the Caribbean Intellectual Freedom* (2019). He is the editor of five collections on Caribbean and Africana thought, including *Caribbean Political Thought: The Colonial State to Caribbean Internationalisms* (2013); *Caribbean Political Thought: Theories of the Post-Colonial State* (2013); (with Yanique Hume) *Caribbean Cultural Thought: From Plantation to Diaspora* (2013) and *Caribbean Popular Culture: Power, Politics and Performance* (2016). He taught at UWI Cave Hill and is now Ruth J. Simmons Professor of Africana at Smith College, USA.

Keane, (Shake) Ellsworth McGranahan (1927-1997) was a St Vincentian poet and jazz musician, who both led his own band and played trumpet in the groundbreaking Joe Harriott Quintet. He moved to Britain in 1952 where he lived until he returned to St Vincent as director of culture from 1972-75. In 1980, he moved to the USA for the rest of his life. His poetry collections include *One a Week with Water* (1979), *The Volcano Suite* (1979) and *The Angel Horn – Shake Keane (1927–1997) Collected Poems* (2005).

Keita, Salif (1949-) is a Malian singer and songwriter with a voice of great purity whose albums combine traditional elements and instruments with contemporary recording techniques, and Afro-pop and jazz elements. He has lived in Paris since the 1980s. His outstanding albums include *Soro* (1987), *Amen* (1991) and *Mouffou* (2002). *La Différence* (2009) explores his situation as an African albino.

King, Bruce A. is an American scholar and writer who has contributed extensively to postcolonial literary studies. His books include *Derek Walcott & West Indian Drama: "Not Only a Playwright but a Company", The Trinidad Theatre Workshop 1959-1993* (1997); *Derek Walcott: A Caribbean Life* (2000), *V.S. Naipaul* (2003) and *The Oxford English Literary History: Volume 13: 1948-2000: The Internationalization of English Literature* (2004).

Kirk, Rahsaan Roland (1935-1977) was an African American tenor saxophonist and multi-instrumentalist, civil rights activist and entertainer famed for playing two instruments at once. Beginning in hard bop, his music extended into the free jazz of the mid-1960s and 1970s. A popular figure, admired for how he coped with his blindness and a disabling stroke, Kirk's outstanding albums include *Rip Rig and Panic* (1965), *Now Please Don't Cry Beautiful Edith* (1967), *The Inflated Tear* (1968) and *Natural Black Inventions: Root Strata* (1971).

Kodaly, Zoltan (1882-1967) was a Hungarian composer of orchestral, chamber and choral music, and an ethnomusicologist who collected and used Hungarian folk music in his compositions. His best know piece is the *Hary Janos Suite* (1926).

La Rose, John (1927-2006) was a Trinidadian much involved in the island's radical politics, who, in London, established himself as a poet, publisher, political activist (in the Black Parents Movement and the New Cross Massacres campaign). His and Sarah White's New Beacon bookshop was a hub for the Caribbean, African American, and African diasporas. New Beacon's publishing focused both on new writing and recuperating Caribbean classics. For an account of New Beacon see Brian W. Alleyne, *Radicals Against Race: Black Activism and Cultural Politics* (Oxford: Berg, 2002).

La Rose, Michael is the son of John La Rose who is a director of New Beacon Books and chair of the George Padmore Institute. He was a band leader and mas' designer of the Peoples War Carnival Band.

Lamming, George (1927-2022) was a Barbadian novelist, poet, essayist and radical, Marxist-influenced intellectual concerned with issues of Caribbean sovereignty. He came to London in 1950, where he was a regular contributor to the *Caribbean Voices* programme. By the time of CAM, his first four novels had all been published: *In the Castle of My Skin* (1953), *The Emigrants* (1954), *Of Age and Innocence* (1958) and *Season of Adventure* (1960). He had also written the first account of Caribbean cultural history from within, *The Pleasures of Exile* (1960). His later novels were *Water with Berries* (1971) and *Natives of My Person* (1972).

Last Poets, The (1968-) were a radical African American performance poetry/ rap group, often with African percussion and later with jazz backgrounds (jazzoetry) with fluctuating personnel. The first line-up was Abiodun Oyewole, Gylan Kain, and David Nelson. Other line-ups included Jalal Mansur Nuriddin a.k.a. Alafia Pudim, Umar Bin Hassan, and Abiodun Oyewole, along with poet Sulaiman El-Hadi and percussionist Nilaja Obabi.

The first Last Poets album was released in 1970 and others followed regularly up to 1977, a handful between then and 1999, and a re-emergence in 2018 with *Understand What Black Is*.

Latif, Yusef (1920-2013), born William Huddleston, Latif was an African American jazz musician and writer, playing mainly tenor sax and flute, but also a wide variety of wind instruments such as rahab, shanai, arghul, koto. As a Muslim, he introduced World/Eastern themes into jazz, and is seen as a pioneer of both New Age and World Music, making at least 100 albums between 1957-2013, including *Cry!/Tender*, *Eastern Sounds*, *Live at Peps*, and *The World at Peace*.

Laurence, Keith O. (1933-2014) was a Trinidadian historian who taught at both UWI Mona and St. Augustine, until1995. His publications focused on 19th century labour and migration. They include *The Settlement of the Free Negroes in Trinidad before Emancipation* (1963); *The Development of the Medical Services in British Guiana and Trinidad, 1834-1963* (1964); *The Establishment of the Portuguese Community of British Guiana, 1834-1863* (1965); *Immigration into the West Indies in the 19th century* (1971); *Indians as Permanent Settlers in Trinidad before 1900* (1985); and *A Question of Labour: Indentured Immigration into Trinidad and British Guiana, 1875-1917* (1994). He also co-edited Volume IV, *The Long Nineteenth Century: Nineteenth Century Transformations for The General History of the Caribbean*, UNESCO series publications (2011).

Lee, John Robert (1948-) is a St Lucian poet, Baptist preacher, professional librarian and formerly information manager at the Folk Research Centre in St Lucia. At one time close to Rastafarianism, he returned to Christianity and describes himself as a Christian poet. He organises an important online hub and e-mailing list for people involved with Caribbean writing. He began publishing his poetry in 1975; his recent collections include *Elemental: new and selected poems* (2008), *Collected Poems, 1975–2015* (2017), *Pierrot* (2020) and *Belmont Portfolio* (2023).

Lewis, C.S. (1898-1963) was a British author of Northern Irish origins, academic and lay theologian. He is best known for his children's seven book series, *The Chronicles of Narnia* (1949-1954), his *Introduction to Paradise Lost* (1942) and the Oxford University Press volume, *English Literature in the Sixteenth Century Excluding Drama* (1954).

Liverpool, Hollis (Chalkdust or Chalkie) (1940-) is a Trinidadian calypsonian and cultural historian, nine times Calypso Monarch champion (between 1976-2017) and famed for his witty and educative ("No smut") calypsos with a political bite. He also holds a Ph.D. in history and ethnomusicology. He is the author of the books *Rituals of Power and Rebellion: The Carnival Tradition in Trinidad and Tobago, 1763-1962* (2001) and *From the Horse's Mouth: An Analysis of Certain Significant Aspects in the Development of the Calypso and Society as Gleaned from Personal Communication with Some Outstanding Calypsonians* (2003). Gordon Rohlehr writes about Chalkdust in *A Scuffling of Islands* (2004).

Lixie (see Erna Brodber).

Lovelace, Earl (1935-) is a Trinidadian novelist, short-story writer, playwright, poet, essayist and one-time journalist. He is distinguished as being one of the region's major writers who, apart from periods of education and writer-residences, has stayed at home. His work is characterised by a focus on characters who find themselves in opposition to social and cultural hierarchies and repressive neocolonial elites and on the mix of creative energies and sometimes nihilistic destructiveness amongst the powerless. His novels include, *While Gods Are Falling* (1965), *The Schoolmaster* (1968), *The Dragon Can't Dance* (1979), *The Wine of Astonishment* (1982), *Salt* (1996) and *Is Just a Movie* (2011). Other publications include *Jestina's Calypso and Other Plays* (1984), *A Brief Conversion and Other Stories*, (1988), and *Growing in the Dark. Selected Essays* (ed. Funso Aiyejina, 2003).

Lowell, Robert (1917-1977) was an American poet who influenced a whole generation of poets (including Derek Walcott) in the English-speaking world with his mix of formal rigour and personal confessionalism about, for instance, his marital affairs. He was invariably in opposition to the American state as a conscientious objector in WW2 (serving prison time) and a fierce opponent of the Vietnam war. He was diagnosed as bi-polar and was institutionalised many times. Among his twenty poetry collections, *Life Studies* (1959), *For the Union Dead* (1964), *The Old Glory* (1965), *For Lizzie and Harriet* (1973) are outstanding.

Lucien, Vladimir (1988-) is a St Lucian poet and critic whose work has been published in *The Caribbean Review of Books*, *Wasafiri*, *Small Axe journal*, the *PN Review*, *BIM* magazine, *Caribbean Beat* and other journals, as well in *Beyond Sangre Grande: Caribbean Writing Today* (2011) edited by Cyril Dabydeen. His first collection, *Sounding Ground* won the overall OCM Bocas Prize for Literature in 2015.

Luck, Ray, a Guyanese born concert pianist, now settled in the USA. See https://guyanachronicle.com/2012/08/05/find-your-niche-in-life-says-professional-concert-pianist-ray-luck/.

Mahfood, Margarita Anita (c. 1931-1964) was a dancer and singer of Lebanese-Jamaican heritage who was the partner of the jazz-ska trombonist, Don Drummond, who worked with Count Ossie and was attracted to Rastafarian culture. She was murdered by Drummond who suffered from bouts of psychosis.

Mais, Roger (1905-1955) was the Jamaican author of *The Hills Were Joyful Together* (1953) *Brother Man* (1954) and *Black Lightning* (1955). His work, particularly the call and response elements of *Brother Man* was important to Kamau Brathwaite as the inspiration of his foundational essay, "Jazz and the West Indian Novel", (1967), collected in *Roots* (Ann Arbor: University of Michigan Press, 1993), 55-110.

Manley, Edna (1900-1987) was a Jamaican sculptor, artist, educator and cultural organiser. She was the English-born wife of Norman W. Manley. Her sculptures were iconic expressions of Jamaican nationhood. She gathered around her a generation of Jamaican writers that included V.S. Reid, M.G. Smith and George Campbell, and organised the occasional anthology, *Focus*.

Manley, Norman (1893-1969) was a barrister, distinguished soldier and athlete, one of the founders and longtime leader of the People's National Party and first premier of pre-independence Jamaica. From a mixed-race, middle-class background, he described himself as a Fabian socialist, but he expelled from the PNP some of its most dynamic, Marxist-influenced members. When he backed Jamaica's membership of the West Indian Federation, lost a referendum on Federation to the Jamaica Labour Party opposition and lost the next general election to Bustamante's JLP, his political career was over.

Markham, E.A. (Archie) (1939-2008) was a Montserratian poet, dramatist, novelist, short-story writer and editor. He settled in the UK in 1956. His memoir, *Against the Grain* is a witty account of his early British days and of his loss of origins when the volcano eruption of 1995 put his home out of bounds. His collection of short stories, *Taking the Drawing Room Through the Customs*, is a sharp reminder that some Black arrivals in Britain came from a well-established Caribbean middle class. As a poet, he was inventive in writing under different names with different personas, including Sally Goodman, a Welsh woman, and Paul St Vincent, from the Black working class.

Marquez, Gabriel Garcia (1927-2014) was a Colombian, Nobel Prize winner and author of such world-famed novels as *A Hundred Years of Solitude*, *The Autumn of the Patriarch*, and *Love in the Time of Cholera*. He was a short story writer, essayist, filmmaker and best-known proponent of the style and philosophy of magical realism in which elements of the fantastic and the real merge. As a leftist and admirer of the Cuban revolution he was forced to go into exile from Colombia to Mexico in 1981.

Marquez, Roberto is a Puerto Rican born and raised in Spanish Harlem, a translator, editor, essayist, and literary critic who taught at Mount Holyoke College since 1989. He has been recognized for his work in the field of Caribbean literary and cultural history. His books include *A World among These Islands: Essays on Literature, Race, and National Identity in Antillean America* (2010).

Marsalis, Delfeayo (1965-) is an African American jazz trombonist and record producer, a member of a family which has produced many jazz musicians from father Ellis and brothers Wynton, Branford and Jason. His best rated album is *Pontius Pilate's Decision* (1992).

Marshall, Paule (1929-2019) was an African American novelist with deep Caribbean connections (her father was Barbadian). Her novels include *Brown Girl, Brownstones* (1959) about Barbadian migrants in New York; *Soul Clap Hands and Sing* (1961); *The Chosen Place, the Timeless People* (1969);

Reena and Other Stories (1983); *Praisesong for the Widow* (1983); *Daughters* (1991); *The Fisher King: A Novel* (2001); and *Triangular Road: A Memoir*. Kamau Brathwaite wrote a critical analysis of *The Chosen Place, the Timeless People* in his *LX*.

Martini, Jurgen is a German scholar and translator specialising in African and Caribbean literatures. He was the editor/publisher of *Missile and Capsule* (Bremen, 1983), which includes KB's essay "Caribbean Culture: Two Paradigms", 9-54.

Masekela, Hugh (1939-2018) was a South African trumpeter, singer and composer and anti-apartheid activist who was forced to spend much of his life in exile. His music was jazz-based but absorbed many Township popular elements. His songs "Soweto Blues" and "Bring Him Back Home" were famed anti-apartheid songs and he had a number-one US pop hit in 1968 with his version of "Grazing in the Grass".

Matthews, Marc (c 1942-) is a Guyanese poet, broadcaster and performer. In the 1960s he spent time in London and was actively involved in the Caribbean Artists Movement. His poetry collections are *Guyana My Altar* and *Season of Sometimes*. As an actor/performer he was involved in dynamic new forms of improvised theatre in Guyana with Ken Corsbie (Dem Two), and All a We, with Corsbie, Henry Muttoo and John Agard. He left Guyana at the height of the Burnham repression and lives in London.

Maxwell, Marina (Ama Omowale) is a Trinidadian poet, novelist, dramatist and theorist of "yard theatre". Her novel *Chopstix in Mauby: A Novel of Magical Realism* was published in 1997 and her collected poetry, *Decades to Ama* in 2005. Her published drama includes *Play Mas* and *Hounsi Kanzo* (1976). *About Our Own Business* (1981) is a collection of her essays.

McAndrew, Wordsworth (1936-2008) was a poet, folklorist and radio broadcaster who had to flee Guyana in 1978, having incurred the enmity of the ruling party. His poetry collections include *Blue Gaulding* (1958), *Meditations on a Theme* (1963), *More Poems* (1970), *Poems to St Agnes* (1962) and *Selected Poems* (1966).

McNeill, Anthony (1941-1996) was a major Jamaican poet whose range of prolific experimentalism was barely seen outside the circle of other admiring poets including Mervyn Morris, Edward Baugh, Dennis Scott, Pam and Michael Mordecai. McNeill suffered from alcohol and drug addictions and periods of mental ill-health. His published collections include *Reel from "The Life Movie"* (1972) *Credences at the Altar of Cloud* (1979) and *Chinese Lanterns from the Blue Child*, published posthumously in 1998. Peepal Tree Press has a 3-volume collected poems in preparation, including around twenty unpublished collections.

Miles, see Davis, Miles.

Millette, James is a Trinidadian historian and one time newspaper publisher and politician. He was involved in the New World Movement but was a critic of Lloyd Best's Tapia House Movement as a supporter of Cheddi Jagan's kind of class-oriented Marxism. He and Gordon Rohlehr set up a radical weekly newspaper, *Moko* in 1970, until Rohlehr withdrew when Millette made it the journal of his political party, UNIP (United National Independent Party). He taught for many years at UWI St Augustine specialising in imperial history, labour history and economics. His publications include *The Genesis of Crown Colony Government: Trinidad 1783-1810* (1971), *Society and politics in colonial Trinidad* (1985) and *Freedom Road* (2007).

Mingus, Charlie (1922-1979) was an African American jazz musician who played acoustic bass and piano, a bandleader and the most outstanding composer for small and large groups since Duke Ellington. His music bridges bebop (he played with Charlie Parker) to the avantgarde of the 1960s, but always with a gospel dynamic. Classic albums include *Mingus, Mingus, Mingus*; *Mingus Ah Um* and *The Black Saint and the Sinner Lady*. He wrote a powerful autobiography *Beneath the Underdog: His World as Composed by Mingus* (1971). He was politically engaged, suffered from depression and had a famously short fuse.

Miss Queenie (1928-1998), Imogene Elizabeth Kennedy was also known as Kumina Queen, a leader of a Kumina group, the most African of the spiritual survivals in Jamaica. It was from Miss Queenie that KB took the title for the Arrivants: "Well, muh ol' arrivance... is from Africa... That's muh ol' arrivants family."

Mittelholzer, Edgar (1909-1965) was a Guyanese novelist, playwright and short story writer. In 1937 he self-published *Creole Chips* and sold it from door to door. His novel of East Indian life *Corentyne Thunder* was published until 1941. In 1948 he left for England with the manuscript of *A Morning at The Office*, which was published in 1950. Between 1951 and 1965 he had published a further twenty-one novels and two works of non-fiction, including his autobiographical, *A Swarthy Boy*. Apart from three years in Barbados, he lived for the rest of his life in England. He was the first Caribbean writer to live entirely by his writing. He died by his own hand in 1965, a suicide by fire predicted in several of his novels.

Moko (with the banner-head, "a serious review" and sold for 10c.) was a radical Trinidadian fortnightly newspaper originally established by Gordon Rohlehr and James Millette, first published in October 1968. Gordon Rohlehr had articles on "The Generation Gap" (No 2, Nov 15, 1968), "Calypso and Morality" (No. 6, 17 Jan., 1969)), "Kaiso '69" (No. 8, 14 Feb., 1969), "Rights of Passage and Masks" (No. 14, April 9, 1969), "Sounds and Pressure" [on Don Drummond] (No. 16, 6 June, 1969), "Sounds and Pressure Part 2" (No. 17, 20 June, 1969), "Film Preview" [on the Beatles Yellow Submarine] (No. 18, 4 July, 1979). UNIP was launched as a political party (the point at which GR exited from Moko) in issue 20, January 16, 1970. From that point on no further named GR articles appear. *Moko* survived until 1973.

Moonsammy/this is probably **Moutousammy, Ernest** (1941-), a Guadeloupian politician, poet and novelist of Indo-Guadeloupian ethnicity. He was a member of the Communist Party of Guadeloupe until the break-up of the Soviet Union. His novels include *Aurore* (1987), *Chacha and Sosso* (1994) and a memoir *A La Recherche De L'Inde Perdue* (2004).

Moore, Colin A. (1942-1980) was a Guyanese who studied at UWI Mona, was involved in setting up the National History and Arts Council in Guyana and went on to become a prominent civil rights activist and attorney in the USA, including the defence of the accused in the Central Park joggers' case. He was banned from entering Jamaica, but when could not be found.

Moore, John (Dizzy) (1938-2008) was a Jamaican jazz and ska trumpeter, always in demand as a session player, who played with the Skatalites and Soul Vendor bands. A graduate of the famous Alpha School for wayward boys, he was attracted to Rastafarianism.

Mordecai, Pam (1942-) is a Jamaican poet, short storywriter, writer for children, novelist, anthologist and publisher. She now lives in Canada. Her poetry collections include: *Journey Poem* (1989), *de Man: a performance poem* (1995), *Certifiable* (2001), *The True Blue of Islands* (2005), *Subversive Sonnets* (2012), *de book of Mary: a performance poem* (2015), *de Book of Joseph* (2022) and *A Fierce Green Place: New and Selected Poems* (2022). Her fiction includes *Pink Icing and other stories* (2006), *Red Jacket: a novel* (2015). She wrote *Culture and Customs of Jamaica* (with Martin Mordecai) (2001). From 1988 to 2005, she published almost a dozen titles, mostly poetry, as the Sandberry Press.

Morgan, Mary E. (d. 2019) was Kamau Brathwaite's sister. She worked as Senior Assistant Registrar at UWI Mona in Jamaica. She has written about the Brathwaites' childhood in "Growing Up at the Round House with Our Brother Kamau" (with Thelma E. Abrams (d. 2019) and Joan A. Brathwaite), in *Bim*, Special Issue, November 2010 (online at https://www.bimlitfest.org/articles/growing-round-house-our-brother-kamau).

Morris, Mervyn (1937-) is a professor emeritus, literary scholar, poet editor and mentor. He was Jamaica's first poet laureate between 2014-17. As a critic he is famed for persuading readers to take the work of the poet Louise Bennett seriously (and not just as a dialect entertainer). He also worked with the dub poet, Mikey Smith, to find ways of transcribing his oral poetry. Morris's own poetry is famed for its succinctness and formal rigour. His four poetry collections are included in *I Been There, Sort Of: New and Selected Poems* and his critical work includes *Making West Indian Literature* and *Miss Lou: Louise Bennett and Jamaican Culture.*

Morrison, Toni (1931-2019) is the distinguished African American author of such acclaimed novels as *The Bluest Eye* (1970), *Sula* (1973), *Song of Solomon* (1977), *Beloved* (1987) and *Jazz* (1992). Probably of all the African American authors in the period of the GR/KB correspondence, she was the one whose work had resonances for Caribbean writers and readers. This was in her focus on the historical shaping of the present, the irreparable enormity of slavery and her use of folk survivals in the culture of the African American South, such as the beliefs in the possibility of flying back to Africa which she explores in *Song of Solomon*. It is clear, for instance, that Kwame Dawes draws inspiration from Toni Morrison's work in constructing the prophetic figure of Clarice in his verse epic, *Prophets* (1995).

Munroe, Trevor (1944-) is a Jamaican politician, university lecturer and political scientist. From 1978-1992 he was the general secretary of the Marxist-Leninist Workers Party of Jamaica, which for a time flirted with extra-parliamentary revolutionary political action. He was a mentor of Bernard Coard, whose group overthrew Maurice Bishop in Grenada. In later years, Munroe has served in the Jamaican senate as a social democratic and constitutionalist politician. His books include *The Politics of Constitutional Decolonisation: Jamaica 1944-1962*; *Jamaican Politics: A Marxist Perspective in Transition*; and *The Cold War and the Jamaican Left, 1950-1955*.

Mutabaruka (Allan Hope) (1952-) is a Rastafarian Jamaican dub poet, recording artist, educator and host of the influential radio programmes, *The Cutting Edge* and *Steppin' Razor*, whose poetry collections include *Outcry* (1973), *Sun and Moon* (1976), with Faybiene, and *The Book: First Poems* (1980) and *The Next Poems* (2005).

Naipaul, V.S. (1932-2018) was the Nobel prize-winning Indian Trinidadian novelist, long settled in England since his arrival as a student in 1950. At the time of the ACLALs conference at Mona in 1971, where Kamau Brathwaite's and Naipaul's presentations were in sharp ideological opposition, and one attendee offered to shoot Naipaul, Naipaul had written *The Mystic Masseur* (1957), *The Suffrage of Elvira* (1958), *Miguel Street* (1959), *A House for Mr Biswas* (1961), *Mr Stone and the Knights Companion* (1963), *The Mimic Men* (1967) and *A Flag on the Island* (1967). Gordon Rohlehr's essay on V.S. Naipaul ("Character and Rebellion in *A House for Mr Biswas*") recognises both the limitations of Naipaul's vision and embraces it as a novel that tells the Caribbean about itself. GR refers to Naipaul with Derek Walcott's renaming as VS Nightfall.

Nettleford, Sir Rex (1933-2010) was a Jamaican academic, Vice-Chancellor of UWI Mona, dancer, choreographer, and public intellectual. He was one of the UWI academics whose research and report in *Caribbean Quarterly* (1960) began the process of reaching out to and bringing Rastafarians in from the position of a persecuted, outcast minority. His seminal book *Mirror, Mirror: Identity, Race and Protest in Jamaica* (1970) considers how to overcome the colonial negativity attached to blackness, whilst his choreography for the National Dance Theatre Company of Jamaica developed its grammar from African survivals in Jamaican culture. Other books include *Outward Stretch, Inward Reach: A Voice for the Caribbean* (1995).

New World Fortnightly, ***New World Quarterly*** were the publications of the New World movement in Guyana. *New World Fortnightly*, edited by David De Caires, went through 50 issues (some double) between 1964 to January 1967. There were fourteen issues of NWQ between 1963 and 1972, with two double issues; it appeared more regularly in earlier years. NWQ covered issues of political economy and economic dependence, politics, history and literature, including original writing. Outstanding issues included the *Guyana Independence Issue* (un-numbered and undated but probably 1966), edited by George Lamming and Martin Carter, and Vol 3 Nos. 1 & 2 (1966-1967), the *Barbados Independence Issue*, edited by George Lamming.

NJAC was the National Joint Action Committee, founded in 1969, and prominent in the leadership of the 1970 Black Power revolt. It put out a newspaper called *East Dry River*. At the time of the revolt its leadership included Geddes Granger (Makandal Daaga) and Dave Darbeau (Khafra Kambom). It remained as an organisation for the next 40 years, stood in elections but won no seats.

Nketia, J.H. Kwabena (1921-2019) was a Ghanaian composer and ethnomusicologist who pioneered the transcription and description of African music. He taught in both Ghana and the USA. His best-known book was *The Music of Africa*, published in the USA in 1974. His work was important to Caribbean researchers who were exploring the African roots of folk and popular music in the region.

Paba (Patrick 'Paba' Anthony, Msgr.) (1947-) is a St Lucian theologian, communications specialist, cultural activist and Roman Catholic priest who, as a young Black priest, is credited with beginning the decolonisation of the Catholic church in St Lucia from its white-led, socially reactionary past and hostility to African Caribbean St Lucian culture. He brought drums, steel pans and guitars into church services and was one of the founding members of what became the Monsignor Patrick Anthony Folk Research Centre, established in 1973 (and tragically destroyed by fire in 2018) which has played a crucial role in preserving Kweyol and the documentation of folk belief systems.

Pascall, Alex (1936-) is a British broadcaster, journalist, musician, cultural activist, oral historian and educator. Grenadian-born, he came to Britain in 1959 and established himself as an organiser and person of influence within the London Black Community. He was involved in the development of the Notting Hill Carnival and was one of the first regular Black radio voices in the UK, presenting the programme *Black Londoners* on BBC Radio London for 14 years from 1974.

Patterson, Orlando, 'Patto' (1940-) was at the LSE in the period of CAM, working on *The Sociology of Slavery* (1967). He had already written *The Children of Sisyphus* (1964), but it is his second novel, *An Absence of Ruins* (1967), with its satire on earlier Caribbean fiction and its echo of Naipaul's "History is built around creation and achievement, and nothing was created in the West Indies", which Brathwaite saw as nihilist. Patterson's third novel, *Die the Long Day* (1972) provoked further argument of a different kind within CAM when John Hearne dismissed the book as mere sociology. As a Jamaican-American sociologist and thinker Patterson has had a distinguished career with notable publications such as *Slavery and Social Death* (1982), *Freedom in the Making of Western Culture* (1991) and *The Confounding Island: Jamaica and the Postcolonial Predicament* (2022).

Philip, Dawad is a Trinidadian-American poet, author of *Invocations* (1980), *A Mural by the Sea* (2017) *Jayden and the King of the Brooklyn Carnival*, (co-authored with Yolanda Lezama-Clark, 2019) and *City Twilight* (2020). After living in Brooklyn for nearly four decades as a poet, journalist and artist, Philip has since resettled in his hometown of San Fernando, Trinidad.

Phillips, Esther (1950) is a Barbadian poet and former lecturer at Barbados Community College, now much involved in the reparations dialogue, having grown up in the village next to Drax Hall sugar estate, still owned by the wealthy Conservative MP Ernle-Ernle Drax. She has coedited the magazine *Bim* since 2007 and was appointed the first poet laureate in Barbados in 2018. Her poetry collections include *When Ground Doves Fly* (2003), *The Stone Gatherer* (2009), *Leaving Atlantis* (2015), *Witness in Stone* (2021).

Phillips, Anthony (Tony) (d. 2018) was a lecturer in history at UWI Cave Hill from 1963-2004. He published papers and articles on the parliament of Barbados, World War 1 and the labour movement. He edited the journal of Barbados Museum and Historical Society between 1988 and 1995.

Pilgrim, Philip (1917-1944) was a Guyanese pianist and composer of "The Legend of Kaieteur" and various short pieces. He was the first Guyanese musician to win a scholarship to the Royal College of Music where he studied between 1935 and 1939. He taught and gave recitals in Guyana, Trinidad and Barbados. He was granted a British Council Scholarship to further his studies in 1944 but died a few days before he was due to leave. "The Legend of Kaieteur" was revived for performance at the first CARIFESTA in 1972.

Post, Ken (1935-2017) was Professor Emeritus at the Institute of Social Studies, The Hague. He taught in Nigeria, England, the USA, and at UWI Jamaica where his immersion in local political life and outreach to Rastafarians made him persona non grata with the government. A Marxist of no particular school he wrote two essential books about colonialism and the Jamaican working class: *Arise Ye Starvelings: The Jamaican Labour Rebellion of 1938 and its Aftermath* (1978) and *Strike the Iron: A Colony at War, Jamaica 1939-1945* (2 vols, 1981), both of which are rich in cultural detail.

Pozo, Chano (1915-1948) was a Cuban musician, percussionist and bandleader and one of the founding figures of Latin jazz, and a bridge to involving jazz musicians like Dizzie Gillespie in Cuban rhythms. As a working class Black Cuban from a tough neighbourhood, his opportunities were restricted in Cuba and he moved to the USA in 1947 where he made his first commercial recordings and played with Gillespie's band. He was shot dead in 1948 by a fellow Cuban.

Prince, Mary (c1788-1833) was an enslaved woman transported to Bermuda, who worked in the salt mines of Turk Island. She was taken to England in 1818, escaped into the protection of Moravian missionaries and the Anti-Slavery society. Her autobiography *The History of Mary Prince, a West Indian Slave, Related by Herself* was first published in 1831. A properly edited and annotated edition edited by Moira Ferguson was published in 1997.

Questel, Victor (1949-1982) was an outstanding poet and critic whose promise was cut short by a tragically early death. His three collections of poetry, *Prelude, Hard Stares* and *On Mourning Ground* were republished as *Collected Poems* (Peepal Tree Press, 2016) with an afterword by Gordon Rohlehr. Questel undertook important work on documenting Derek Walcott's journalism.

Ra (Sun Ra) (1914-1993), born Herman Blount, was an African American jazz composer, band leader and pianist who had a long history in traditional forms of jazz before putting together his Arkestra in the late 1950s (a band which contained loyal disciples and which still performs long after his death). Over the next forty years, in many albums and elaborately costumed public performances, Sun Ra evolved an experimental form of "cosmic jazz" employing the metaphor of interplanetary travel and Black Egyptology, which forecast Afro-Futurism. Classic albums include *Jazz in Sihouette* (1959) *The Heliocentric Worlds of Sun Ra* (1966), *The Nubians of Plutonia* (1966), *Atlantis* (1973), *Space is the Place* (1973) and *Languidity* (1978).

Ramchand, Kenneth (1939-) is a Trinidadian writer, editor, literary critic, one-time senator, who is Professor Emeritus of English at UWI St Augustine, and at Colgate University in the USA. His *The West Indian Novel and its Background* (1970) is a foundational work in the development of Caribbean literary studies and its establishment at UWI. He was a regular columnist in the Trinidad press, concerned to reach out beyond the campus. As a Trinidadian of Indian heritage who espoused the idea of a "Creole" national identity that left behind primary African and Indian affinities, he was at times at odds with Kamau Brathwaite's mission to recover the African presence in Caribbean culture. In recent years he has led the Friends of Mr Biswas organisation, setting up a museum and cultural centre at Seepersad Naipaul's former house in St James, Port of Spain.

Ranglin, Ernest (1932-) is great Jamaican guitarist and composer in ska, reggae and jazz. He played lead guitar on countless classic reggae tracks and amongst the thirty or so albums he recorded in his own right, *Below the Bassline* (1996) and *Memories of Barber Mack* (1997) are outstanding.

Rattray, R.S. (1881-1938) was a pioneering Africanist who as a district officer in the colony of the Gold Coast (Ghana) researched Ashanti religion, customs, law, art, beliefs, folktales, and proverbs. His books, which still have documentary value, include *Ashanti Proverbs: the primitive ethics of a savage people: translated from the original with grammatical and anthropological notes* (1916), *Ashanti* (1923), *Religion and Art in Ashanti* (1927), *Ashanti Law and Constitution* (1929) and *Akan-Ashanti Folk-Tales. Collected and translated by R. S. Rattray* (1930).

Reiss, Tim (1942-) is an American academic who taught at New York University, now Professor Emeritus, who matches interests in Classical and Renaissance literature, philosophy, and history with Caribbean culture and political theory. Long a friend and supporter of Kamau Brathwaite, his books include *Against Autonomy: Global Dialectics of Cultural Exchange* (2002), and he edited *For the Geography of a Soul: Emerging Perspectives on Kamau Brathwaite* (2001) and *Sisyphus and Eldorado: Magic and Other Realisms in Caribbean Literature* (2002).

Rilke, Rainer Maria (1875-1926) was an Austrian poet and novelist whose poetry was a major influence on European Modernism. His collections in translation include *The Duino Elegies, Sonnets to Orpheus* and *Letters to a Young Poet. The Duino Elegies* explore the themes of suffering and redemption.

Risden, Winifred (Winnie) (d. 2017) was the former Jamaican Information Service Executive Director, who served as Director at the Jamaica Broadcasting Corporation. In her younger days she worked in theatre (LTM) and contributed a review to *Savacou*. She wrote a critical review of Brathwaite's *Masks*, ('Review of Masks', *Caribbean Quarterly*, 14, 1 & 2 , March-June (1968), 145) charging it with being a "public" poem that offered nothing to the heart.

Ritter, Erika is a dedicatee of several Kamau Brathwaite poems.

Roach, Eric (E.M.) (1915-1974) was a Tobagan poet who before the emergence of Carter, Walcott and Brathwaite was unquestionably the region's most recognised poet. Published in *Bim, Kyk-over-al* and broadcast on *Caribbean Voices*, it was not until the 1992 publication of *The Flowering Rock: Collected Poems 1938-1974* (Peepal Tree) that the scope of Roach's achievement and development could be clearly seen. This collection, based on the research work of Danielle Gianetti, was edited by Kenneth Ramchand. Roach was the author of the 'Tribe Boys vs Afro-Saxons' review of *Savacou 3 / 4,* to which GR responded in "West Indian Poetry: Some Problems of Assessment". Roach committed suicide in 1974.

Robinson, A.N.R. (1926-2014) was Trinidad's third prime minister (1986-1991), and third president (1997-2003). Initially a member of the PNM, he left after the suppression of the Black Power uprising of 1970 and formed the Democratic Action Congress. Later, he allied with other parties to form the National Alliance for Reconstruction. He was prime minister at the time of the Muslimeen attempted coup of 1990, when he was shot and beaten after ordering the army to attack the parliament building where he and other MPs were being held.

Rodney, Walter (1942-1980) was a Marxist, Pan-Africanist Guyanese historian, writer on politics and development, and a political activist. As one of the leaders of the Working People's Alliance, he was assassinated by the Guyanese government. Before returning to Guyana, Rodney had taught and been expelled from Jamaica for making contact with urban youth, out of which came his book, *The Groundings with My Brothers* (1969). He was a professional historian whose *A History of the Upper Guinea Coast 1545–1800* (1970) and

A History of the Guyanese Working People, 1881–1905 (1981) are still standard texts. Rodney also wrote for the widest possible readership in books like *How Europe Underdeveloped Africa* (1972).

Rollins, Sonny (1930-) was one of the great African American jazz musicians of the post bebop generation. A tenor saxophonist, he was both the writer of countless modern jazz standards and regarded as an outstanding improviser. He had a particular love for calypso-influenced tunes, reflecting his parents' origins in the Virgin Islands. He made over fifty albums between 1953-2016. His classic albums include *Tenor Madness, Saxophone Colossus, A Night at the Village Vanguard, Way out West, Newk's Time, Freedom Suite, The Bridge* and *G Man*. In later life, jazz critics came to admire his live performances more than his studio records, where his period of greatest invention was in the 1956-64 period.

Rudder, David (1953-) is a Trinidadian calypsonian, soca singer and social critic much admired by Gordon Rohler. Between 1988-2015 Rudder released more than thirty albums, the first, *Haiti*, with Charlie's Roots still regarded as an outstanding innovation in Trinidadian music, with the album *1990* (1990) similarly regarded. Rudder's songs have pan-Caribbean, decolonising sentiments, often fiercely critical of political corruption in Trinidad. "Almost overnight David Rudder became a national hero of the order of Marley in Jamaica, Fela in Nigeria and Springsteen in New Jersey," wrote Daisann McLane in *Village Voice* of Rudder in his first calypso year.

Saad, Neuza holds a degree in Dance from the Federal University of Bahia in Brazil and taught at the Federal University of Bahia. She is the author of *Danca afro: sincretismo de movimentos* (1992).

Salkey, Andrew (1928-1995 was a Jamaican novelist, poet, editor and writer for children, who by the time CAM was formed, had already published *A Quality of Violence* (1959), set in Jamaica; an early London novel which deals with LGBTI themes, *Escape to an Autumn Pavement* (1960); a quartet of popular novels for children: *Hurricane, Earthquake, Drought* and *Riot*; and an influential anthology, *West Indian Stories* (Faber, 1960). He was regularly involved in the BBC *Caribbean Voices* programme. He went on to write around thirty books and edit several more significant anthologies. He settled in the USA for the last 20 years of his life.

Sander, Reinhard W. (1944-) is a retired Professor of Comparative Literature who taught at the University of Puerto Rico, Rio Piedras, and at Hampshire College and at Amherst, Massachusetts. His important books on early Caribbean writing include, *The Trinidad Awakening* (1988); as editor, *From Trinidad: An Anthology of Early West Indian Writing* (1978); and as co-editor, *Ousmane Sembene: Dialogues with Critics and Writers* (1993), and *Twentieth Century Caribbean and Black African Writers* (1992/1993/1995).

Sanders, Pharoah (1940-2022) was an African American tenor saxophonist who was at the far end of the 1960's avantgarde in pushing the range of sounds the instrument was capable of making. He came to prominence playing with John Coltrane's group and then with his own Afro-centric spiritual recordings, such as *Tauhid*, *Karma* and *Jewels of Thought*. Over the next sixty years he released almost 100 albums, and in later years his spiritual jazz became more melodic and found a new, younger audience. His *Floating Points* with the London Symphony Orchestra was a best-selling album in 2021.

Sandoval, Arturo (1949-) is a Cuban American jazz trumpeter, composer and band-leader who defected from Cuba to the USA in 1989.

Santamaria, Mongo (1917-2003) was a Cuban percussionist who made over fifty albums between 1952-1998 in a variety of Cuban and Latin American dance styles, including rhumba and salsa. He left Cuba in 1950 and worked for the rest of his life in the USA. He worked with jazz musicians like Cal Tjader, had a huge hit with his version of Herbie Hancock's 'Watermelon Man'. Later in his career he played with the Fania All-Stars. His style was rooted in African cross-rhythms.

Satchmo, see Louis Armonstrong.

Savacou was the title of the journal of the Caribbean Artists Movement, originally involving Kenneth Ramchand and Andrew Salkey as editors. Later it became very much a Kamau Brathwaite project and went through 14 numbers: Vol 1 no. 1, June 1970 was devoted to the subject of slave societies; No. 2, September 1970, was a literary issue with an emphasis on history, with articles by Kamau Brathwaite, Derek Walcott, Kenneth Ramchand, Gordon Rohlehr and C.L.R. James, among others; No. 3/4 was a Special Issue, Dec 1970/March 1971, subtitled New Writing 1970. It was consciously pan-Caribbean and contained prose fiction and poetry, established writers and new voices from what Brathwaite would call the revolution in Caribbean arts, such as Bongo Jerry, Ras Dizzy, Alfred Fraser and Anthony McNeill. It was the issue of *Savacou* that sparked Eric Roach's dismissive review of poets like Bongo Jerry and Gordon Rohlehr's lengthy and considered rebuttal, "West Indian Poetry: Some Problems of Assessment", which first appeared in *Tapia*, No 23, Dec 26, 1971 and was collected in *My Strangled City* (1992, 2019); *Savacou 5*, June 1971 was subtitled "Essays around the Idea of Creolisation"; *Savacou 7/8*, January/June 1973 was an 80th birthday tribute to Frank Collymore, in poetry and prose, extracts from *Bim* and new work from younger Barbadian writers; *Savacou 9/10*, 1974, was subtitled *Writing Away From Home*, edited by Andrew Salkey and John La Rose. It covered writing from Britain, the USA and Canada; *Savacou 11/12*, September 1975 (edited only by Edward Brathwaite) had studies of Orlando Patterson, Edouard Glissant, and Brathwaite's "Caribbean Man in Space and Time"; *Savacou 13*, Gemini 1977 was subtitled "Caribbean Woman" edited by Lucille Mathurin-Mair. It contained poetry, fiction and criticism, including early poems by Lorna Goodison; *Savacou 14/15*, 1979, was subtitled "New Poets from Jamaica", edited by EKB – it contained poetry by Goodison, Opal Palmer, Pam Mordecai, Christine Craig and others.

Scott, Dennis (1939-1991) was a Jamaican poet, playwright, actor (he was Lester Tibideaux in the Cosby Show), dancer in the Jamaican National Dance Theatre, an editor of *Caribbean Quarterly* and teacher. His first collection, *Uncle Time* (1973) was one of the first to establish the serious use of nation language in lyric poetry. His other poetry collections include *Dreadwalk* (1982) and *Strategies* (1989). His posthumous collection *After-Image* (2008) was edited by Mervyn Morris. His plays, acknowledged as one of the major influences on the direction of Caribbean theatre, include *Terminus, Dog, Echo in the Bone.*

Scott-Heron, Gil (1949-2011) was an African American singer, songwriter and poet, whose songs have a jazz inflection and a spoken-word poetry feel with a radical political content that had an influence on the emergence of hip-hop in the 1980s. Scott-Heron's classic albums include *Pieces of a Man* (1971), *Free Will* (1972), *The Mind of Gil Scott-Heron* (1978). Other less well-received albums followed, but cocaine and crack addiction and two prison sentences interrupted his career. After a gap of 16 years, *I'm New Here* was released to acclaim in 2010.

Sekou, Lansana (1959-) is a poet, short story writer, editor and publisher from St Martin (Dutch sector). He has published over 20 collections of his poetry, radical and Black in feeling. His publishing house, House of Nehesi, founded in 1980, has published work by George Lamming, Kamau Brathwaite, Amiri Baraka, Shake Keane, Howard Fergus, Yvonne Weekes and his own poetry. He is an advocate for the independence of St Martin.

Selvon, Samuel (1923-1994). Selvon had arrived in London from Trinidad in 1950, already an accomplished journalist and short story writer whose work was regularly broadcast on the *Caribbean Voices* programme. By the time of CAM, he had written six novels and a collection of short stories, including *A Brighter Sun*, *An Island is a World* (1955); *The Lonely Londoners* (1956); *Ways of Sunlight*, short stories (1957); *Turn Again Tiger* (1959); *I Hear Thunder* (1963) and *The Housing Lark* (1965). Selvon emigrated to Canada in around 1978 and died on a return visit to Trinidad.

Senghor, Léopold Sédar (1906-2001) was a Senegalese poet, cultural theorist and politician who was one of the founding figures of Négritude. As a politician he advocated for full political and social rights for Africans within a federal French overseas framework, later for a federation of former French colonial states in West Africa, but by 1960 he became President of an independent Senegal, established a one-party state and imprisoned opponents. As a cultural theoretician he was one of the founders of *Présence Africaine*, and the influential anthology *Anthologie de la nouvelle poésie nègre et malgache* (1948). His own poetry collections include *Chants d'ombre* (1945), *Hosties noires* (1948) and *Éthiopiques* (1956). *Nocturnes* (1961) was translated into English by Clive Wake.

Shepp, Archie (1937-) is an African American tenor saxophonist, band leader and arranger, educator, and playwright who continues to play into his eighties. Shepp was the crucial link between the 1960s "New Thing" avant-garde and the older traditions of jazz, including the collective improvisation of New Orleans and the marching bands, but also with an ear for modernist funk and African rhythms. He was a Black Power militant but never had an issue with including white musicians in his bands. His essential albums include *Four for Trane*, (1965), *Fire Music* (1965), *Mama Too Tight* (1967), *The Way Ahead* (1968), *The Magic of Ju-Ju* (1969), and *Attica Blues* (1972) – though few Shepp albums are without interest.

Simmons, Harold (Harry) (1914-1966) was a St Lucian artist, folklorist, historian and mentor to Derek Walcott and the artist Dunstan St Omer. Simmons was instrumental is rescuing St Lucia's folk arts with their African and Creole roots from the disapproval of the Roman Catholic church. He published numerous articles in local papers and edited the *Voice of St Lucia* newspaper. His death by suicide is a major theme in Derek Walcott's autobiographical poem, *Another Life* (1973) in Part Four "The Estranging Sea", where Walcott credits Simmons with teaching him to see his island.

Simone, Nina (1933-2003) was an African American singer, songwriter, pianist and political activist who took a Black nationalist view in the struggle for civil rights in the USA, whose work ranged between jazz, r&b, gospel, blues and pop. She recorded regularly between 1959-1972, much less frequently thereafter (though *Baltimore* in 1978 was well received) as a result of being out of favour with white-led record companies and personal difficulties, including being diagnosed as bi-polar. Her best known songs include "Mississippi Goddam" and "My Baby Just Cares for Me".

Small, Richard (1943-) is a Jamaican lawyer, who was a race equality activist in London during the 1960s, and involved in many movements and organisations. He was a close political associate of C.L.R. James, acting as his political secretary from 1965. He was involved with CAM and New Beacon and Bogle L'Ouverture Press.

Smith, Keith (1945-2011) was a Trinidadian reporter and editor and an immensely popular columnist with a notable personal style. As the *Caribbean Review of Books* recorded in their obituary "The Keith Smith column ... mixed personal anecdote and humour with social and political observation, street smarts and folk wisdom, delivered in a prose style his regular readers could recognise sometimes by a mere sentence."

Smith, M.G. (Michael Garfield) (1921-1993) was a Jamaican anthropologist and poet, most famed for the development of the plural society theory as a way of understanding the tensions within Caribbean societies as former colonies created out of (forced) imported labour with different ethnic and cultural identities and divided by race and class. As a poet he was part of the circle around Edna Manley, was published in Caribbean magazines but his work was not collected until 2003, in *The Kingdom of Light*. His important academic publications on the Caribbean (he also studied African societies) include *West Indian Family Structure*; *Kinship and Community in Carriacou*; *Dark Puritan*; *The Plural Society in the British West Indies*; and *Culture, Race and Class in the Commonwealth Caribbean*. Douglas Hall wrote a biography *A Man Divided: Michael Garfield Smith - Jamaican Poet and Anthropologist 1921 – 1993*.

Smith, Mikey (Michael), (1954-1983) was a Jamaican poet and performer with anarchist, Rastafarian views whose poem/performance "Mi Cyaan Believe It" was the title of the album put out by Island Records in 1982. Smith worked with the Jamaican poet Mervyn Morris to transfer spoken word to text for the book, *It A Come: Poems by Michael Smith* ed. Mervyn Morris (London: Race Today Publications, 1986). Smith was killed by stoning when he heckled a meeting of the conservative Jamaican Labour Party on Stony Hill. In response Kamau Brathwaite wrote "Stone" in *Middle Passages* (Newcastle: Bloodaxe Books, 1992), 49-54.

Smith, Raymond T. (1925-2015) was an English social anthropologist who for a time taught at the Institute of Social and Economic Research at UWI Mona. His books included *The Negro Family in British Guiana* (1956), *British Guiana* (1962), *Kinship and Class in the West Indies* (1988) and *The Matrifocal Family: Power, Pluralism and Politics* (1996). He was critic of the plural society approach, putting more emphasis on class structures.

Soyinka, Wole (1934-) is a Nigerian playwright, poet, novelist, critic and literary theorist who was awarded the Nobel prize for Literature in 1986. For periods he has had to live in exile as a fierce critic of military dictatorships, elite corruption and the conduct of the civil war against Eastern Nigeria, when he was imprisoned. Though an atheist, he has worked creatively with the divinities of Yoruba myth. He has written at least 27 plays between 1957-2011 (including *The Lion and the Jewel*, *Kongi's Harvest* and *Madmen and Specialists*), three novels (*The Interpreters*, *Season of Anomy* and *Chronicles from the Land of the Happiest People on Earth*), five memoirs and six collections of poetry and a dozen works of non-fiction of literature, culture and politics.

Sparrow, Mighty, Francisco Slinger (1935-) is probably the best known and most admired of all Trinidadian calypsonians. He has won Trinidad's Carnival Road March competition eight times, Calypso King/Monarch eight times, and has twice won the Calypso King of Kings title. The prime of his career was probably between 1956-1980. A dozen or more of his songs are permanent records of shifts in Trinidad's cultural and political life ("Jean and Dinah", "Congo Man", "Dan is the Man in the Van", "Capitalism Gone Mad"). He is the subject of Gordon Rohlehr's book, *My Whole Life is Calypso: Essays on Sparrow* (2015).

Springer, Pearl Eintou (1944-) is a playwright, theatre director, poet, librarian and devotee of Orisha religion in Trinidad. Her publications include *Out of the Shadows* (1986), *Focussed* (1991), *Moving Into the Light* (2000) and *Loving the Skin I'm In* (2005) – all poetry; *Survivor: A Collection of Plays for Children and Young Adults* (2016), and as editor of *The New Aesthetic and the Meaning of*

Culture in the Caribbean; the dream coming in with the rain: proceedings of the Carifesta V Symposia, Port of Spain, Trinidad, August 1992 (1995).

St Omer, Dunstan (1927-2015) was St Lucia's most distinguished artist and muralist. He has painted murals throughout St Lucia, including the notable Holy Family Mural at the Church of the Holy Family in Jacmel, Roseau (1973.) These church murals initially created controversy for his depictions of black divinity. St Omer is "Gregorias" in Derek Walcott's *Another Life* (1973).

Stewart, Robert is the American author of *Cut Cane: Poems from Jamaica* (Savacou, 1988), who taught and lived in Jamaica for "a major proportion of his life".

Striker, Mighty (1930-2011) was a Trinidadian calypsonian, Percival Oblington, who was at the height of his career between 1949-1970. He won the Calypso King contest with "Don't Blame The PNM" and "Can't Find A Job To Suit Me" in 1958, and became the first person to retain the title in 1959 with "Ban The Hula Hoop" and "Comparison". He returned to taxi-driving after 1970 but later wrote *The True History of Calypso*, published in 2000.

Sutherland, Efua (1924-1996) was a Ghanaian poet, playwright, educator, and cultural activist who influenced the development of Ghanaian drama as both a writer and the founder of theatre groups and other national and community projects. She came to Britain in the 1940s and contributed to the BBC's *West African Voices* as a writer and reader. She returned to Ghana in 1951 where at one point she worked with Kamau Brathwaite. Her plays include *Edufa* (1967) and *The Marriage of Anansewa* (1977).

Tapia House Movement was a label that connected together a newspaper *Tapia* (September 1969-) which became the *Trinidad and Tobago Review*; an actual building which, tragically, was burnt down in 1982 with the loss of invaluable archives; a political party which fought elections with minimal success; and a group of people who generated ideas and actions which raised possibilities for decolonisation and nation-building much superior to any of the political parties that held power. Founded by Lloyd Best out of the New World Movement, Tapia's ideas focused on self-reliance, the formation of participative, democratic institutions that broke away from the inherited Westminster political structures that excluded people from involvement except at elections, opposed autocratic "doctor politics" (the leader as hero) and politics dominated by ethnic sub-loyalties. Many of Gordon Rohlehr's literary essays first appeared in *Tapia* and later *The Trinidad and Tobago Review*.

Taylor, Caldwell was Grenada's Ambassador to the UN (1980 to October 1983), and Deputy Minister for Foreign Affairs (1982 to 1983). He feared for his life from those in the PRG who murdered Maurice Bishop, but opposed the American invasion. He is founder and editor of *Big Drum Nation*.

The Bomb is a weekly Trinidadian newspaper, a scandal sheet that was at its peak in the 1970s under the editorship of Patrick Chookoolingo (qv), that is still appearing to this day.

Thiongo, Ngugi wa (1938-) is a Kenyan novelist, playwright, literary critic and memoirist. Many suspect that only his consistent radicalism, critiques of continuing Western imperialism and neo-colonialism (which led to him being imprisoned by the Kenyan government), has prevented the award of the Nobel prize for literature his stature warrants. It was Edward Brathwaite's meeting with Ngugi which led to his naming as Kamau by the latter's mother. In his commitment to decolonising African writing, Ngugi stopped writing in English and wrote in Kikuyu, his mother-tongue. His best-known novels include: *Weep Not, Child* (1964), *The River Between* (1965), *A Grain of Wheat* (1967, 1992), *Petals of Blood* (1977), *Caitaani Mutharaba-Ini* (*Devil on the Cross*, 1980), *Matigari ma Njiruungi*, 1986 (*Matigari*, 1989), *Murogi wa Kagogo* (*Wizard of the Crow*, 2006), *The Perfect Nine: The Epic of Gikuyu and Mumbi* (2020). *Decolonising the Mind: The Politics of Language in African Literature* (1986) is where he sets out his case for writing in Kikuyu.

Thomas, Clive Y. (1938-) is a Guyanese economist, academic and political activist. He was one of the founding members of the New World Group in Guyana in the 1960s, and later one of the group who, with Walter Rodney, Eusi Kwayana and Rupert Roopnaraine, founded the Working People's Alliance in 1974 to counter the racial divisions in Guyana's politics. His books include *Plantations, Peasants, and State: A Study of the Mode of Sugar Production in Guyana* (1984) and *The Poor and the Powerless: Economic Policy and Change in the Caribbean* (1988).

Thomas, J.J. (1841-1889) was a pioneering Trinidadian linguist, anti-racist and incisive critic of British colonial assumptions. His two important books are *The Theory and Practice of Creole Grammar* (1869), the first text to show that Caribbean creoles were rule-driven languages, and still an invaluable source on the French-influenced creole of 19th Century Trinidad; and *Froudacity: West Indian Fables by James Anthony Froude* (1889) a skewering of the British historian's odious racism and inaccuracy in his *The English in the West Indies, or The Bow of Ulysses* (1888). Both Thomas's books were republished by New Beacon Books.

Thomkins, Thomas (1572-1656) was a Welsh composer and organist who composed mainly choral music for the English church. He was a staunch royalist who wrote *Sad Pavan: for these distracted times* following the execution of Charles I.

Thompson, David (1961-2010) was the sixth prime minister of Barbados from 2008-2010 until his early death from cancer.

Thomson, James (1834-1882) was a Scottish poet and journalist whose most famous long poem, *City of the Dreadful Night* (1874) was, as a deeply pessimistic vision of the underside of the 19th century city, a precursor of

20th century modernism's portrayal of the city, for instance Eliot's 'Prufrock' and *The Waste Land*.

Toni, see Morrison, Toni

Torres-Saillant, Silvio is a Dominican Republic academic who teaches in New York. His books include *An Intellectual History of the Caribbean* (2006); *The Dominican-Americans* (1998); *Caribbean Poetics: Toward an Aesthetic of West Indian Literature* (1997; Peepal Tree Press 2013); *An Introduction to Dominican Blackness* (1999) and *The Once and Future Muse: The Poetry and Poetics of Rhina P. Espaillat* (2018).

UNDP was the United Nations Development Programme.

Walcott, Harclyde is a Barbadian academic, theatre director, filmmaker, photo-journalist and author of *imagining and other poems* (Bridgetown, 2015).

Walcott, Derek (1930-2017) was a Saint Lucian poet and dramatist. A towering figure in world literature, he was awarded the Nobel Prize for Literature in 1992. His first poetry collection, *25 Poems*, was published in 1948; his last, *Morning, Paramin* (illustrated by Peter Doig) in 2016. At the time of the first mention of Walcott between Brathwaite and Rohlehr in 1967, Walcott had written *In a Green Night: Poems 1948-60*; *Selected Poems* and *The Castaway and Other Poems*. Walcott had also reviewed Kamau Brathwaite's *Rights of Passage* in the *Trinidad Sunday Guardian*, 19 March, 1967, reprinted in *Derek Walcott: The Journey man Years*, Vol. 1 (Rodopi, 2013), 222-226.

Walcott, Margaret (nee Maillard) (1932-2014) was the co-founder of the Trinidad Theatre Workshop, the Chairperson of the Queen's Hall in Port of Spain and the second wife of Derek Walcott.

Walcott, Roderick (1930-2000) was a St Lucian playwright, twin brother of Derek Walcott. In the latter part of his life he lived in Canada. His plays include, *The Harrowing of Benjy* (1957), *The Banjo Man* (1958), *A Flight of Sparrows* (1966), *Malfinis* (1967), *The Trouble with Albino Joe* (1966), and *Shrove Tuesday March: a play of the Steelband* (1966). Several of them are still quite regularly produced.

Walmsley, Anne (1931-) is an editor, critic and author, who specialised in Caribbean art and literature. She is widely recognised for her work as Longman Caribbean's publisher. Her school anthology, *The Sun's Eye: West Indian Writing for Young Readers* (1968) was notable for the wide and contemporary range of Caribbean writing it drew on. She was actively involved in and wrote the definitive history of CAM: *The Caribbean Artists Movement: A Literary and Cultural History, 1966–1971* (1992). Her other books include *Art in the Caribbean* (2010). She lives in London.

Warner-Lewis, Maureen (as Maureen Warner) (1943-) is a linguist and historian of the African heritages in the Caribbean. Born in Tobago, after teaching in West Africa she spent much of her working life at UWI Mona in Jamaica. Her books include *Guinea's Other Suns: The African Dynamic* *in Trinidad Culture* (1991), *Yoruba Songs of Trinidad* (1994), *Trinidad Yoruba: From Mother Tongue to Memory* (1996), and *African Continuities in the Linguistic Heritage of Jamaica* (1996); *Central Africa in the Caribbean: Transcending Time, Transforming Culture* (2003) and *Archibald Monteath: Igbo, Jamaican, Moravian* (2007). Her guide to Kamau Brathwaite's *Masks*, *Notes to Masks* was published in Nigeria in 1977.

Washington, Salim is an African American tenor saxophonist and educator. His albums include *Love in Exile, Harlem Homecoming, Live at St Nick's, Dogon Revisited* and *Sankofa*. He wrote *Clawing at the Limits of Cool: Miles Davis, John Coltrane and the Greatest Jazz Collaboration Ever* (2008).

Webb, Barbara teaches Caribbean, African and African American literatures at Hunter College. She is the author of *Myth and History in Caribbean Fiction: Alejo Carpentier, Wilson Harris, and Edouard Glissant* (1992). She has published articles on African American and Caribbean women writers. Her research interests include postcolonial theory, transnational and transcultural expressive forms, and theories of creolization.

Webster, Ben (1909-1973) was an African American tenor saxophonist who rose to prominence with the great Duke Ellington band of 1940-43 with tunes such as "Cottontail" and "All Too Soon". His track "Chelsea Bridge" is a good example of what GR describes as a sound which is almost just breath. He recorded at least 50 albums between 1953 and his death, including, *Soulville* and *The Soul of Ben Webster*. In 1964 he moved to Denmark where he lived until his death.

Weston, Randy (1926-2018) was an African American jazz pianist who was notable for developing a style that made connections with Africa. His recording career spanned from 1954-2018. Classic albums include *Blues to Africa* (1975) *The Spirits of Our Ancestors* (1991) and *Nuit Africaine* (2004).

White, Sarah (1941-2023) was an anti-racist campaigner, cultural activist, publisher and bookseller. She founded New Beacon Books in 1966 with her partner John La Rose. Their London house at Albert Road was one of the centres for visiting writers from Africa, the Caribbean and Latin America and a base for the Caribbean Artists Movement.

Wilkinson, Lester Efebo (1947-) is a Trinidadian poet, playwright and cultural activist. His best known play is *Bitter Cassava*. He was Artistic Director of the theatre company, Mausica Folk Theatre (1979-1989).

Williams, Aubrey (1926-1990) was a Guyanese artist who came to the UK in 1952. His work is notable for its use of Amerindian motifs. Discussions and examples of his work can be seen in *Guyana Dreaming: The Art of Aubrey Williams*, compiled by Anne Walmsley (Dangeroo Press 1990) and *Aubrey Williams* (Institute of International Visual Arts, 1998).

Williams, Eric E. (1911-1981) was the "doctor" who led Trinidad and Tobago to independence in 1962 and became its first Prime Minister. He was famed for his mission to bring historical awareness to Trinidadians at the "University of Woodford Square", but his premiership was marred by expressions of hostility to Indian Trinidadians and an increasing authoritarianism. He was an important historian, particularly for *Capitalism and Slavery* (1944), *The Negro in the Caribbean* and *British Historians and the West Indies*. Gordon Rohlehr wrote a critical analysis of the weaknesses of Williams's intended masterwork, *From Columbus to Castro* in "History as Absurdity" in *My Strangled City and Other Essays*.

Williams, Lavinia (1916-1989) was an African American dancer and dance educator who was instrumental in setting up schools of dance in Guyana, Haiti and the Bahamas. She was born in the USA of Caribbean parents. She was one of the important contributors to developing distinctively Caribbean styles of dance.

Wynter, Sylvia (1928-) is a Jamaican novelist, playwright and a major social and cultural theorist in the field of race and gender. She was an early editor of *Jamaica Journal*. Her novel, *The Hills of Hebron* (1962), and one of her plays, *Maskarade* (1973) have been republished. *We Must Learn to Sit Down Together and Talk About a Little Culture: Decolonizing Essays 1967– 1984* (2022) collects her Caribbean essays before her move to the USA.

Zap Pow (1969-c 1979) was a reggae band formed by Michael Williams (d. 2005), Dwight Pinkny, Max Edwards, Glen D'Costa, Joe McCormack, Dave Madden and later Beres Hammond. Some members of the band reformed in 2010 and released *Zap Pow Again* (2017). The albums from their first formation include *Zap Pow Now* (1970) and *Revolution* (1971)

Zea Mexican. See Doris Brathwaite.

INDEX

ABOUT THE AUTHOR

Gordon Rohlehr was Emeritus Professor at the University of the West Indies at St Augustine, Trinidad. Unquestionably one of the Caribbean's finest critics and thinkers, his territory covers both literature and popular culture, particularly Calypso. His publications include: *Pathfinder: Black Awakening in "The Arrivants" of Edward Kamau Brathwaite* (Tunapuna: College Press, 1981); *Cultural Resistance and the Guyana State* (Casa de las Américas, 1984); *Calypso and Society in Pre-Independence Trinidad* (Port of Spain, 1990); *My Strangled City and Other Essays* (Longman Trinidad, 1992); *The Shape of That Hurt and Other Essays* (Longman Trinidad, 1992); *A Scuffling of Islands: Essays on Calypso* (Lexicon Trinidad Ltd, 2004); *Transgression, Transition, Transformation: Essays in Caribbean Culture* (Lexicon, 2007); *Ancestories: Readings of Kamau Brathwaite's "Ancestors"* (Trinidad: Lexicon, 2010); *My Whole Life is Calypso: Essays on Sparrow* (2015) and *Perfected Fables: A Bookman Signs off on Seven Decades* (2019). New editions of *My Strangled City and Other Essays* (2019) and *The Shape of That Hurt and Other Essays* (2020) were published Caribbean Modern Classics by Peepal Tree. His death in January 2023 was met by an outpouring of expressions of love, grief and admiration.

ALSO AVAILABLE BY GORDON ROHLEHR

My Strangled City and Other Essays
ISBN: 9781845234379; pp, 308; pub. 2019; £19.99

Gordon Rohlehr's critical work is outstanding in the balance it achieves between its particularity and its breadth – from the detailed unpacking of a poem's inner workings, to locating Caribbean writing in the sweep of political and cultural history – and the equal respect he pays to literary and to popular cultural forms. His "Articulating a Caribbean Aesthetic" remains a stunningly pertinent and concise account of the historical formation of the cultural shifts that framed Caribbean writing as a distinctive body of work. Indeed, along with Kamau Brathwaite, Sylvia Wynter and Kenneth Ramchand, no critic has done more to establish the subject of Caribbean writing and its distinctive aesthetics.

These essays, written between 1969 to 1986, first published in radical campaigning newspapers such as *Tapia* and *Moko*, and first collected in 1992, were the work of a young academic who was both changing the university curriculum, and deeply engaged with the less privileged world outside the campus. Rohlehr catches Caribbean writing at the point when it leaves behind its nationalist hopes and begins to challenge the complex realities of independence. Few critics have written as clearly about how deeply the colonial has remained embedded in the postcolonial.

What shines in Rohlehr's work is not merely its depth, acuity and humanity, but its courage. He writes when his subject is still emergent, without waiting for the credibility of metropolitan endorsements as a guide to the canon. "My Strangled City", a record of how Trinidad's poets responded to the upsurge of revolutionary hopes, radical shams, repressions and disappointed dreams of 1964-1975 is an indispensable account of those times and the diversity of literary response that continues to speak to the present. And if in these essays Trinidad is Rohlehr's primary focus, his perspective is genuinely regional. His native Guyana is always present in his thoughts and several essays show his deep interest in the cultural productions of a "dread" Jamaica, and in making insightful comparisons between, for instance, reggae and calypso.

The Shape of That Hurt and Other Essays
ISBN:9781845234645; pp. 342; pub. 1992/2021; £19.99

In this phrase from Anthony McNeill's poem "For the D", Gordon Rohlehr finds the perfect title for the deep questioning of the conjunction between politics and aesthetics that these essays, mainly written in the 1980s and 90s, explore. He charts the fine balance between hope and despair that Caribbean writers from Martin Carter in the corrupt autocracy of Burnham's Guyana, Kamau Brathwaite surveying the desolation of Kingston, Jamaica during internecine cross community political warfare, and the soca/calypsonians of Trinidad in the midst of the Muslimeen attempted coup d'etat of 1990 respond to the "turmoil of new worlds coming into existence". Rohlehr is never less than an astringent truth-teller in confronting the darkest years of postcolonial disappointments when the hopes of independence were being buried by the neo-colonial policies of the new/old political elites and sections of the oppressed abandoned the politics of renewal for the insurrectionary despair of crime and terror. But Rohlehr's focus on the dread political climate is only a part of his wider investigation into the aesthetics of literary form, of how writers, notably Brathwaite, Carter, Kendel Hippolyte, George Lamming, Victor Questel, and Dennis Scott, and soca/calypsonian David Rudder, amongst others, have found ways to transmute the region's at times inchoate energies into art of the highest order. His reading of Lamming's Season of Adventure and Brathwaite's The Arrivants points to the sources of renewal in the Caribbean world, and his attention to then little-known writers such as Hippolyte and Questel is another sign of his critical independence, his courage in establishing a canon of relevance long before metropolitan publishing and academia offer their blessing. Rohlehr has little time for the fashions of "theory", of the kinds of post-colonial criticism that has flourished mainly in the metropolis. His virtues are in seeing relationships between writing and the world, writing and other texts, in reading closely and imaginatively, and looking for real evidence to support a point of view. When he sees that missing, as in a couple of critical approaches to Kamau Brathwaite, he attacks with a fine mixture of Trinidadian picong and the lash of the deftest stick-fighter. Whilst these essays were written almost thirty years ago, they are as necessary as they ever were as a model of how to connect aesthetics and politics, how to move seamlessly between literature and popular oral forms, and as still the most pertinent critical work on foundational writers such as Carter and Brathwaite. If the Caribbean is currently in a state of comparative social and political quiescence, Rohlehr's unwavering stare into the apocalyptic turmoil of those times is a necessary reminder that the reasons for that turmoil are still very much present, volcanic, if simmering and not yet blowing.

Perfected Fables Now: A Bookman Signs off on Seven Decades
ISBN: 9781845234508; pp. 288; pub. 2019; £19.99

Since the mid-1960s, Gordon Rohlehr has been an incomparable recorder
and analyser of Caribbean literature and culture and their intersection
with history and politics. His work on the emergence of Caribbean
writing from its colonial shell and his analysis of calypso as the voice
of Trinidadian consciousness establishes him as essential to our time
as William Hazlitt was to the early 19th century in documenting and
characterising the turbulent spirit of his age. Radical, but never willing
to compromise his sense of what was fraudulent or power-seeking amongst
his fellow travellers, Rohlehr is the best touchstone we have for both
what the Caribbean has achieved and of its struggling, neo-colonial
fragility in the face of the new imperialism of economic and cultural
globalism.

Now – though who knows? – in putting together what he says is his last
book, Gordon Rohlehr doffs the costume of the carnival figure of the
"Bookman", the recording Satan of the devil band, who walks with his book
in which he writes down the names of the damned. And here we have the
clue to the fact that along with the serious analysis of calypso, his summing
up of what is essential in the work of Derek Walcott, Earl Lovelace and V.S.
Naipaul, and the essays of remembrance for those like Walcott, Lloyd Best,
Pat Bishop, Tony Martin and others who have made their earthly exits,
there is a devilish humour at work. This comes out particularly in an essay
that joyfully demolishes an attempt to characterise the Caribbean in any
other than its own terms – as a new Mediterranean, for instance – and the
subservience of Trinidad's rulers to the neo-colonialisms of tourism,
visiting American ships and the U.S. embassy. What is often salutary, if
uncomfortable, is to be reminded by the long span of Rohlehr's observations that problems seen as contemporary were being identified by the
nation's calypsonians sixty years ago.

Rohlehr's voice is always distinctively personal, though the Bookman
has rarely revealed much of himself, but in one of the concluding essays he
writes about his Guyanese upbringing from the 1940s to the 1960s in a way
that is both very funny and sad and gives an understanding of what has
shaped his vision.

Musings, Mazes, Muses, Margins
ISBN: 9781845234652; pp. 184; 2020; £13.99

There is nothing quite like Gordon Rohlehr's *Musings, Mazes, Muses, Margins* in Caribbean writing; probably its nearest neighbours are Kamau Brathwaite's *The Zea Mexican Diary* and *Trenchtown Rock*. Over a period of more than forty years, Rohlehr, supreme public critic of the post-colonial Caribbean, its creative writing and the historian and deep analyser of calypso, has been paying quiet attention to his inner consciousness, a fictive journeying that has much to say about outer personal and wider Caribbean realities. It is a book that ranges over a variety of forms – diary, recorded dreams, poems, a kind of flash fiction, polemics, prophecies, and philosophical reflections – all enriched by a lifetime of reading, thinking and articulate writing. As befits the slippery connections between inner and outer worlds, Rohlehr's writing is distinguished by an infectious humour and a delight in puns.

In the act of questioning what the years of "wuk" have achieved, Rohlehr asks himself and us the most profound questions – not the unanswerable metaphysics of "What are we here for?" but the material, ethical question of "To what end do we exist?" In the context of a Caribbean of disappointed post-colonial hopes, Rohlehr both confronts an existential void and records the increments of creativity and achievement that offer future hope.

The book begins with the Guyanese child, born with a caul over his face, gifted with a prophetic vision deeply immersed in the African being that is part of his inheritance. He records how he was told – beyond his memory – how family members "steamed" his eyes to destroy something embarrassing to a colonial, lower-middle class family. The visions and intuitive knowledge disappeared, but if the family elders believed that they were cauterising something to destruction, they failed utterly to kill the visionary dreamer, the Daniel Lyonnes-Denne, who is one part of the triumvirate that also includes the public Gordon and the reticent Frederick.

In his previous books, Gordon Rohlehr confronted the Caribbean world head-on. Here, he approaches from the margins, and who is to say his dream-work doesn't tell just as powerful truths about Caribbean reality?

ABOUT PEEPAL TREE PRESS

Peepal Tree Press has been decolonising bookshelves since 1985 with our focus on Caribbean and Black British writing. We are a wholly independent publisher and part of the Arts Council of England's national portfolio since 2015. In 2024, we established a partnership with HopeRoad Publishing.

Peepal Tree's list features fiction, poetry and non-fiction, including academic texts and creative memoirs. By the end of 2024, we will have published 490 books by 320 different authors, including those published in our anthologies. Most of our titles remain in print. Our books have won the Costa Prize, T.S. Eliot, Forward, OCM Bocas, Guyana and Casa de las Americas prizes.

From the beginning, women and LGBTI authors have been fully represented in our lists. We have focused on the new by publishing many first-time authors and have restored to print important Caribbean books in all genres in our Caribbean Classics Series. We have also published overlooked material from the past as a way of challenging received ideas about the Caribbean canon.

You can find curated bundles of books on our website on such topics as Slavery, Indo-Caribbean and LGBTI writing; find books by country such as writing from Barbados, Guyana, Jamaica, St Lucia and Trinidad. In "Discover", find lists of books, short essays and notes on books under a vast number of headings – from books that have things to say about childhood and youth, the plantation, imaginary Caribbeans, to food and horse-racing and much else.

As an ACE funded organisation, Peepal Tree supports writer development projects both nationally (Inscribe) and locally (the Readers and Writers Group in Leeds).

We see decolonisation as about overthrowing and repairing oppressive, economically exploitative and racist power relationships. Many of our books explore the halting, difficult process of overcoming four hundred years of colonialism in the Caribbean in the post-independence period. But we also see decolonisation as needing to happen in Britain. We are committed to ending British amnesia over the destructiveness of empire and colonialism, including our role in the irreparable damage of nearly three centuries of slavery , and promoting an understanding of how Britain's long relationship with the Caribbean has contributed to the making of British society in ways that persist into the present. As a publisher, we have taken a stand on supporting Palestinian rights for freedom from a colonial occupation and denial of statehood.

We hope that you enjoyed reading this book as much as we did publishing it. Your purchase supports writers to flourish. Keep in touch with our newsletter at https://www.peepaltreepress.com/subscribe, and discover all our books at www.peepaltreepress.com, and join us on social media @peepaltreepress